CHANGE YOUR MIND, CHANGE YOUR WORLD

Richard Gillett

A Fireside Book

Published by Simon & Schuster
New York • London • Toronto • Sydney • Tokyo • Singapore

FIRESIDE
Simon & Schuster Building
Rockefeller Center
1230 Avenue of the Americas
New York, New York 10020

Designed by Chris Welch
Manufactured in the United States of America

10 9 8 7 6 5 4 3

Library of Congress Cataloging-in-Publication Data is available.

ISBN 0-671-73538-1

CONTENTS

▼

Part 3 The Belief Manual   199

TO MY FAMILY

ACKNOWLEDGMENTS

▼

Thank you—

to Theresa Carr who typed the manuscript many times.
to all those involved in the development of wordprocessors
to my ancestors for all the rich influences I could choose from
to my parents for their love
to my father for his scientific understanding
to Kathryn, Arthur, and Alex for taking my elsewhere concentration with such good grace
to the authors of all the books in the reading list
to Heinz Wolffe, Paul Sempft, Nadine Scott, Sherrie Horner, Frank van Lerven, Anthony Jones, and Denys Kelsey, who taught me about different forms of psychotherapy and communication

Thank you to Gurumayi Chidvilasananda who shows by her example that it really is possible to transcend limited beliefs and to love without conditions.

INTRODUCTION

If you think you can, you can; If you think you can't, you can't.
—Henry Ford

Throughout history, great and wise people from every culture have held the basic understanding: what we believe we will somehow create. This book explores the mechanisms behind this amazing process, and shows how to use these same mechanisms to create the most fulfilling beliefs we can.

Ralph Waldo Emerson said that what we think is what we create, and he called this principle the "law of laws." James Allen said, "The outer conditions of a person's life will always be found to reflect their inner beliefs." More recently the idea of creating your own reality has been in vogue in New Age thinking and various therapies. In fact, the basic philosophy that your life is created according to your belief has a pedigree of thousands of years through the recorded words of some of the greatest masters of wisdom.

The Upanishads, Indian texts dating back almost three thousand years, say that everything that happens in our own world is a reflection of how we think:

> One's own thought is one's world.
> What a person thinks is what he becomes—
> That is the eternal mystery.
> —Maitri Upanishad

In the Old Testament one of the maxims of the wise says:

> As a man thinketh in his heart,
> So *is* he.
> —Proverbs 23:7

In the Dhammapada (written about 500 B.C.), Buddha states:

> We are shaped by our thoughts;
> We become what we think.
> When the mind is pure, joy follows,
> Like a shadow that never leaves.

On several occasions Jesus is said to speak of the belief that is necessary for self-healing. "Thy faith hath made thee whole," he says to Bartimaeus, the blind beggar (Mark 10:52).

Shakespeare said:

> For there is nothing either good or bad
> But thinking makes it so.
> *Hamlet,* (Act II, Scene II)

Goethe, the great German literary figure, writes of the connection between a firmly held belief and the mysterious response of circumstance:

The moment one definitely commits oneself, then providence moves too. All sorts of things occur to help that would never otherwise have occurred. A whole stream of events issues from the decision, raising in one's favor all manner of unforeseen incidents, meetings, and material assistance, which no man would have dreamed would come his way.

Reading such words from great teachers sometimes leaves us thinking, well, that might be true for them, but for me living in the ordinary world in the 1990s, I have to accept something much smaller. Not so! It depends on what we believe.

This book presents strong evidence that our beliefs about ourselves and the world alter our perception, our memory, our hope, our energy, our health, our mood, our actions, our relationships, and eventually even our outward circumstances. This is the psychology of how we create self-fulfilling prophecies. When we see how we do this, then we can create positive self-fulfilling prophecies based on unlimiting beliefs. This makes us supremely independent beings with an extraordinary capacity to determine our own happiness. If only we could believe it!

In my practice as a psychotherapist, I often ask myself how can I and my client believe the very best and then put this belief into practice so single-mindedly that it becomes true. I have found that my old psychotherapeutic assumptions have often gotten in the way of this.

When people look too much at what is wrong with them, it seems there is no end to the search for reasons to explain the sense of inadequacy they feel. I remember being asked in a psychotherapy group to recall a pleasurable childhood experience. To my amazement, I could not think of one. Years later, I tried the same exercise on myself, and I could remember dozens of good and happy experiences. I realized that the first time, I had been suffering from a common psychological belief: "I have been hurt by my childhood." My mind had then selectively remembered all the times of hurt and selectively forgot the moments of pleasure so the belief could be maintained. That example, shocking to me at the time, shows how a belief can manipulate reality. Those with extensive psychotherapeutic training or experience nearly always had greater difficulty remembering pleasure from the past.

Though therapist and client may have the best of intentions, psychotherapy very easily becomes over-focused on the negative. Many people in psychotherapy keep on looking for what is wrong with them until they develop an inpregnable belief in their own limitations.

Many "positive thinking" books, on the other hand, are so positive they are unbelievable. I've found the most creative middle ground between these two extremes is to recognize the beliefs or mind-sets which limit us and are in the way of true positive thinking. There are methods of getting these limiting beliefs out of the way without interminable journeys into the past. Then positive thought can go deeper, becomes believable, and can really work to change our reality.

Why is this so hard to do? The major impediment to unlimited positive thinking is "victim-consciousness." When we think of ourselves as victims of circumstance, we forfeit confidence, innate strength, creativity, and the belief that we can change. Unfortunately the philosophy of Western psychotherapy has bolstered victim-consciousness. Even therapists who fervently believe in the idea of autonomy may inadvertently foster helplessness.

Psychotherapy and Victim-Consciousness

Nearly all psychoanalytic theory shares one belief, that our present suffering is caused by events from the past which are buried in our unconscious. In other words, either we are the victim of our past or else we are the victim of our unconscious. The underlying belief of the psychoanalyst was a direct influence of the medical model. At the time of Sigmund Freud, this model implied that the patient was neither responsible for his illness nor his healing (i.e., was a victim) while the doctor was responsible for cure (i.e., was the rescuer). Freud also believed that inner desires and instincts were intrinsically anti-social. In other words, if we let go, we become victims of our instincts, and if we repress ourselves, we are victims of society.

In most modern psychotherapies, the client is still usually seen as a victim of his past and his unconscious, and the therapist is still the rescuer, in that he has special access to the client's unconscious. If the important stuff can only be reached with the aid of the therapeutic expert, the client is not empowered to take charge of his own life—he does not even know what he is really thinking! The critical question here is, does the therapist access the wisdom of the client's unconscious, or does the therapist teach the client how to access his or her own wisdom?

Some modern psychotherapy has tried to avoid the medical and psychoanalytic model of diagnosis and labeling. But when the focus is on what's wrong with us, labeling is inevitable. It does not really matter whether we are called "anal retentive" or just "mean." Such feedback tends to accentuate our own belief in our problems and limits; we become what we focus on. Negative labels, even if accurate and well-meant, can easily enhance victim-consciousness. Once we identify with the names that we are called, we begin to see them as reality and act through the screen of these limitations; we become victims of our own labels.

A man might say to himself, "How can I be loving when my mother gave me so little?" It may indeed be hard for that man to be loving and one can be sympathetic to his difficulty. But once he labels himself as "unloving" *and* gives himself a historical reason for it, he is in danger. Knowing the reason from the past can be the final excuse for making the limitation acceptable and permanent.

Self-reliance

It is not *how* we got our limiting beliefs that's so important— it's *why we cling to them* even when we know they cause us (or others) pain. This book explores the secret advantages of staying limited. A woman who believed she was unattractive prided herself on being "above appearances" and had a reason to avoid the difficulties and threats of relationships. A man who saw himself as a failure prided himself on his specialness and had a great excuse for avoiding work. There are hundreds of subtle advantages enmeshed with each limiting belief.

When we see the apparent perks of holding on to limiting beliefs about ourselves, it is very liberating! Because then we know that our limitation is not just a fact caused by the unalterable past—it is, on the contrary, a choice governed by the present.

This choice can be made with great self-reliance. It can also be made more quickly than is usually believed. In contrast to some traditional psychotherapeutic assumptions, this book argues the following points:

- We are not victims of our unconscious, our past, our instincts, or society. We are self-reliant beings whose strength has become obscured temporarily through believing limited thoughts.
- Through logical and understandable mechanisms, what we believe will become reflected in our lives.
- Many of these beliefs are conscious. Rather than being repressed, most beliefs are simply not actively thought about because we take them for granted.
- Many of these beliefs can be explored *without* a therapist.
- Understanding the past is often used to *keep* present limitations, rather than to *transcend* them. It is more fruitful to explore how we maintain negative attitudes than to research their origins.
- After removing limiting beliefs, the fastest and most profitable form of therapy is to practice positive unlimited beliefs, in thought and in action.
- Emotional catharsis only temporarily relieves tension, unless it is combined with an understanding of the beliefs that created the situation.
- Many feelings are created out of beliefs based on misinterpretations of reality. It is often important *not* to trust our feelings. It is useful to be able to discern when a feeling

is a manipulation of a limiting belief system and when it is a spark of our own expansive inner intelligence.

Many of these ideas have been stated in different forms over the centuries. In our present era, psychotherapy has created its own rules and its own reality just as any discipline, culture, or family does. It is hard to see this because we are all steeped in the same beliefs. Usually the assumptions can only be seen retrospectively. Only a hundred years ago it was generally believed in the West that masturbation caused insanity. Many psychiatric hospitals used metal devices which were locked over the genitals to stop masturbation. Almost everyone believed what to us now is an extraordinary idea. What will they say when they look back in a hundred years time at present psychotherapy?

Going beyond victim–consciousness highlights the meeting point between psychotherapy and spirituality. For if we believe we are nothing more than a number of parts (like ego and id, or mind and emotions) we will always feel a victim of one or other of them, e.g., "I can't help how I feel". . . . "My mind is always in the way". . . . If we believe, on the other hand, that there is some kind of transcendent power within us (whether we call it the "inner self" or God), then we never need feel victimized by a subdivision of ourselves or our past. The same applies to labeling. We can never avoid labeling altogether because language is based on labels. But we can choose to identify with the inner self of unlimited potential rather than with the limiting label. The innermost self can always transcend the divisions we create. The only valid rescuer becomes the inner strength that is already within us. Though we may suffer mental pain, we are never permanently damaged because the power of healing is already within us.

This book focuses on how to rid ourselves of the limiting beliefs that are in the way of an expanded vision of ourselves. It does not argue whether the expanded vision is "true" or not. When we see that whatever we believe becomes manifest in our lives, we might as well believe the very best. We learn to believe the best of ourselves and of others, not out of blindness to faults, but out of well-founded hope in creating the most positive self-fulfilling prophecies. Truly, as we change our minds, we change our world. We find that as we remove the old, dusty curtains of outworn beliefs, we are illuminated by a quality of light that we did not know even existed.

Part 1

▼

*B*ELIEF ANALYSIS

We would rather be ruined than change;
We would rather die in our dread
Than climb the cross of the moment
And let our illusions die.

—W. H. Auden

Chapter 1

▼

MIRACLES

THE POWER OF BELIEF

Throughout history there have been great stories of people who, despite all odds, succeeded in achieving their dreams. The strength of their beliefs seemed to carry them through impenetrable obstacles. Similarly, there are many stories of people blinded by narrow beliefs whose lives have been limited according to the confines of their minds.

The power of belief even extends to matters of life and death. When I was first studying psychiatry, I looked after a man whose wife had just left him. He became so depressed that he would sit motionless and mute, and on the rare occasions when he moved, it would take him literally three minutes to cross a room. He believed that his body was rotting inside and that he stank. He truly believed that the stench could be perceived by the people he avoided. He was sure that the end was near and, in fact, he wanted to die.

Within ten days of coming to the hospital, he was dead. Autopsy revealed multiple thromboses in his legs, and heart—it was as if his blood had simply stopped moving. His lungs, liver, and kidneys were riddled with seemingly unresisted infection. His belief in rotting and death turned out to be a dreadful self-fulling prophecy. I have never seen a case like this before or since and it is certainly unusual in the literature. There are many cases of depressed people believing they will die; they do not die. Perhaps their belief is not strong or deep enough. On the other hand, it is well-documented in other cultures that witch doctors and voodoo practitioners can cause death if the recipient of the curse believes they can.

People may die "exactly on schedule" after being told the time of their death by an authority they believe in, whether it's a witch doctor in Africa, or a modern doctor anywhere, answering the dangerous question: "How long do I have to live?" When a doctor tells a patient "You probably have six months," it can be a sentence of death. If the patient believes it, she might fulfill the belief to the day.

There are also many well-documented cases of people surviving diagnoses of "terminal" illness through their own belief. Niro Markoff Asistent describes in her book *Why I Survive AIDS* how through changes of self-concept and as a result of acting on these changes, the "impossible" occurred: her HIV positive test results became HIV negative. Several researchers have shown a correlation between hope or will-to-live and measurements of immune response. Summarizing the qualities of "exceptional patients" (those patients who can change a "terminal" illness either in quality or direction), Bernie Siegel, surgeon and author of *Love, Medicine and Miracles,* notes that such people refuse to be victims and succeed in maintaining a belief in their own inner healing power.

Quite often, beliefs about the body are not held consciously and may be highly symbolic. Colin Parkes, who worked at the Tavistock Institute in England, found that elderly wives or husbands are three times more likely to have a heart attack in the six months after losing their spouses than nonbereaved people of the same age. The hearts of the widowed seem literally to break.

Beliefs, whether conscious or hidden, whether direct or symbolic, have a powerful effect on our bodies and minds. Some writers view beliefs as a form of continual self-hypnosis. Some yogis in deep meditation (a form of self-hypnosis) can alter at will body functions that western medicine used to consider totally automatic, such as heart rate. In the same way, we hypnotize ourselves with less deliberate beliefs which over time change our bodies and our vitality. If a man believes "I am inadequate," he actually starts to feel weaker. It is a physical sensation. Then he says to himself, in effect, "Well, I must be inadequate because I feel so weak." The more he imagines himself as weak, the weaker he feels. This process is used positively in visualization techniques in which the body is pictured as healthy in order to cure an illness. O. Carl Simonton and Stephanie Matthews Simonton had considerable success using these techniques with people who had life-threatening diseases. In the Simontons' first published results, they treated 159 patients who had been told that their malignancies were medically incurable. On average, survival time was doubled compared to the national average. Four years later, 63 patients were still alive and of these, in over 40 percent there was no evidence of disease (22 percent), or else the tumors were in regression (19 percent).

Beliefs and Perception

These stories illustrate the potency of personal belief. If our beliefs can have such a powerful effect over the physical realities of our bodies, it is hardly surprising that our beliefs can also affect our minds and the way we perceive things. In fact, one way we maintain our limited beliefs is by perceiving the world in accordance with our beliefs.

In a well-known psychological research paper, by Wilson in 1968, three groups of people were asked to estimate the height of one particular lecturer. The first group was told that he was a professor, the second group that he was a lecturer, and the third group that he was a student. On average, the professor was estimated to be 5 inches taller than the student, even though they were both, in reality, the same person.

Belief affects perception similarly in the familiar experience of noticing that people look different when we like them and when we don't. If you believe that someone is horrible, then they start looking horrible to you. If you are in a battle with someone who has a spot on his chin, the spot seems to get bigger and bigger. Finally, you are so mad at him that all you see is a walking pimple. How we see and hear things is filtered through our beliefs until our perception fits our preconception (see chapter 4).

In another piece of research, subjects were asked to walk down an immensely long and completely dark corridor. They were asked to stop only when they could discern a red light marking the end of the corridor. One hundred percent of normal subjects claimed they saw a red light even though the experimenters had tricked them—there was no red light! This was a classical example of illusion created by expectation.

Belief and Interpretation

Not only our perception but also our interpretation of events is deeply affected by our beliefs. Suppose, for example, a man walks into a room of people that he knows; everybody is busy, however, and because of this, ignores him. As he has a tendency to believe that people don't like him, he starts to think, "Aha—they're not talking to me because they don't like me," and his belief seems to be confirmed.

Belief, Action, and Reaction

Once the belief seems to us to be true, we are likely to act on it. Our action creates a reaction which further confirms our belief according to the pathways of self-fulfilling prophecy (see chapter 5). The man who thinks his acquaintances ignored him because they didn't like him, retaliates or protects himself by ignoring them. If his coldness continues, it may well create a self-fulfilling prophecy—they begin to dislike him. In this way he has created his own reality. If, however, he believed in the first place that he was basically likable and that they were simply busy, then he might be perfectly friendly to them, in which case they would probably be friendly to him. He would have created a more pleasant reality.

Even when our actions are less obvious, our beliefs still affect others through our body language. The expressions in our faces, how we position our bodies, and our patterns of body tension all convey messages to other people (see chapter 6). Other people read the messages even though they are not conscious of them, and this then affects how they relate to us. Someone can walk into a room looking miserable, solemn, or sulky and people respond by keeping away. If that same person walks in with a bright smiling face, people will respond positively. It is unconscious and automatic.

The Tenacity of Belief

Once we hold a belief it tends to stick with us, unless we challenge it, for the rest of our lives. For example, a woman had a childhood in which she experienced her mother as angry and threatening. Over time she formed the belief: "The world is a threatening place." During her childhood her world was indeed a threatening place. As an adult, however, her belief was an out-of-date, though understandable, overgeneralization which had an enormous effect on the quality of her life. First of all, the old belief affected her perception and interpretation of events. Because of the strength of her belief and her oversensitivity to anger, her mind would often exaggerate the "threat signals" coming from others, or else she would misinterpret an innocuous phrase or facial expression as being angry or threatening. These misperceptions and misinterpretations would lead her to react to people with belligerence which would, of course, make people angry. In this way she continued to create her own reality based on her belief. This was amply supported by her own feelings: As she believed the world was threatening, she often felt frightened; because she felt frightened, she believed the world was threatening.

In such a way an initial belief can become a lifelong conviction. The tricky part is that we are often not aware of the connection because we are so used to living with it. This woman, for example, had never consciously thought "the world is a threatening place." Rather, it was an unchallenged assumption which caused her to react automatically with suspicion, irritability, or anger. Without her knowing it, this perpetuated a misconception and greatly limited the quality of her life.

These automatic or "preconscious" assumptions create automatic responses which can be counterproductive. For this reason, it is useful to know what our inner beliefs are. The first half of this book is designed to help notice and understand automatic, unchallenged beliefs. Some automatic beliefs are highly positive and beneficial. Those that are not, those that limit the quality of our lives, can be challenged and changed using the techniques described in the second half of the book.

Chapter 2

▼

FALSE CONVICTIONS

HOW WE CREATE LIMITING BELIEFS

The way we see the world is based on our senses, our language, our innate prejudices, and our personal history. These four *screens* or representations are always between us and what we perceive to be outer reality. We cannot help but experience the world through these distorting lenses.

Distortions of the Senses

There is no such thing as seeing the world "realistically," because our very sense organs and brain mechanisms are highly selective in the extent and quality of information they handle. For example, we can see wavelengths of light only between about 400 and 700 millionths of a millimeter. This is a tiny proportion within the vast band of electromagnetic waves of X-ray, gamma-ray, ultraviolet, visible light, infra-red, microwave, and radio wave. In other words, most electromagnetic information simply passes us by.

The small portion of the total electromagnetic spectrum that we are able to pick up is coded through our eye and brain into what we think we see. But other creatures with different coding systems will see "reality" differently. A goldfish can look through its bowl and see the infra-red remote-control beams that operate TVs and videos. If a goldfish took to burglary, it would have the advantage of being able to see the infra-red beam of an intruder alarm system.

The housefly has a flicker fusion frequency of 300 per second, which means it can separate 300 different images per second. The human flicker fusion frequency is comparatively very slow. A fly watching a film would see a series of still slides, while a fly watching TV would see the TV scanner building a picture twenty-five times each second. In one sense the fly on the wall has a more accurate picture of reality than we do.

Reality is truly in the eye of the beholder. Nowhere is this better exemplified than in the strange case of the disappearing crab spider. This spider hides itself from insects by changing color to match the petals of the flower in which it lies in waiting. However the spider is highly visible to birds, which have better visual discrimination. Even when camouflaged, the spider retains two bright red spots that are designed to frighten birds. Birds see these red dots and recognize the spider as dangerous. But insects cannot see this particular shade of red and so do not see the spider at all, and consider the flower harmless. Bird and insect each see reality according to their visual capacities, and the spider is content.

Our hearing, too, is limited by the capacity of our ears, which can hear only wavelengths between 20 and 20,000 cycles per second, and have limited sensitivity and discrimination. Elephants can come to each other's aid over huge distances by emitting infrasounds—sounds too deep for the capacity of the human ear. Some bats can detect a midge 20 yards away in total darkness by emitting ultrasounds (up to 200,000 cycles per second) and monitoring infinitesimal differences in the sounds bouncing back. This sonar effect can alert tiger moths, which scream back in ultrasound and jam the bat-sonar so that they can escape the sharp teeth of the bat. On the same night, a barn owl might catch a moving mouse in total darkness guided only by sound.

These examples illustrate the relativity of our senses. When you hear that a tsetse fly can smell the breath of a buffalo 2 miles away, you may not be envious, but it shows how different are the worlds sensed by different beings. Since much of what we believe tends to be based on trusting our senses, it reminds us to understand that our senses, for all their magic, are limited and highly selective encoders of information.

Distortions of Language

Richard Bandler and John Grinder tell of a Native American language in northern California called Maidu, which divides the basic color spectrum into three colors. In Maidu there is a name for red, a name for green-blue, and a name for what we would call orange-brown-yellow. In English the rainbow is usually seen as divided into seven colors. So in English a yellow object and a brown object will be seen as different, while in Maidu they are the same color. In physiological reality, the human being is capable of 7,500,000 discriminations of color between different wavelengths of light. So where we draw our lines between colors is arbitrary. Yet it is such dividing lines between things which are the basis of language. The divisions and generalizations of one language create a different picture of reality from the divisions and generalizations of another. An example is the number of divisions within an important concept of a culture: the Eskimos have many different words for different kinds of snow; in Sanskrit, the language of ancient India, there are over fifty words for "consciousness"; while in Luganda (one of the languages of Uganda spoken by the tribe of Baganda) there are over forty different words for *banana*. To them a *matoke* is a completely different thing from a *gonja*, while to Americans, they are both just bananas. No matter which language you speak, the divisions are matters of convention which determine how we organize our thoughts and how we classify the world. Once we have mastered our first language, we cannot help seeing the world through the limiting screen of our linguistic divisions.

Innate Prejudices

People are born with certain characteristic tendencies. For instance, some people are born more fearful than others; whatever happens in their history, they have a tendency to be nervous. Studies comparing identical twins reared together with identical twins reared apart, suggest that some aspects of personality (such as extraversion) are at least partially inherited. There are many cases of identical twins separated at birth who have no verifiable contact with each other, and who choose the same toothpaste brand, the same cigarettes, who make the same life choices at similar times in their lives, and who even call their children by the same names. Whatever the mechanism, it is clear that there are deep factors beyond this life's personal experiences that affect how we see and react to the world.

Physiological distortion, innate prejudice and linguistic distortion are hard to alter. All languages distort and it is difficult to change our eyes or our ancestors. Our own personal prejudices based on our experiences, on the other hand, are more easily amenable to change, and they account for much of our distorted view of the world. This distortion occurs because we automatically generalize from one experience to all experiences.

Generalization from Personal Experience

If you cut your hand with a knife it is normal to generalize: "Knives are sharp. It's a good idea to be careful with knives." Generalizations are usually completely automatic and many of them are very useful. Try, for instance, holding up one hand about a foot in front of your eyes and then, as you look at it, move it one foot farther away so that it is two feet from your eyes. For most people, the hand looks the same size at both distances. Some people find that the farther hand looks a little smaller. In fact, the images projected onto the retina at the back of the eye are very different: The image of the hand one foot away is four times the area of the image of the hand two feet away! The brain, automatically compensates, effectively making the farther hand larger so that it appears the same size as the nearer hand. This phenomenon is called *size constancy*. Imagine what it would be like if we didn't compensate—someone walking toward us would get bigger and bigger. There was a tribe of forest pygmies who had never seen a clearing and who had therefore never used distance vision, nor developed size constancy. When they were first introduced to a large clearing made by European explorers, they were amazed that the men in the distance were not only a strange color, but incredibly small.

For most people with experience of distance, size constancy is a completely automatic and useful generalization which makes more distant objects larger, so that their size seems constant at any distance. The problem with any automatic generalization, though, is that it only works when conditions are regular or expected.

A generalization about life is like a fixed compartment or a square box. If life does not fit the box, we distort it until it does. This is elegantly illustrated by the "Ames room" (page 32). Adelbert Ames was an American psychologist who was famous for building unlikely rooms. His "Distorted Room" had one side much longer and higher than the other, but the room was painted with such cunning that it looked like a normal rectilinear room when viewed from a particular point (see figure 2). Ames had been a painter and knew how to make perspective realistic; in the distorted room the actual image on the back of the eye was the same as that created by a rectilinear room, so it was natural for the brain to assume it was perceiving a normal room. In effect, the brain has made the generalization that whenever such an image ap-

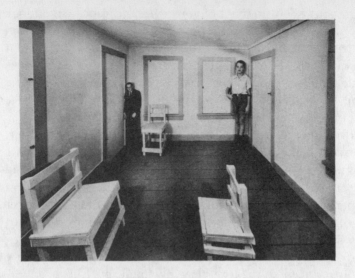

This boy and man are normal sized people and no trick photography has been used. Because the "distorted room" is so constructed that it casts the same image on the retina of the eye as a normal rectilinear room, we assume the room is a normal shape.

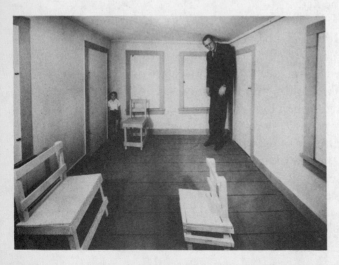

The same man and boy have changed places. The left corner of the room is actually twice as far away as the right corner.

(Both photos:Eric Schaal, *Life* Magazine © Time Warner Inc.)

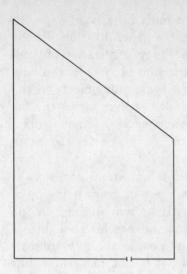

The actual shape of the room seen from above. The person at the far (upper) left corner is twice the distance from the viewing hole as the person at the far (upper) right corner.

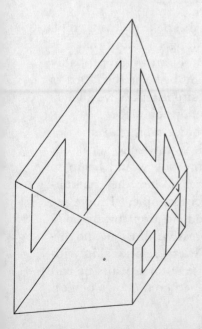

3-D drawing of Ames' distorted room. The ceiling actually slopes sharply upwards to the left while the floor slants downwards to the left. The far left hand corner is twice the height of the far right hand corner.

pears on the retina of the eye, it must be a box shape. In most cases this is a very reasonable generalization. In the particular case of the Ames room, the generalization of "rectangularness" does not fit, but it creates no problem so long as the room is empty. However, if you put objects in the room, weird things begin to happen: Anything in the far corner "shrinks" because size constancy no longer works, because the brain thinks that the far corner is the same distance away as the near corner.

This illusion neatly illustrates the limitations of generalization. Any generalization keeps a person from being open to the constant changes of reality. If we remain fixed on our belief, we will try to fit life into square boxes which will distort reality into illusion. Since life and people are so extraordinary, variable and unpredictable, it is not surprising that psychological generalizations are especially effective in distorting reality.

Generalizations from Parents

If a boy's father beat him whenever he spoke out as a child, the generalization that the father is dangerous and that it is therefore unwise to speak out in front of him would probably be useful. It is already a generalization because the father is almost certainly not dangerous in all situations. Nevertheless it is a reasonable and protective assumption.

If however the generalization becomes more extreme, for instance: "Men are dangerous and it is unwise to speak out in front of men in general," then the boy would begin to distort reality and to limit his choices. When the generalization becomes more extreme still, for example, "People are dangerous and I will never speak out in front of anybody again," then he lives with an oppressive illusion and his choices are crippled. It may affect every relationship with every man for the rest of his life. Quite automatically he will assume that men are threatening whether they are or not.

He will misinterpret benign expressions as hostile. He will even find a negative motive for a kind action: "He only gave me that because he wants to control me." In short, he cannot see reality because it is distorted by his belief.

However, the fact that he holds such a belief will not be apparent to him because he is so used to living with it that it becomes part of him; the generalization becomes an assumed truth about reality which is not normally questioned or even seen. It is as if he is looking through colored spectacles and forgetting, after a few months or years, that he is even wearing spectacles. Others may notice that his behavior is inhibited, shy, anxiety-ridden, or repressed without ever knowing the belief behind this behavior. He may then label himself with one of these adjectives, and believe that it is an unchangeable part of his character.

Generalization from experience is one of the main ways we learn and is probably both impossible and unwise to avoid. One of the first generalizations that we make as babies is that our parents are all-knowing and all-powerful models of perfection. This is not surprising when we consider that as babies we are completely dependent on our parents for physical care (food, cleaning, and physical warmth) and emotional care (stimulation, sensitivity, and emotional warmth). To a baby, the giant parents perform miracles: they can make things appear and disappear; they can create food and good feeling; they have the power to give or withhold anything the baby needs or wants.

From the generalization of the parent's perfection a number of assumptions naturally follow:

If my parent, who is perfect, disapproves of me, there . must be something wrong with me.

or

If my parent, who is perfect, rejects me or is cold to me, there must be something wrong with me.

or

If my parent, who is perfect, leaves me (even for a few days) there must be something wrong with me.

In all these situations, the child ends up with the conclusion "I'm a bad person," or "I'm not good enough" and, as we shall see (in chapter 7) this is one of the fundamental limiting beliefs of adult life.

Because the parent is seen as perfect, it is natural for the child to take the behavior of its parent as a model. Although children may later rebel against some of the overt attitudes of their parent, they will not usually rebel against the attitudes they have unconsciously copied. If there is a limitation on laughter or touching or assertion in the household, for example, the child will grow up with an automatic, unconscious belief that such a quality is to be restricted. Such limitations in people will usually stay with them for the whole of their lives, unless they challenge them in some way.

Copying is especially strong from boy to man and from girl to woman. A little boy looks up to his father as the model of masculinity and a little girl looks up to her mother as everything a woman should be. A father may not need to say to a boy: "It's babyish to cry"—the boy picks up his attitude and unconsciously copies, just as his own son will copy him. Thus the patterns of what is believed are passed on from generation to generation, and in this way cultural norms are maintained.

Generalizations from Culture and Country

Our country of origin has a strong impact on how we think. An example is the amount of assertiveness that is tolerated in Northern Europe as compared to America. In England it is not acceptable to be strongly assertive in many situations; when an American man comes to England he may be disapproved of because he is forthcoming. When an Englishman goes to America, he may also be disapproved of because he is reserved. The training is so ingrained, so automatic, and yet so strong that neither party realizes that a division is created by different behavioral beliefs. As long as we live in our own country, we don't see the idiosyncrasies of our behavior because everyone else behaves in the same way. We assume it is natural. It is only when we meet someone from another country that we think "Hmm, they're odd." One cause of culture shock is that when we change countries we are thrown into a new set of belief systems. If we do not understand the new codes and priorities of our host country, we can easily become frustrated and judgmental.

A story is told of a Dutch farmer in Portugal who produced ten times as much milk as his Portuguese neighbor who had the same area of land. When the Dutchman proudly researched the matter, he discovered that the reason for the low productivity next door was simply that the Portuguese man did not milk his cows very often because he was busy having a good time with his friends. The Dutch farmer thought the Portuguese farmer was stupid because he produced a tenth of the quantity of milk and wasted so much time. The Portuguese farmer thought the Dutch farmer was stupid because he spent all his time working and not having any pleasure.

The underlying belief of the Dutchman was based on centuries of Protestant work ethic. Although his parents were not religious and he never went to church, his automatic belief was that life *should* be hard, and that pleasure was relatively unnecessary. He learned these beliefs before he could consciously remember and therefore it became so much a part of him that he did not notice it or oppose it. The underlying belief of the Portuguese man was based on a mother who, like many Portuguese mothers of that time, gave him everything he wanted. Both beliefs created limitations— a choice of milk or honey, rather than both.

Generalizations from Class

Each social class carries an unwritten book of beliefs. In general, the older the society, the more deeply embedded is the class structure and the beliefs that go with it. Common lower class beliefs are:

I will never be successful.
I will always work for somebody else.
Mental work is not real work.
My boss does not really work and is using me.
It is normal to resent my boss.
I should do as little work as possible.
Real work is physical.

Most of these beliefs are held covertly: The person is not aware of these thoughts. An example is a friend of mine who saw himself as lower class and who had a hidden belief that he could not be successful. Although he was brilliant at business, every time he got near to what he saw as the top, he would drink or make an unusual mistake or find some way of throwing away his position.

Many researchers have studied the correlation between child-rearing habits and class. John and Elizabeth Newson noted that in the lower classes, authority was used more arbitrarily, while in the higher classes the child was more often given space for his or her own thoughts and feelings. Perhaps these results are related to the dislike of authority, the fear of independent thinking, and the avoidance of personal responsibility found more commonly in those brought up in a lower class environment.

A client of mine in Holland had not particularly thought of himself as lower class though his father was typically lower class in attitude. A few years ago he bought his own restaurant and bar and invested his money in a property in Amsterdam. He received much good advice from his friends about ways to increase customers, but kept making decisions that simply put people off so that every month he lost more and more money. Whatever good advice he got seemed to make absolutely no difference—in fact, it was hard to avoid a sense that he resented the good advice. He could make no headway until he was challenged on his own beliefs. Finally, after months of being stuck with his sense of failure, he admitted that he did not believe that it was possible for him to be successful in his own business. In fact, he did not believe he could ever be very successful at anything. It was not "fitting" for him to make much money and it was not "right" for him to employ somebody else.

Intellectually, he disagreed with every one of these beliefs, but the beliefs had been formed before the age of reason and questioning, when he was a little boy trying to emulate the seeming perfection of his father. He suddenly realized that if he gave up any of these beliefs he would feel terribly disloyal to his father whom he loved dearly. The sense of disloyalty caused him great anguish even though his father had been dead many years. As these thoughts and feelings came to light, he realized he had been loyal to some limited ideas of his father, not the spirit of his father. His loyalty to these ideas had cost him a great deal of freedom. From these realizations, he felt freer, and within months his business was profitable.

Generalizations on Gender Behavior

Men and women, even those who see themselves as liberated, are often trapped in belief systems about their sex. For example, it is generally more acceptable for a man to be aggressive, while it is more acceptable for a woman to cry. Though they may challenge these ideas intellectually, it is difficult to transcend them. Not being assertive or not being tender becomes an ingrained pathway of behavior.

Many therapists have the experience that men are just as capable of tenderness and women are just as capable of assertion. Tough, taciturn men who have never allowed themselves to "break down" feel enormously relieved to be able to cry without restraint and to be openly tender with those they love. The only thing that has really broken down is their old limiting belief of what a man is.

Women who have held back their opinions for years, suddenly find they have a powerful voice and feel worthy of being listened to. Both find pleasure in discovering and liberating another side of themselves, previously hidden behind a limiting belief.

Men are supposed to be better at math, driving, logic, and physics, while women are supposed to be more compassionate, artistic, intuitive, and nurturing. While any of these attributes may hold true for an individual, as generalized beliefs they have prevented thousands from enjoying their potential.

Generalizations from Body Image

Many people have discovered how hard it is to change their body image even when they have changed their body. If a boy was small and bullied at school, for example, even if he later grew to six feet four, he may still somehow think of himself as small. Rationally, of course, he knows he is not small, but somehow he sees himself as small or he acts small. He is still carrying around the old belief that says: "I'm little, people are going to hurt me." If you have ever tried dieting, you know that even if you succeed, it is hard to believe that you have succeeded. If you lose weight and look in a mirror, you may find that you look exactly the same, because your body image has not adjusted and alters your perception of the image in the mirror. Then when you see that you do not look any different, it is easy to lose hope and start eating again. It is actually harder to change your belief about your body than it is to change your body.

Generalizations from Education

Children are strongly influenced by each other, and peer-beliefs spread through classrooms. If a boy escapes the home lesson that it's unboyish to cry, he will probably get it at school. Students may also be very influenced by their teachers' attitudes. Many adults have told me how their thinking or their life changed (either negatively or positively) from the input of a teacher. One man had been treated with such sarcasm by a teacher that he had decided it was unwise to speak out his ideas; this belief persisted as a generalized reticence in all groups or meetings.

Most professionals have their underlying beliefs. Physicists enjoy exactitude, while sociologists believe in social causes. Academics believe in the pure pursuit of knowledge and sometimes look askance at businesspeople who believe in market forces. Doctors used to believe exclusively in the external force of disease, implying the helplessness of the patient and the curative power of the doctor. The patient's own capacity for self-healing was ignored. This medical model tended to make the doctor seem "above" the patient. Some doctors, without even realizing that they did so, treated their patients as if they were stupid. Many patients used to accept this attitude because it fit their beliefs that the doctor is better because he or she knows more. In this way a mutual agreement of superiority/inferiority went on for decades quite automatically and often unnoticed. But these beliefs can shift. Now, as the belief in the medical model changes and people see themselves as more and more involved in their own health and sickness, the doctor becomes more of an adviser or a helping partner.

Generalizations about Aging

It is impossible to escape a great deal of propaganda on our supposed loss of power as we get older. There are all kinds of ideas on what we can and can't do at certain ages—"I'm too young to . . ." or "I'm too old to. . . ." People see themselves as deteriorating as they get older. This seems to be an incontrovertible fact of life. But in reality, unless a person suffers from a disease such as Alzheimer's, apart from some loss of short-term memory (which isn't a problem as long as a notebook is available), most older people do not need to lose their mental powers. As for their physical powers, the body can be kept lithe, strong, and sexual into old age. What is required, though, is practice. If mind or body fall into disuse, they quickly atrophy. Ironically the most common reason for their disuse is the person's belief that their peak is past. If we believe we are going downhill, we tend to use our mind and body less, and if we use our body and mind less they deteriorate. Thus the belief becomes a prophecy.

With each of these beliefs, we learn that only this much is possible. Usually, no one actually says this, but by observation of what we see in the examples around us, we receive the repeated warnings: "Do not expect too much"; "You cannot do that"; "You cannot have that"; "You cannot be that."

Occasionally we meet somebody, an unusual person, who seems able to transcend the usual barriers, and we say to ourselves: "That's an exceptional person" or "That's a great man" or "That's a great woman." In this way we can discount our own possibilities and our own greatness by assuming the unusual person to be special.

Why, you might ask, do we hold on to such limiting beliefs even when, in some cases, we are fully aware that they make us smaller than we are? This question takes us to the next chapter.

Chapter 3

▼

GREAT LIMITATIONS
THE ADVANTAGES OF LIMITING BELIEFS

A major part of psychotherapy and psychoanalysis has been directed to understanding the history of people's conditions. In the last chapter this was described in terms of creating generalized beliefs. But understanding the history, even when combined with cathartic release of feeling, is not enough to liberate us or change our beliefs. Far more important is understanding why we hold onto our beliefs even when we know full well that they limit us and make us unhappy. Once we know how they have such a hold on us, then we can challenge them.

The danger of focusing on history is that it gives us an acceptable reason for perpetuating the limiting belief. Once you say to yourself: "Well, I am like this because this and this happened to me," you have not only given yourself a fixed limit, you have also given yourself a reasonable excuse for that limit, so it becomes more acceptable to you. There are so many people who understand their problems and the origin of their problems, but who cannot seem to change their everyday life.

Once we see that our beliefs, even the most limited ones, confer advantages on us, we have a chance of tackling them seriously. When I worked with alcoholics I would always ask: "What does drinking give you?" Some would offer many reasons, such as "It makes me relax," or "It gives me relief from feeling lonely," or "It's the only way I can feel okay enough to talk to people," or "It stops the pain." With those people, I would know there was at least some chance for them to stop drinking.

If they answered: "Nothing—it is ruining my life," I would reply, "There must be some advantage for you—otherwise you would not continue." If there was a constant denial of any advantages, I would know there was little chance of a successful recovery because they were not facing the reality of the temptation. Likewise, each limiting belief is an addiction to a way of thinking and being. If we do not face the reality of why it's tempting to keep the belief exactly as it is, we are unlikely to be realistic in changing it. We use our beliefs to make us look good (and others look comparatively bad). That is the *ego advantage*. Our fixed beliefs give us an illusion of safety, a sense of excitement, less responsibility, and less work. What's more, they help us predict the uncertainties of life, sometimes with surprising accuracy.

The Ego Advantage

Somehow, with great dexterity of mind, any belief, however narrow, can be converted into a personal superiority. We have an extraordinary capacity to flatter ourselves. Take the situation of the man who has difficulty in crying or being tender: It is usually much easier for him to think to himself "I'm a man"; "I'm not weak"; "I'm strong"; "I can take it," than it is for him to admit his own difficulty with, or even disapproval of, tenderness. It is easier to say: "I know what's best for me" than to admit you are frightened of change because you have an old belief that change is dangerous. It is easier to consider "I am above money" or "money is dirty" than to face the possibility that you cannot successfully sell goods because you do not really believe you are good enough. Quite often underlying beliefs are lightly hidden beneath a sugar-coating of ego, which makes the belief palatable. It is this coating that initially disguises the belief. With it, the worst liabilities can become marvelous assets, for example:

"I'm unassertive"	becomes	"I'm good-natured."
"I can't keep to a task"	becomes	"I am very free."
"I depend on others"	becomes	"I'm loving."
"I exploit others"	becomes	"I'm astute."
"I am vindictive"	becomes	"I believe in justice."
"I avoid work"	becomes	"I am clever."

At the same time as we convert our limitation into a virtue, we judge others who do not share our limited belief. The man who has difficulty being tender calls the man who weeps "soft." The woman who is frightened of change calls the person who changes freely "inconsistent" or "untrustworthy." The man who cannot sell his product thinks of the successful salesperson as a "money-grabber."

In these ways, by making ourselves and all who agree with us superior, and those who disagree with us inferior, we create divisions, strife, disharmony, and suffering. The process is identical whether the initial belief is about ourselves or others, because whatever we believe about others is based on what we think of ourselves. If a man believes others are selfish, for example, the obvious ego advantage is that he can see himself as not selfish by comparison and therefore above them. But on a slightly deeper level, he focuses on the selfishness in others only because he is selfish himself—but he calls this selfishness in himself "good competitive spirit." The ego will make an advantage out of anything! This connection between beliefs about self and others works through the mechanism of projection described by many philosophers and later by Freud. It is another way of saying that we cannot help but to see others through the screen of our own limited beliefs.

Sometimes the ego advantage and the judgment of the other are not apparent. A person may not be consciously aware that he disapproves of the human body and may have no conscious thoughts of being "above" others who are more physical. His belief may be expressed by avoiding physical activity and contact or through difficulty enjoying a physical appetite for food or sex. A person may not be aware that she is "above money" but perhaps finds herself reluctant to deal with financial issues.

The judgment of the other often goes underground. For example, because ideas about men and women are fast expanding, the man who has difficulty crying might also believe that it is unacceptable to call a man "soft" because he cries. In this case the overt judgment is inhibited and such a man, seeing another man cry, is left with a feeling of disgust, discomfort, or of wanting to get away as soon as possible. He cannot be comfortable with a crying man until he has, in some way, dealt with his belief about what a man is.

With some beliefs, it is hard to imagine that there could be an ego advantage. Take the belief "I'm a failure, I'm not good." How could that boost the ego? The answer is that there really is a pride in failing successfully. The implied statement, "Look at me. I've done it again" is a request for recognition. The failure prides herself on the cynical knowledge that it's not really worth trying and that she is the one that is wise enough to know that effort is senseless. The failure prides herself on being special. She judges successful people as uncaring (about failures like her) or as fools for playing a game which will eventually end in no good. People are proud of their greatest limitations. It requires humility to let go of the pride invested in a belief.

When it is hard to understand what the ego advantage could be, it is a useful exercise to ask ourselves what is our judgment on people who we see as different from us. For example, when I asked a man who held the belief "I am unintelligent," what that did for his ego, he looked at me as if I were stupid. "So what is your judgment of intelligent people?" I asked.

"They waste their time thinking rather than doing. They're pie in the sky, they're not down to earth. They're weak," he said.

"Anything else?"

"Yes, impotent."

"So, what about your ego? How are you superior?"

"I'm a doer. I'm down to earth. Strong, potent." He smiled.

The flip side of our judgment is our pride. Rationally this man knew that intelligent people were not necessarily weak or impotent. He had met strong, potent, intelligent people before. But at a level just beneath the rational, at the preconscious level, his pride in his limitation was evident. He smiled when he recognized a superior attitude he had not been aware of before.

The Illusion of Safety

As long as we stay within the confines of our belief systems, we are afforded a feeling of security. There is no need for the anxiety of uncertainty because any new input will be rejected before it is effective, or else distorted to fit the parameters of our beliefs.

This remains true even when our beliefs appear to cause us danger. For example, women who believe "men are violent" or "I deserve to be mistreated by a man" tend to choose violent men over and over again. Although they are genuinely fearful and do not like pain or humiliation, the "old situation" provides a paradoxical sense of security.

The familiarity of a repeated situation, created by a belief, somehow feels like home. We know the score. We know the rules of the game. Spiritual teachers say that it's necessary to repeat situations until we master what we need to learn. There is certainly a curious attraction to repeat experiences that fit in with a limited belief, and this continues until we learn to change the belief.

A woman told me about her belief that she was "a panicky person." She tended to panic over "little things." I asked her what advantage this belief gave her. She looked blank at first, then gave me a quizzical look, and then answered. "Familiarity, I suppose," she said. "It's strange to say this, but there's a kind of comfort in being in a state I know so well, even though it's panicky. This sounds even more strange," she added, "but when I panic, I don't need to worry—I don't need to worry about important things."

When we analyze, challenge and give up a belief system, it does, initially, make us anxious. It opens us to new possibilities and more variety. We do not know where life is going to lead us. It takes courage to challenge our beliefs seriously.

Excitement

There is also a certain kind of addictive excitement in repeating situations, even when they are limited. A certain woman always chose tough, taciturn men with jutting jaws, just like her father. Even after she had been unhappily married to six of them, she was tempted by a seventh. "He is so exciting," she said. Though she knew her pattern well and understood its origin from her therapy, the excitement was too tempting to be denied. Other men, who could have helped her break this pattern, seemed boring. The old mental pattern seems to have a life of its own and manufactures feelings which seem to confirm its desirability.

Each mental pattern carries a certain energy of attachment. The repeat situation carries an excitement which tempts us very strongly to go ahead and do it, once again. This can be so even when the situation is in other ways very painful. It is another reason why men and women choose partners who abuse them terribly, and do this over and over again.

Sometimes the only way out of this repetitive cycle is to try out a new situation even though it seems, at first, completely unattractive. The new, less limiting pattern is often an acquired taste. For this reason, new unlimiting beliefs need to be practiced in action (see chapter 17).

Less Responsibility, Less Work

Holding a limiting belief about ourselves or others exonerates us from action. If you believe you are shy, for example, then you have a reason not to make contact with anybody. If you are a woman who believes "men are brutes," then you have a reason not to try to be tender toward a man—and it's his fault. If you believe that you are not worthy of happiness, then you do not need to do the hard work of arranging happiness in your life. It is easier to be inactive and miserable. Whether our beliefs are about ourselves or others makes little difference. With great creativity the mind can translate any limiting belief into a reason to take less responsibility and do less work. For example:

"I am not a lovable person"	I can be a slob
"I'm a limited person"	It is not worth trying
"I could never have that"	I do not need to bother to try to get it
"I don't have much to give"	I don't have to give
"I'm weak"	I won't do it
"I'm thin/fat"	I don't need to bother to look good
"I'm ugly"	I don't need to try to make relationships
"I'm too old"	I don't have to exercise any more
"I'm a bad friend"	I don't have to make the effort of friendship

"I'm not important"	I don't have to work to succeed
"I'm a total failure"	I don't have to work at all
"People are basically bad"	I can be bad
"They (any authorities) know more than I do"	I don't need to risk trusting my opinion
"They don't understand"	I don't have to try to make contact
"People are out for what they can get"	I don't have to be generous

If we are leading our lives in a narrow way in accordance with a narrow belief, then there are not so many things we have to do. We have less responsibility, or less response-ability. If you believe you had a terrible mother, for example, and you write off half the human race by believing "women are terrible" then you have a reason not to *respond* to women. It is as if you wipe them out, you only really deal with men, and your response-ability is halved.

Any belief that you have about yourself, any fixed label, carries the implication that you are a victim. You may consider yourself to be, for example, too tense, too inhibited, uncreative, boring, bad-tempered, over-dependent, untalented, or unlucky. Any label we place on ourselves holds a power over us. For once we believe we "have" a characteristic, we behave in accordance with that characteristic, and prove that the characteristic is true. It also proves that we are victims and that we do not have free choice. For a man who considers himself to be shy, for example, the belief in shyness will create a feeling of dread of meeting people. He will imagine the discomfort and perhaps failure of an awkward meeting. Focused this way on his own difficulties during the meeting, he will not move out with interest or curiosity towards the other. This makes the meeting awkward, and thus acts as one more confirming example of his inability. He can then say to himself: "You see I am shy—I can't help it."

It takes work and effort to expand our beliefs. There is

also work involved in holding to a fixed belief. The difference is that holding to a belief involves the routine repetitive work of following a well-worn path, while expanding or changing a belief involves the creative and exhilarating work of forming a new path.

Accurate Predictions

Most people like to know what is going to happen to them. The advantage of a fixed limited belief is that it appears to be verified over and over again, and therefore provides a sense of satisfied prophecy and certainty. The mechanisms of prediction are as follows:

First, our interpretation and perception of events are distorted to fit into our system of belief. If you don't like somebody, for example, they look uglier and your interpretation of their motives is tainted with suspicion.

Secondly, we selectively remember and perceive events that fit our beliefs, and selectively forget and ignore events that do not fit. If you think the world is an awful place, you will notice and focus on the one dead leaf in a bunch of beautiful flowers.

Thirdly we make life choices that fit our belief. For example, if you are a woman who believes "men are brutes," you will have a tendency to marry brutes. If you are a man who believes women are manipulative, you will tend to choose manipulative women.

Fourthly, implicit in every belief is a self-fulfilling prophecy. I have always found that there is a rational explanation to how a belief gets translated into reality. For the woman who believes "men are brutes," the self-fulfilling prophecy goes something like this: "He's a brute; therefore I resent him and I'll never be vulnerable." His reaction to her resentment and invulnerability is to become invulnerable himself and hard: a brute.

The self-fulfilling prophecy of the man who believes

"women are manipulative" goes something like this: "Women are manipulative, therefore I won't trust her." Because she feels treated with suspicion, she keeps her distance from him. Intimacy therefore disappears and they are left with a relationship of emotional dishonesty and mental manipulation. The part she takes in that process proves that "women are manipulative."

Of course, people are hardly ever aware of the mechanism behind their self-fulfilling prophecy. Events happen that seem to vindicate the belief—the man *does really* act like a brute, and the woman *does really* manipulate, and both are unaware of the little strings *they* pulled to create or manifest that reality in the other. In the same way the shy person is unaware that he created the awkwardness in order to hold to his belief.

We will do almost anything to keep our beliefs intact. Our sense of power and individuality is bound up with our beliefs, even though, if we examine our beliefs, the vast majority are not really ours—they are somebody else's. We like reality to conform to our ideas, even when our ideas are limited. We are proud of being right and we will make sure we *are* right even if it means sacrificing pleasure. It takes humility to give up being right about a trifle, it takes courage to give up predictability, and it takes curiosity to look beyond what we think we know.

This section looks at some of the mechanisms through which beliefs are maintained and converted into reality. The next chapter looks at these maintenance mechanisms in more detail. By analyzing our beliefs in such great detail, we see the phenomenal manipulations required to maintain a limited belief—and then the belief begins to lose its power.

Chapter 4

ADAPTING THE WORLD
BELIEF MAINTENANCE

*I*t is more work to maintain a belief than a car. The difference is that we don't usually notice the work on a belief because it is done automatically. There are a number of clever strategies for maintaining beliefs even when they obviously (to someone else) disagree with reality. It is amazing what we will do to keep our precious beliefs intact.

Life Choices

To some extent we choose situations and people that fit our preconceptions. A woman who believes that change is dangerous will choose secure relationships and secure working situations so that she does not have to test out change. A man who believes he is stupid will choose manual work or repetitive mental work requiring little creativity or initiative—in this way he never develops his mind and is able to retain his belief.

People assiduously avoid situations and evidence which might contradict their beliefs. This can be very subtle. Take the man with the belief "men are dangerous." Let's say that he *does* meet men who are kind and generous. He may accurately perceive their kindness and he may be quite clear, intellectually, that of course not all men are dangerous, that some are actually quite nice. However the fixed belief has become attached to an equally fixed habit of avoiding speaking out in front of men. And since he never risks speaking out, he never really tests whether men are dangerous or not. "Yes, he is kind," he might think to himself, "but I wonder what he would be like if I let him know my true opinion?" The belief is never really challenged. In this case the life choice is not to avoid kind men but to avoid challenging any man. In such situations, the choice is hardly ever consciously realized. This does not mean it is deeply buried in our unconscious; rather, the behavior has simply become as automatic as breathing.

On a subtler level still, we attract situations which fit our beliefs through our facial expression and body language. For example, a woman with wide-open eyes, slightly caved-in chest, raised shoulders, and shaking hands is proclaiming through her patterns of muscular tension and the stance of her body: "I'm scared—protect me." This message acts as an aphrodisiac on all those men who believe "I am the great protector." Like moths drawn to the light, these men will pursue her, one after another.

Beyond the powerful expressions of body language, it is possible that thoughts, especially thoughts combined with feelings, have an effect on attracting the ones we want to meet. Though no wave or any other form of thought transmission has ever been measured, the empirical evidence for the effect of thoughts is interesting (see chapter 6, page 77).

Justification from the Past

The history of the origins of some of our beliefs has been the stuff of psychotherapy and psychoanalysis for years. Unfortunately it is all too easy to use this information as the supreme justification for keeping our limits. Focusing on things that went wrong in the past adds fuel to our belief and reinforces our limitations. Take for example the belief that being assertive is too dangerous. A woman with this belief may have been brought up in an atmosphere where little assertiveness was expressed. Alternatively, she may have been brought up in a home atmosphere in which assertiveness was expressed very negatively, by a violent drunken father. Such explanations from the past can be useful to *understand* the belief. But it is all too easy for them to become *justifications* for the belief. Once the belief is fixed, moments of positive assertion from the past are selectively screened out from the memory.

If you believe, "The best part of my life is now over," you may have powerful and emotive supporting memories for this idea, for example:

"After my mother had children, she gave up work completely and resented us for her lost ambition—she never got over this."

"When my father was forty-five, he was disappointed about his work and thought it was too late for him to change."

"My grandfather was alone and miserable as an old man."

At the same time, you will almost certainly have screened out the memories of friends, aunts, uncles, or acquaintances who lived fulfilling lives well beyond the age at which you believe "the best part of my life is over."

We mold, select from, exaggerate, or distort the past to make it support our current belief. The process is so automatic, however, that we do not even realize our own bias. When negative aspects of the past are accentuated, so is our belief in the immutability of our limits.

Justification from the Present

Similarly, evidence from the present is carefully selected, molded, or exaggerated to fit our beliefs. If you believe "change is dangerous," your mind will automatically be on the lookout for changes in ourselves and others that go wrong. Then, as soon as there is an intimation of an unplanned result, the mind jumps in—"Aha, look what happened when she tried to change. . . ." Meanwhile, ten other examples of positive change have simply been ignored.

SELECTIVE EVIDENCE

Our minds are tuned by our selective attention to all phenomena that fit our beliefs while we avoid all phenomena which contradict our beliefs. If you believe that "people are out for what they can get," you will notice every moment of selfishness and ignore or forget any moments of genuine care. If you believe that you are unlovable, you will selectively focus on the times when relationships go wrong or you are rejected.

A woman who held the belief, "Happy moments are always ruined," discovered that she was actually not aware of happiness until it went wrong. For example, she had three-quarters of an hour of "great" tennis after which her hip started to hurt. Immediately she said to herself: "Ah, you see, there it is again, as soon as things go well, something goes wrong." But she was not aware of the great tennis until *after* her hip hurt. In the first three-quarters of the hour, she had screened out the pleasure. In the last quarter hour she had focused on the pain and contrasted it (bitterly) with the selective memory of pleasure. All these automatic maneuvers highlighted her belief that pleasure is always ruined.

One of the most obvious examples of selective evidence can be seen on people's bookshelves. Look at someone's selection of books and you can usually diagnose a few belief systems. It's not so much that their bookcase supports their books, it's their books that support their case. The selection of books fits in with the broad ways in which the world is seen, giving the owner an impression of solid evidence for his beliefs.

An example of this occurred in the long debate on whether the syndrome of schizophrenia was primarily hereditary or environmental. Scientists and psychiatrists with a hereditary point of view wrote review articles showing hereditary predominance; scientists with a more environmental point of view concluded that the environment (especially the family) was more influential. Part of the difference was evidenced by selecting out papers and literature that fitted their point of view. Part of the difference was also created by interpreting exactly the same evidence—even identical figures—in different ways to fit the preconceptions. For example, using a 0.8 percent figure for the incidence of schizophrenia in the general population and a 12 percent figure for the chance of schizophrenia occurring in the offspring of one schizophrenic parent, a conclusion can be emphasized in two different ways: the environmentalist can say that the offspring have only a 12 in a 100 chance of being similarly affected; the genetecist can say that having a schizophrenic parent increases the child's chances of being schizophrenic by fifteenfold.

Selective inattention is the technique, usually quite unconscious, of not noticing what is inconvenient for the belief. For example, not noticing someone's concern when you believe that people don't like you, or not noticing anything beautiful when you're in a bad mood.

Sometimes inconvenient events *are* noticed but later denied. Such denial may also be unconscious—it is as if the memory has simply been erased. I experienced this when I was a general practitioner. Laboratory and X-ray results had just come back on a man with respiratory problems; cancer of the lung had been confirmed. I told him the diagnosis. Naturally he was shocked. We spent twenty minutes talking about what the diagnosis meant for him, and his fear of dying. As he was very nervous about his wife's reaction, I suggested that he and his wife come in the following day so that we could talk together. When they arrived the next day, it was clear that he had not told his wife anything. Then, to my surprise, I realized that *he* had absolutely no knowledge that he had cancer or any other serious illness. The information had apparently vanished.

DISTORTION OF PERCEPTION AND INTERPRETATION

This is the automatic technique of kneading contradictory perceptions until they fit reasonably into the belief. A kind voice can be perceived as bitter, goodnatured laughter as sarcastic, a questioning frown as disapproving, a loving look as controlling. Once we form a generalized belief, we view the world through the prism of our preconception, and the preconceived notion takes precedence over reality. Anyone with children knows that if a child believes that he or she will not like a certain food, no amount of saying "but you haven't even tried it" will make a difference. When the mind is made up that the food will not taste good, it will not taste good.

We adults are pretty well the same, only better at hiding it from ourselves. One of the examples that most people can relate to is our ability to change our perception of someone's face according to what we believe about that person. If we think a woman is angry, we can make her face appear angry by a simple reinterpretation of visual data. When we love someone, they look beautiful. When we hate them, they look ugly.

If you believe that you are getting ill or likely to get ill, the smallest physical discomfort, which might normally be ignored, becomes reinterpreted as the herald of illness. Your perception of the discomfort can also become exaggerated into pain, so that your belief in illness is supported. Perception of discomfort and pain is very closely related to state of belief. Research on people's subjective feeling and tolerance of pain shows a close relationship between anxiety (about illness, death, or loss of function, for example) and the severity of subjective sense of pain.

Pleasure, too, depends on our beliefs. Those who hold the old Protestant belief that pleasure is wrong, of minor importance, or not for this world, diminish their perception of their own bodily pleasure. This usually occurs through the mechanism of muscular tension—bodily pleasure requires a certain degree of muscular relaxation to be experienced fully (see chapter 16).

THE RATIONALIZATION OF CONTRADICTORY EVIDENCE

This is a misinterpretation of the motives for an action in order to uphold a belief. If you believe "Nobody cares about me," and if you meet somebody who genuinely does care (and you are able to perceive this through the screen of your disbelief), you might then say to yourself: "Well, he's only being nice to me so that he can get his own way in the end." Rationalization is the last ditch attempt, when all else has failed, to make the aberrant world fit the confines of a belief system.

If a man believes "women are untrustworthy," any action whatsoever that she takes can be interpreted in that light. Let's say that she is generous, without ulterior motive. This can be sensed partly by the look in her eyes, the color in her face, and the tone of her voice. It is not that these signs are consciously computed as evidence, but that we are all equipped with an automatic unconscious understanding of the basic body language that constitutes genuineness. In the face of this evidence, in order for the man to maintain his belief in her untrustworthiness, he has three possible strategies. He can ignore his perception altogether (selective inattention); he can alter his perception, for instance, making her voice sound hard (distortion of perception); or he can misinterpret her motives (rationalization). He might, for example, tell himself, "Those dewy eyes were turned on because she's trying to seduce me so that she can get something out of me." He may be totally convinced that his interpretation is right. If he acts on this conviction (for instance by rejecting her), her voice, face, and eyes are likely to get harder in defense of herself. As soon as she is defensive in this way, he senses it—accurately, this time—and now has a reason not to trust her. He has created his own reality. This process can all take place in the space of thirty seconds without a single word spoken.

Justification by Imagination of Future Results

Most beliefs carry with them the assumption that they will go on forever. The insomniac thinks "I will never be able to sleep well." An overweight person thinks, "I may be able to lose weight from time to time but it will always come back— I will never have a beautiful body."

The projection of the belief into the future is maintained by imagination. A future picture is visualized or a total scenario imagined. The imagined result then has a powerful effect on our present capacity. Such projections into the future can be put to conscious, positive use, as has been done by many athletes. One of the reasons for the success of the East German athletes in the Olympics was their systematic use of visualization techniques. They had been taught to imagine themselves, in great detail, running every moment of the race until they felt the tape on their chests as they won. The power of visualization has been harnessed in techniques of self-healing and many have ascribed their recovery from "terminal" illness to determined visualization. It is also one of the tools that can be used to change limited belief systems (see page 175).

Used negatively, the effect of imagination is no less powerful. In the case of "shyness," a person imagines what will happen when she meets someone: awkwardness, being tongue-tied, looking like a fool. Her imagination feeds her feeling of shyness and both imagination and feeling vindicate her belief and give it the power to affect her life.

The Manufacture of Supporting Feeling

Our beliefs may create powerful feelings within us. Someone who believes that people are just selfish and competitive generates a feeling in himself of being threatened, or else feels aggression related to the need to compete first and grab what he can. These feelings can occur in the absence of any external competition. Yet because he trusts his feelings, his sense of being threatened or feeling competitive seems to prove that his belief is true. If he believes "they are against me," his belief will create a feeling of uneasy suspicion. Again, because he tends to trust his feelings, his suspicion seems to prove his case.

Many schools of psychotherapy have emphasized the importance of trusting our feelings. In part, this was a healthy reaction to too much analytical thinking, and expression of feeling was seen as liberating from the restrictions of the mind. From this developed a psychotherapeutic belief system that feelings are primary or more important. But many feelings are no more than emotional representations of the restrictions of the mind. There is an old story from the East of a man who mistook a piece of old rope for a snake and felt great fear. His feeling was generated by his misinterpretation of reality. The feelings generated by racial prejudice work similarly. A person has to have the prejudice—the misinterpretation—before he or she can feel the hate. Feelings are easily manufactured from attitudes. It is useful to be able to discriminate between a feeling that is a dramatic reflection of a limiting belief system and a feeling that is a valuable or wise reaction.

The power of emotion to validate belief is far-reaching and often deceptive. A woman with the belief "I don't deserve much, I'm an inferior person," will generate feelings of inferiority. She feels lower, smaller, and may carry her body in such a way that she looks smaller (rounded shoulders, slumped head, retracted jaw). The feeling of being lower than others, the feeling of inferiority has a strong effect over months or years. In effect, she says to herself: "Well, if I feel inferior, I must *be* inferior," and her belief is once more confirmed and deepened.

Often, the feeling generated by a belief will contribute to a self-fulfilling prophecy. Racial prejudice is one of the clearest examples, where the feeling of hatred generated by a limiting belief about people creates a violent reaction that vindicates the belief. Mahatma Gandhi and Martin Luther King, Jr., deliberately set out to break this vicious circle by their example of nonviolence (see chapter 9).

Even when feelings are not openly expressed they may still create self-fulfilling prophecies through others' reactions to facial expression or body language, as in the example of the woman whose body said, "I'm scared—protect me." In other words, feelings, whether openly expressed or not, can alter not only our perception of reality, but also reality itself.

▼

Chapter 5

I TOLD YOU SO

THE SELF-FULFILLING PROPHECY

*O*ur beliefs are supported by our selective interpretation of the past, our selective view of the present, and our selective projection into the future. All these evidences constantly tell us:

My life was limited
My life is limited
My life will be limited.

Past, present, and future are misperceived and reinterpreted to fit our beliefs. In this way our perception of reality is distorted, but reality, as seen by someone else, remains unchanged.

This chapter now goes on to show that we also actually *change* reality in accordance with our beliefs! This is the process of self-fulfilling prophecy. Most prophecies have three basic stages;

Belief creates action
Action creates reaction or result
Reaction or result confirms belief.

For example, a man with the *belief:* "People don't really care," will often take the *action* of keeping his distance from people and minimizing his involvement. Their commonest *reaction* to this is to minimize their involvement too. In this way, his belief is *confirmed*—people, in his world, don't really care.

A woman who believes that lack of sleep ruins the next day will tend to worry about the next day after a poor night's sleep. This worry prevents her getting fully involved in the day's activities, and this results in greatly limited enjoyment and satisfaction. Therefore, "Lack of sleep ruins the next day." When people give up the belief that a certain number of hours sleep is required to feel good the next day, they find that they are not so affected by the amount of sleep they have. But it is a difficult belief to give up because of the effect of the self-fulfilling prophecy, which seems to prove, beyond all shadow of doubt, that the belief is a true reflection of reality.

Some beliefs can be divided into many components. For instance, "I am a helpless victim of circumstance" may have the following components (among many others):

"I cannot really change my life"
"I cannot do what I want"
"I am at the mercy of negative experiences in my past"
"I am at the mercy of unconscious drives"
"I nearly always have bad luck"

Each of these subsidiary beliefs has several possible self-fulfilling prophecies. An example of each follows:

"I cannot really change my life." Therefore I give up trying to make changes. Therefore I have little experience of changing. Since I tend to believe what I experience, it appears evident that I cannot really change my life.

"I cannot do what I want." So it seems there is no point in trying. Therefore I don't try, or at least not very hard. Therefore I don't succeed. So I cannot do what I want.

"I am at the mercy of negative experiences in my past." When similar situations arrive in the present I avoid them. My

avoidance is a result of past pain. Therefore it seems that I am at the mercy of negative experiences from my past.

"I am at the mercy of unconscious drives." Therefore I repress my impulses. They will then tend to get stronger or more distorted, so that when they do come out, they are more destructive. Therefore it seems that I am at the mercy of unconscious drives.

"I nearly always have bad luck." Because of this belief I tend to limit my enthusiasm and my eagerness to react. Therefore I will miss opportunities and people will respond less positively to me. Therefore I nearly always have bad luck.

All these self-fulfilling prophecies, when combined, seem to prove the belief in personal helplessness. Every belief has a strong potential to be materialized, vindicated or affirmed. This is even true of what we call *character*. Though character is merely a description of our habitual ways of acting, it gives the appearance of fixed reality because habits are difficult to change.

Psychological literature contains many systems of classifying character types. All classifications are relatively arbitrary; there are as many characters as there are infinite combinations of thousands of beliefs. Certain rather gross caricatures, however, are useful for stimulating thought, even though they hardly ever exist in pure form. The following division is taken from Alexander Lowen and John Pierrakos, the founders of bioenergetic therapy, adapted here to examine the prophecies that are fulfilled. Every classical personality is also a complex self-fulfilling prophecy.

The Dependent Personality Habit

The *dependent* type (sometimes called "oral" in psychoanalytical literature) looks to others to provide a sense of worth and emotional care. Her underlying preconscious belief is "nobody loves me," and this is combined with an inner sense of incapacity, weakness, and helplessness. Such a life stance creates a number of self-fulfilling prophecies. If she finds someone to depend on, she will begin to hate the caring partner as vehemently as the alcoholic hates the bottle—it is a constant reminder of her incapacity. When faced with such bitterness, combined with carrying the weight of a dependent, the caring partner is sooner or later going to react either by hating back or by leaving. Either way the dependent's belief is vindicated in objective reality: "Nobody loves me," and she is right—nobody does.

Her belief in her helplessness is fulfilled by her avoidance of effort, which results in her working far beneath her capacity, or else staying unemployed, either of which makes her feel helpless in that she is not in charge of her own destiny.

Her belief in her weakness is fulfilled by her avoiding physical effort, which enables her body to remain relatively weak. Her belief in her inability is fulfilled by her not trying, hence her lack of practice, and hence her continuing inability.

The Power-Play Personality Habit

This character type (also known as "psychopathic" in psychological literature) believes that life is about power, about who controls whom. This person sometimes has a childhood history of involvement in family politics, from which he generalizes that what matters is winning and that it is normal to use others for this end. This creates a self-fulfilling prophecy in this manner: "The only thing that matters is who has control. Therefore I will control you before you control me (because, of course, you are like me and want to control me)." The people who get controlled or maneuvered against are likely to react by defending themselves in some way. In other words, they start fighting back. As soon as they do this, the power-play man can say to himself: "Ah, you see, they're trying to control me as I knew they would. I told you, life is about power and control." His point is proven and his belief is strengthened.

The Seductive Personality Habit

The seductive personality is a variant of the power-play type. In psychoanalytic literature the male is sometimes known as the "Don Juan" type or else the "phallic-narcissistic character," while the female is known as the "hysterical personality." They, too, believe that life is about power and control. The difference is that their means of achieving power is through seduction and by being more attractive and desirable than others of the same sex. Classically, they do not deeply enjoy their sexuality but only use it as a means to the end of holding power over another.

The seductive woman holds the belief: "Men reject me, men hurt me, men do not love me." This may be a generalization from a belief about her father who she feels rejected her. It is rarely conscious and is covered with a statement of intended action which is also rarely conscious: "I will never let myself be hurt again; I will avoid intimacy by keeping the power; I will hurt him before he can hurt me; they (men) are going to suffer for what my father did." Thus she seduces and rejects man after man, never getting too involved herself. She proves that "men do not love me" because no man is ever given a chance to get near. She proves that life is a play of control, first by choosing men who play the game, and secondly because the man's reaction to the seductive power game is to try to win the game himself. So life becomes a play of who controls whom on the game board of sexual politics.

For the seductive man the process is identical: his attempted conquest of woman after woman proves his case that women do not love and that relationships are no more than a game of power. Both seductive men and women are intensely competitive with members of the same sex—often the competition is in attractiveness, desirability, and the number, or quality, of sexual conquests. Such competition, which gets in the way of intimacy, fulfills the belief that it is not possible to be intimate with someone of the same sex.

Change occurs through seeing, clearly, how the behavioral habit of seduction and competition fulfills the prophecy of the belief in lack of love and intimacy. When we see exactly how we sustain the habit, then we have more power to challenge it.

The Rigid Personality Habit

This character type asserts his own opinions, and stands up for himself with strength and determination. However, he tends to be inflexible and unfeeling, and sees life as rather fixed and limited. This creates a simple self-fulfilling prophecy. He says, in effect: "Life is rather limited. Since life is so limited, I don't think I'll get too involved" (either with external things or his own inner life). Since he's not too involved, he doesn't have very many exciting experiences. Therefore life, in his world, is limited.

The Good Behavior Personality Habit

The good behavior type has put a tremendous amount of energy into conforming. She relies on others' opinions and likes to obey the rules. Her underlying belief is: "I'm not good enough." We will see in chapter 7 that all limiting beliefs have a flavor of "I'm not good enough." In this character habit, however (unlike the other four mentioned), the flavor is particularly conscious. Related to feeling inferior is the belief: "I cannot trust my inner impulse—I'm basically wrong inside" and from this follows: "I must resist my own impulses." This last belief can be so strong that all sexuality is resisted unless it is "forced on her" by another—in which case it's not her fault and she is not being "bad." (This is why this habit has the psychoanalytic name of "masochism.")

Each belief carries its own accurate prophecy. "I'm not good enough" makes her try harder and harder to conform to others' wishes. This takes her further and further away from her own feelings and wishes, which creates in her a lack of self respect and a judgment that she is not her own person. This judgment makes her feel deeply that she is not good enough.

The "I must resist my own impulses" belief leads to bottling up many feelings. Over time, she builds tremendous resentment towards those she is conforming to. By the time this is expressed (if ever), it is indeed destructive. Therefore "I must resist my own impulses" becomes a realistic conclusion.

The Up-in-the-Clouds Personality Habit

The up-in-the-clouds type (known in psychological literature as "schizoid") makes a split between life on the outside and life on the inside. Ordinary external life is seen as an unfortunate necessity which is acted out separate from any real inner feeling. The inner fantasy life is what is valued and this aspect (which may be artistic and creative) is often kept private.

The basic belief of the up-in-the-clouds type is: "The world is a dangerous place and I don't want anything to do with it. People are untrustworthy, and I don't want anything to do with them. I would rather live in the clouds—clouds don't hurt you." The world and people have become generalized as alien and untrustworthy, and a habit is formed of avoiding them. The habit fulfills the belief as follows: "People are untrustworthy and reject me," he believes. He therefore avoids people, or is suspicious of them or hates them. When people sense these feelings coming towards them they naturally tend to avoid him and reject him. Therefore people in his world are "untrustworthy and reject" him. Though he is not aware of this process, his underlying beliefs are proven time after time.

Entire character types, then, are constructed on beliefs that generate their own fulfillment. I have yet to find a belief that does not contain a prophecy of its own fulfillment. The more powerfully a belief is held, the more it will be fulfilled. When this same process is used for positive unlimiting beliefs (see chapter 14: "Unlimiting Beliefs: Changing the Present"), we can deliberately create positive self-fulfilling prophecies and inspiring nonvicious circles.

Besides these fairly logical understandings of the mechanisms of belief fulfillment, beliefs have more subtle effects, which are the subject of the next chapter.

Chapter 6

▼

DID I DO THAT?

THE SUBTLE EFFECTS OF INTENTION

*I*f you are afraid that a dog will bite you, it is more likely to bite you. Everybody knows this, and the mechanism of how this belief becomes reality is usually assumed to be the dog's capacity to read body language, to "smell" the fear. It is also possible that both animals and human beings have the ability to detect thoughts, desires, and intentions by as yet unmeasurable means.

Body Language

One of the differences between four-legged animals and human beings is that, in our upright stance, we expose the most vulnerable parts of our body—the front of the neck, chest, belly, and genitals. When people are frightened, quite automatically they will tend to protect their fronts—some will pull their shoulders forward and arch their backs as if protecting their hearts. Some will fold their arms in front of them or close their jackets. It is natural in moments of tension or fear to try to put something safe in front of us. Body language is usually not consciously relayed or perceived. Yet it is perceived and processed. You may not know that you know body language signs, but you will find yourself reacting unwittingly. For example, you see a salesman who is nervous about himself or his product and he is doing up a nonexistent button on his jacket. You do not think you notice his body language, but you do not buy his product because, somehow, you don't trust his confidence. His body language has, unknowingly, helped him to fulfill his belief: "I don't think I can sell this."

Much detailed body language is conveyed through facial expression. If a woman believes that her relationships are going well and she feels good about herself, her face will convey that good feeling. The people she relates to will respond to her expression with good feeling, which will support her belief that these relationships are going well. On the other hand, if she believes the relationships are going badly and feels bad about this, it will show on her face, which will make others feel bad, which will equally support her belief. People, even seemingly insensitive people, are perceptive to the smallest changes of expression. Wilhelm Reich, John Pierrakos, and Alexander Lowen, the pioneers of bioenergetics, developed an understanding of how feelings and psychological defenses are translated into patterns of body tension. They found that for every psychological defense there is a corresponding muscular "armor." For example, the "up-in-the-clouds" or "schizoid" types (mentioned at the end of chapter 5), tend to experience excessive tension in the deep muscles of all the limbs and constriction of the arterioles in the extremities of the body. In other words, in accordance with the split between the inner private world and the outer social world, the up-in-the-clouds type appears to block energy from reaching the extremities of the body. We interact with the world mostly via our hands, face, feet, and genitals. The up-in-the-clouds type tends to have cold hands and feet, a pale expressionless face, and limited sexual energy. This, combined with rather wooden movement due to excessive muscular tension, creates its own self-fulfilling prophecy: Because she lacks expression, she makes little impression and tends to disappear into the background. Hence, the interaction and warmth that come back to her are minimal. Therefore her belief that the world is cold and rejecting is vindicated; and therefore it continues to make sense for her to focus on the safe inner world and ignore the seemingly cold, rejecting outer world. Her body language has made the world according to her belief.

Fatal Attractions

We choose situations and people that fit our beliefs, often unconsciously, through body language. Attractions and repulsions occur daily through a hidden language that reflects our inner beliefs.

If a woman believes she is ugly, this belief will affect how she moves her body, her facial expression, and the dilation or constriction of blood vessels in her face which will determine whether it is pale or glowing. It will affect how she combs her hair, how she dresses, and how she applies make-up. It will affect the whole pattern of muscular tension in her body. In such ways people who believe themselves to be ugly, *make sure* they are ugly. Conversely, people who believe they're attractive become attractive.

How our faces and bodies look may reflect our strongest beliefs: beauty is as deep as our belief. How we look has a powerful effect on how others react to us in family, business, or any other setting. Although make-up cannot cover up a sour expression, sometimes making an effort at looking better makes us feel better about ourselves, and thus affects our expression and our energy (see chapter 17, Better Without: Taking Positive Action).

While people in general can be attracted or repelled by how we look, there are also specific types that we tend to attract or repel according to our beliefs. Without knowing it, we attract people that fit our basic life scenario. A controlling man will be attracted by a dependent woman and a dependent woman will be attracted by a controlling man, both without realizing why. He may only be aware of falling for those eyes that look up at him, that delicate head that looks down coyly and that body that seems to ask for guidance. She may be attracted by the firmness of his jaw and his unemotionality which seems so strong.

Such a man might automatically be repelled by a "strong" woman, while a dependent woman would feel repelled by a "weak" man. These attractions and repulsions occur so quickly and so unconsciously that we end up aware only of our likes and dislikes, not realizing that they are a reflection of our beliefs mediated through the language of the body.

Muscle Tension

Our body expression has a powerful feedback effect on ourselves, as well as others. If, for example, you see your hand shaking, your "nervousness" is confirmed. If your body tenses through fear that you are not good enough, the tension then affects your ability and makes you "not good enough."

Sometimes tension occurs through a belief that certain expressions are wrong. Electro-myographic recordings of the tension levels within muscles show that when a person wants to express a thought or feeling but stops short of doing so, the tension level increases in the muscles that would normally have been used in the expression. A freely expressed sound involves the movement of air from the lungs through the throat, mouth, and lips to the air outside. When we block our expressions, we automatically hold our breath, tighten the muscles around the throat, clench the jaw, tense the tongue, and tense the lips. Quite literally we "keep our mouth shut," "hold our tongues," and have "stiff upper lips." When such tension patterns become habitual, they eventually become permanent. It may actually become physically impossible to open the mouth fully after years of holding in the jaw, so what started as the belief "I can't express myself fully," becomes, over time, a physical reality.

Another common reason for tension is fear of making a

mistake or looking like a fool. The more inept we think we might be, the more we tense our muscles, and the tenser we are, the more inept we are in physical, emotional, or mental expression. Physical performers know very well how fear of failure leads to muscle tension, which affects coordination and causes failure. Nearly everyone has had the experience of speaking well and with emotional freedom when relaxed, but of speaking haltingly and with little freedom of expression when tense.

Muscular tension is intimately related to how we feel and has a large effect on the quality of our actions, affecting both our own self-image and others' perception of us. It is a crucial link in many self-fulfilling prophecies.

Other Effects on the Body

The effects of belief on our health is very clearly documented, for the "belief factor" is a standard part of statistical tests on new medical treatments. The effectiveness of all new drugs is measured by comparing them to a placebo—a medication that looks exactly the same but has no active ingredients. It is a universal finding that people on placebo drugs do better than people on no drug at all. The effect of belief on our health, and even over life or death, is potent (see chapter 1).

I have worked with several women who desperately wanted to become pregnant. Sometimes we discovered an underlying belief, "I am not worthy of being pregnant," and for a few of these women, this was due to guilt over an abortion. One woman I knew had a stillbirth, then a healthy baby and then a miscarriage. It was only in her fourth pregnancy that she felt hopeful—she felt that she had now paid her dues for two abortions she'd had many years before. I have seen four women, all of whom could not get pregnant, become pregnant within two months of understanding and challenging their belief in their unworthiness to be pregnant.

There are, of course, women who cannot get pregnant for

physical reasons. The line between limiting beliefs and external/medical realities can be fuzzy and quite confusing. Some medical "realities" do change with belief and some do not. For further discussion on this, see the section in chapter 21, "So, What is Real."

Energy Fields?

On countless occasions I have noticed that as soon as an old belief is cracked, new opportunities seem to arise to match a new belief. For example, someone challenges their lower-class beliefs, and the next day a new job opportunity comes up. A woman finally realizes and allows herself to feel that she wants a man, and in the next week, after years of being alone, she finds a man she wants. A man realizes that he is worthy of talking equally to an old friend and an hour later meets him "by chance" in the street.

Such occurrences can easily be seen as coincidences. Carl Jung coined the term *synchronicity* to designate a meaningful coincidence, for instance between a psychic and a physical event. He thought that a cause of these meaningful coincidences "is not even thinkable in intellectual terms." Since then, however, there has been a great deal of scientific research and evidence on such subtle phenomena.

Can we influence other people "energetically" without words, body language, or any other communication through the five senses? If you begin to believe that you are an attractive person, you will begin to find that people are attracted to you. Apart from improving your looks and the intricate mechanisms of body language, does your belief have a direct effect on others?

Can we create opportunities directly through our beliefs? When we change a belief, new opportunities do arise—partly because we're making new self-fulfilling prophecies, and partly because we see opportunities that we didn't even notice before. But some occurrences are difficult to explain this way.

A man who tried to start his own business could raise no money despite good business plans negotiated with many banks. When he changed his inner belief in his ability to do business and be successful, a complete stranger, whom he did not meet personally, offered capital to start his business. Another businessman found his business gradually going downhill over years until he suddenly changed his inner belief that he would fail. A day later he received a large unexpected offer which enabled him to change the trend. Within two weeks, sales were mushrooming with requests and offers from old connections that were thought to be lost. The proximity of two events (one psychic and one physical) can never be proven to be anything more than coincidence. Science, however, does cast light on whether it is possible for beliefs directly to affect events on an empirical level.

The Evidence for the Subtle Effects

In the past fifty years, psi phenomena (psi is short for psychical and is a general term for allegedly paranormal human abilities) have been thoroughly investigated. For our beliefs to affect events and people directly, without mediation by any known physical force or sensory input, requires both transmission and reception of unknown forces. The transmission has been called PK, or psychokinesis, the apparent ability to influence other people, objects, or events by will and without any known or measurable physical force. The reception has been called ESP, or extrasensory perception (the apparent perception of information not obtained through the five senses).

There have now been thousands of ESP experiments on apparently psychically gifted individuals. Because of scientists' disbelief, these experiments are the most rigorous and repeated of any branch of experimental psychology. No one has tried a statistical critique on these results for over thirty years, because the figures both for ESP and PK are overwhelmingly conclusive. An excellent summary of this evidence has been written by Hans Eysenck and Carl Sargent, "Explaining the Unexplained" (see reading list).

ESP in Everybody?

After studying the evidence it is impossible to deny that certain gifted people exhibit the as yet unmeasurable powers to transmit and receive information or energy. The more interesting question is: do we all have it? One of the first definitive answers to this question came from Dr. Gertrude Schmeidler of the City University of New York who in 1942 divided experimental volunteers with no known special ESP abilities into believers and nonbelievers. The believers thought that ESP was at least a possibility while the nonbelievers thought that ESP was impossible. Dr. Schmeidler found that the believers scored consistently above average in guessing cards that were placed in another room. What was surprising, though, was that the nonbelievers scored consistently *below* average. If there was no ESP effect, their scores would have been average. This meant that the nonbelievers were using ESP to influence their results negatively! These experiments were repeated many times over nine years. In total, 300,000 guesses were made by 1308 subjects. The overall difference between the groups of believers and nonbelievers was so marked that the odds of it being a chance occurrence were over ten million to one. Here was a statistical verification of "creating your own reality." These results have been repeated by many different researchers in the last 40 years. The results have been summarized by the American researcher, John Palmer (see reading list).

Many ESP experiments have attempted to correlate ESP ability with other criteria. Contrary to popular belief, there's no correlation between gender and ESP. ESP ability has been found to be stronger in the extroverted, in children, in those under hypnosis (or alpha rhythm), and in cases where there is great desire or emotional impact.

Anecdotal evidence points to the possibility that psi phenomena are far stronger when personal energy is focused in strong desire. But sometimes desire may not be consciously realized. Is it possible to engineer important coincidences through our own unconscious psi abilities?

Rex Stanford, an American parapsychologist, postulated that "meaningful coincidences" could be caused by a person gathering information and manipulating events through "nonintentional" psi. This conclusion was based on a number of experiments, one of which tested both for unconscious ESP and PK.

In this experiment, men were told that they were taking part in a pursuit rotor tracking experiment. Rather like the cars on moving roads in video arcade machines, a pointer had to be kept on a moving track. The only problem was that the track moved very slowly, which made the task incredibly boring. What the volunteers were not told was that Stanford had placed in the same room a "random event generator," a machine designed by the physicist Helmut Schmidt to create random positive or negative electrical pulses. The machine was set to distribute ten pulses randomly into six different channels. If seven out of ten pulses went down one channel at the same time (which was highly unlikely), then the volunteer would be immediately taken off his tedious task and shown erotic photographs instead.

For the volunteer to escape the boredom would require unconscious ESP to know both that it was possible to escape, and how to do so. It would also require unconscious PK to influence the random event generator. The fact that twenty percent of the subjects did, in fact, escape, suggests that ESP and PK could be used, unwittingly, to satisfy needs. If people can affect a machine through their unconscious minds, it is also possible that they can affect the infinitely more complex and sensitive mechanisms of other people.

Further experiments have shown that nonintentional psi

scores tend to be lower when there is a conflict, anxiety, guilt, or repression. This accords with a common clinical experience. It often occurs that a client wants something yet does not dare feel the desire fully, through fear of disappointment, through belief that it's not really possible, through guilt, or through anxiety. In these cases the desire remains a distant dream which does not come true. When the client then deals with the doubt, fear, or guilt and dares to feel the strength of the desire, what he wants is much more likely to happen. Sometimes this happens through his conscious actions and unconscious body language, but sometimes "chance" events occur that cannot be explained by these mechanisms.

Theorists on psi phenomena have looked for correlations with quantum physics. Since Albert Einstein's theory of relativity, scientists accept that matter is a form of condensed energy. If we could delve into the atoms of any material, we would find that 99.999 percent is empty space between sub-atomic "particles." The other 0.001 percent is "matter" but this itself turns out to be nothing more than fluctuations in energy patterns. In other words, if we get microscopic enough, there is simply nothing there.

Einstein and others went on to postulate that an observer within this fluctuating mass of moving energy can affect an event taking place, independent of distance and, probably, time. Nobel laureate Brian Josephson said that if no psi events had ever been reported, they might have been predicted to occur from extrapolating our knowledge of quantum physics. Olivier Costa de Beauregard went even further to state that the basic axioms of quantum physics demand that psi events *must* occur.

To test the hypothesis of psi being independent of time, the physicist, Dr. Helmut Schmidt, used his random event generator to create random numbers on magnetic tape. This process was observed by nobody. The numbers determined whether clicks would be heard in the left or right ear by volunteers wearing earphones. Statistically the number of clicks in each ear should have been equal. The volunteers were asked to try to increase the frequency of clicks in one ear rather than the other through will power. To many people's surprise, it was found that the volunteers could influence the proportion of clicks in one ear *days after* the mechanical storage. What the volunteers heard was later correlated independently with what had been stored on tape. In order to do this, Schmidt concluded that the subjects had to use PK to influence the random event generator sometime in the past! The experiments have been repeated on the Schmidt machine and by other experimenters using different machines. No one has been able to fault Dr. Schmidt's machine, his scientific method, his statistical analysis, or his integrity. If there is no error in interpretation, these results show that an observer influences reality, independent of time.

Alternatively, it could be argued that Dr. Schmidt's desire for a result unconsciously influenced the random event generator. But even if this is so, he would have had to influence the machine, which was observed by no one, through his own psi powers. It has indeed been found that experimenters who believe in psi are more likely to get stronger psi results than experimenters who do not, even when exactly the same experimental method is used. As Einstein and quantum physics would predict, there is simply no such thing as an independent observer.

Schmidt's, Stanford's, and Schmeidler's results suggest that no matter how rigorous an experimental design, the scientist's beliefs may affect the results (especially if the scientist desires to prove a point). In the same way, our beliefs, in immeasurable ways, affect the people and the events around us. The experimental results are both disturbing and hopeful—disturbing because they imply that reality is unfixed; hopeful because they suggest that we have far more control over our circumstances than we might imagine.

Chapter 7

I CAN'T, I'M NOT GOOD ENOUGH

CLASSIFICATIONS OF COMMON LIMITING BELIEFS

*E*very single limiting belief has two components. The first one is:

I Am Not Good Enough.

Each limiting belief, whether about ourselves or others, carries with it a judgment on the self. Each limitation is flavored with self-deprecation: "I'm inadequate"; "I've failed"; "I'm a sinner"; "There's something wrong with me"; "I'm not good enough"; "I'll never be good enough."

If a person believes she is too tense or too afraid, she believes she is not as good as relaxed or calm people. If he believes he is too thin or too fat, he believes that he is not good enough because he is outside of the norm and the ideal. If she believes, "That couldn't possibly happen to me," she is saying, in effect, "I don't deserve it, I'm not good enough." Even when she has a judgment about the human race in general, that judgment applies to her also.

Here is a list of fairly common self-judgments. Each one is a way of saying, "I'm not good enough." As you read through them, check off or write down any that you connect to. This is the beginning of your personal process of Belief Analysis.

I'm Not Good Enough

I'm not a lovable person.
I do not deserve to be loved.
I'm not worthwhile.
I don't deserve to have the best.
I am a limited person.
That couldn't possibly happen to me.
I could never have that.
I am poor. I never have enough money (I don't deserve
    it).
I don't have much to give.
I am not important.
I am inferior/a failure.
I am a bad mother/father/lover/worker/friend.
I deserve to be punished.
I do not deserve to succeed.
I do not deserve to have him/her/a good relationship.
It is not okay for me to have everything I want.
I cannot accept myself as I am.
People are basically bad (therefore I'm basically bad).
People are tainted with original sin (therefore I'm
    tainted).

Some judgments of self are disguised by the direct blaming
of others, for example, "They don't understand me." Why
don't they understand? "Because they do not care enough
about me (because I'm not good enough to be cared for or
understood)."

The accusation, "People are out for what they can get,"
includes the accuser: "I go for what I can get; therefore I
am selfish/inadequate at giving—I am not good enough. And
if other people go for what they can get out of me, then they
don't care much about me." And the doubt lingers, "perhaps
I am not good enough to be cared for."

Self-judgment and conceit are wrapped up together and
bound inextricably, as has been pointed out many times in

psychoanalytic literature. If he never shows anger, then he is proud of his control yet judges his weakness. If she cannot find the right partner, then she is too good for them and yet she is not good enough. If "they don't understand" it's because they are less intelligent than her, and also because she is not worthy of being understood. If he thinks "They're out to get me," it's because he's both special and terrible.

The judgments of self, disguised or not, have a profound effect on our basic self-confidence. "I'm not good enough" carries with it an abdication of personal authority that is often handed over to "they who know more than I do; (and are therefore better than me)". Though this may not be consciously recognized, authority is automatically handed over to the one who seems to know best.

They Know More Than I Do; (Therefore They Are Better Than Me)

My parents
my older brother/sister
books/newspapers/TV
doctors
lawyers
experts
the church
my boss
my therapist
all famous people
know more
than I do

All these authorities may in reality know more about certain areas than we do. If we respect ourselves we can acknowledge this with no loss of personal authority, but if we believe in our smallness, then we place external authority in a position above us or better than us. A familiar example is that of the doctor. If the patient places the doctor in a position above herself, she will tend to follow the doctor's words with little understanding of the limitations of the doctor's knowledge. Patients in this self-belittling position will rarely question the doctor, swallowing pills without knowing the side effects, and swallowing advice without understanding. These patients have least respect for their own healing processes and, as has been pointed out by Bernie Siegel, tend to deteriorate and die sooner in serious life-threatening diseases.

Patients with greater self-respect see the doctor as a servant, in the best sense of the word, who is being paid by the patient (directly or through insurance or taxes) to give certain specialized information. From this information the patients make their own decisions about whether treatment is worth the side effects, about hospitalization, or about the risks of their various life choices. The doctor's greater knowledge in a certain area does not make him or her superior. Patients who question their treatment (and who are sometimes termed "difficult" by their doctors) have a greater chance of survival in life-threatening diseases, according to researcher Leonard Derogatis and others. They refuse to see themselves as victims.

At an early age, older brothers and sisters usually know more and are stronger than their younger siblings. It is hard for the younger ones to escape the conclusion: "They are better." Such a belief often gets fixed into adulthood even if the younger sibling is both stronger and wiser. The conclusion is even harder to resist with parents who, at the start of the child's life, are seen as magical giants of extraordinary power. There are men and women who, at the point of going beyond what their parents have done, throw away success because they cannot tolerate being "more" than their parents.

Books and media are seen as authoritative, even by people who have had the experience of being grossly misrepresented. The written word takes on a certain power of permanence: in black and white, it must be right.

People will usually be able to find a "they know more/ are better than me" phrase. As I've said, all limited beliefs contain a judgment of self, which has a powerful effect, not only on our self-confidence, but also in perpetuating our lack of attainment. It creates the excuse for staying the same, for not reaching out for new qualities and personal accomplishments. For, if "I'm not good enough," then "I can't."

The other universal in all limiting beliefs is:

I Can't, I'm a Victim of Circumstance.

"I can't" implies helplessness, being a victim of something that's beyond our control, whether it's our own characteristics or someone else's actions. I have divided these circumstances into four broad areas:

I can't because I'm a victim of my characteristics
I can't because I'm a victim of others
I can't because I'm a victim of my past
I can't because I'm a victim of the inevitable way life is

Most people have many beliefs under each category. As you read through the beliefs that follow in the rest of this chapter, check or write down any that you connect to, even if intellectually you don't altogether think you should agree with them. You will get more value from this list if you allow yourself to be irrational. Bear in mind that no beliefs are completely rational: Even Newton's laws of physics, gospel of certainty for centuries, had to be modified by Einstein. In the parentheses are examples of the things you may stop yourself from doing, becoming or even hoping for. You may want to fill in better examples from your own experience.

I'm a Victim of My Characteristics

I can't (paint) because I am uncreative
I can't (let go) because I am too tense
I can't (speak to him) because I am shy
I can't (do it) because I am inhibited
I can't (jump) because I am afraid
I can't (interest them) because I am too boring
I can't (fight him) because I am too weak
I can't (get up early) because I am lazy
I can't (control myself) because I am bad tempered
I can't (live with her) because I am too sensitive
I can't (care for him) because I am not a loving person
I can't (enjoy this kind of work) because I am too talented
I can't (do this) because I am not talented enough
I can't (hope to win) because I am unlucky
I can't (understand such things) because I am not intelligent enough
I can't (do the details) because I am not conscientious enough
I can't (embrace people) because I am not warm enough
I can't (succeed) because I am not good at business
I can't (get through) because I am a bad communicator
I can't (stand up for myself) because I am too dependent
I can't (give my opinion) because I am unassertive

These are just some examples of beliefs about personal characteristics. The list could be endless. The characteristics that we think we have are often no more than other people's observations about our past behavior. Once the generalization of a characteristic is made, we then make sure we behave according to the characteristic, which proves that we *"have"* that characteristic. Once we believe we have a characteristic, once we label ourselves, we become victims of the label and limit our free choice.

I'M A VICTIM OF MY DESIRES, MY INNER SELF, MY UNCONSCIOUS

This is a subdivision of "I'm a victim of my characteristics" and reflects some common negative concepts about the inner self:

> I can't (feel good about myself) because man is tainted with original sin.
> I can't (express myself) because my inner impulses are antisocial.
> I can't (be a loving person) because I'm angry inside.
> I can't (be assertive) because there's a dangerous animal inside me and if I let it out it will cause damage.
> I can't (show my true feelings) because my inner self is negative.
> I can't (be calm) because I can't help having a bad temper.

Many of these beliefs are cultural and will be seen again under the specific cultural beliefs of psychology and religion later in this chapter.

I AM A VICTIM OF MY PHYSICAL CONDITION

This is another subdivision of "I'm a victim of my characteristics" and contains some of the hardest-to-shift ideas, since they seem to be based on physical reality.

> I can't (feel good) because I'm an insomniac.
> I can't (help you) because I'm too tired.
> I can't (make love) because I don't have much sexual energy.
> I can't (look good) because I'm thin.
> I can't (do the job) because I'm weak.
> I can't (feel good about myself) because I'm fat.

I can't (expect to finish this job) because I get sick easily.

I can't (heal myself) because only a doctor/osteopath/ herbalist can cure me.

I can't (do it any longer) because I'm too old.

I can't (do that) because I'm too young.

I can't (make good relationships) because I am unattractive.

For the real power of belief over body, see chapter 1. Some physical characteristics seem to be definitely unchangeable— for further discussion on this, see the section in chapter 21, "So, What is Real?"

I Am a Victim of Others

If we can't take refuge in the inner circumstances of our apparent characteristics, an alternative is to believe we can't because of the outer circumstances of life:

I can't (love) because love is dangerous; I might get hurt.

I can't (be happy) because I can't find the right partner.

I can't (be forgiving, loving, kind or generous to him/ her) because the communists/capitalists/blacks/ whites are our enemies.

I can't (explain it to them) because they don't understand.

I can't (be kind or generous) because people are only out for what they can get.

I can't (be friendly) because they always rip you off.

I can't (be comfortable with her) because she never gives me what I want.

I can't (accept him) because he never gives me what I want.

I can't (like myself) because nobody loves me.

I can't (say what I feel) because she or he wouldn't like it.

I can't (talk to people) because nobody wants me.
I can't (feel free) because my family stops me.
I can't (do more interesting work) because I cannot change or leave my institution.
I can't (trust him) because men are . . .
I can't (trust her) because women are . . .
I can't (enjoy my life) because he is . . .
I can't (be happy) because she is . . .
I can't (be fulfilled) because I am alienated from society.
I can't (be happy) because I am oppressed by society.

When a belief about another is used as an excuse for staying the same, as in the examples here, then one belittles oneself. We are saying in effect: "I can't—I'm not good enough to transcend the influence of another."

I AM A VICTIM OF LOYALTY

One way we maintain belief in the restrictions by others is through the unquestioning practice of loyalty:

I can't (be successful) because I must remain loyal to the lower class.
I can't (respect him or his belief) because I must remain loyal to my church.
I can't (leave the area) because I must remain loyal to my community.
I can't (act differently) because I must remain loyal to my country.
I can't (think differently) because I must remain loyal to my parents.
I can't (treat others as equals) because I must remain loyal to my profession.
I can't (really enjoy life) because I must remain loyal to my husband or wife.
I can't (change my ways) because I must remain loyal to my family.

I can't (make fundamental changes) because I must
remain loyal to my ancestors.
I can't (change at all) because I must remain loyal to
my identity.

Loyalty in itself may of course be a highly positive asset; it
all depends what we are loyal to. If we are loyal to anything
that is restricted, we will share that restriction. It is perhaps
for this reason that many of the greatest sages were loyal
only to one thing: God, universal energy, or the inner (un-
restricted) self. "Loyalty" is often used as an excuse to avoid
change and the threat of being called disloyal is a common
method of keeping the questioner silent or within the fold.
Most of the above loyalty statements are not consciously
recognized. We limit thinking or behavior without seeing that
these limits are in exact accordance with a limited model.

A Jewish woman of forty-five found that she was unable
to enjoy her life despite considerable family and professional
success. Part of the reason, she discovered, was that she had
an inner belief that to enjoy herself would be disloyal to her
family, her ancestors, and the Jews, all of whom had suffered
in Europe under Hitler.

Loyalty to our identity incorporates every single belief
there is. Most of us are incredibly loyal to our conceptions
of our identities, which are usually based on how others have
seen us. The statement "that's not really me" implies a disloyalty to who we think we really are. If we remain loyal to
our idea of our identity, then we cannot change at all.

I'm a Victim of My Past

It is easy for the present to be blamed on the past. Often,
our future expectations are limited by our concepts of what
happened to us:

I can't because I was never given any love
I can't because my father was mean/negative/distant

I can't because my mother gave me so little
I can't because I suffer from my limited upbringing
I can't because I suffer from my past lives
I can't because I suffer from karma
I can't because no one told me how to
I can't because I suffer from my poor education
I can't because I inherited these characteristics

Explanations from the past can be used to excuse present inactivity, unwilligness, lack of hope, or any personal characteristic. This is true of every culture, though in modern Western culture this type of rationalization carries a particularly psychological flavor.

I Am a Victim of the Inevitable Way Life Is

We believe certain statements about life or the world to be self-evident truths. All the following beliefs are limiting self-fulfilling prophecies:

I can't (enjoy myself) because hard, self-denying work is the only virtue.
I can't (be kind) because the end justifies the means.
I can't (be happy) because life is full of sorrow.
I can't (expect anything else) because the world is full of evil.
I can't (enjoy what I have) because there isn't enough to go around.
I can't (fully enjoy my body) because the physical world is inferior.
I can't (be intuitive) because the only valid information is discovered by the five senses.
I can't (forgive myself) because God is punishing and vengeful.
I can't (hope for change) because it is not possible to change the world.

I can't (have meaning in my life) because the only reality
   is physical.
I can't (do it) because there isn't enough time.
I can't (feel any hope) because life is accidental.
I can't (enjoy my life) because life is a hard struggle.
I can't (be fulfilled all the time) because everything must
   have its opposite.
I can't (be hopeful) because God has a bad sense of
   humor, doesn't care, and/or has made some pretty
   bad design errors.

Although when we read through a list like this, each belief
can be seen as only a possible understanding of how life
works, when we actually hold the belief it seems different:
the belief feels as though it *is* reality. If you believe that life
is accidental, for example, you will see the fortuitousness of
events everywhere and see meaningful connections only as
coincidences. If you believe that God has a bad sense of
humor or has made some big mistakes, you will focus predominantly on what is wrong with the world, and at the
same time minimize the liberty of human choice. If you believe "the world is full of evil," you will see it everywhere.

Many of the beliefs about the "inevitable way life is" orig-
inate from philosophical constructions, from religions, and
from other cultural influences, which are considered next.

Cultural Beliefs

Some beliefs clump together into larger, more encompassing
beliefs. Looking at these more central beliefs, it becomes clear
that each one is connected to an aspect of our culture, based
on the history of our philosophies and societies. The central
beliefs that follow are predominantly Western, though most
of them exist in related forms in other societies.

THE PHYSICAL WORLD IS INFERIOR

This central belief, that life in this world is inferior, includes many common subsidiary beliefs. The body, sexuality, desire, instinct, and animal impulses may all be seen as inferior, negative, or tainted with sin. The spirit and mind are seen as superior. Such beliefs may be expressed in different ways:

People are bad.
People are tainted with original sin.
The only important thing in life is the spirit.
The most important thing in life is the intellect.
Sex is an unfortunate need.
My body is an inefficient, badly designed machine.
I get sick easily.
My body is fat/thin/blemished/ugly or ill.
I am poor.
I cannot trust my feelings.
Being assertive is dangerous.
My natural impulses are antisocial.
My inner self is negative.

For nearly three thousand years many of the Judeo-Christian traditions have taught that this life is a preparation for the afterlife, that what really matters is the future and whether we finally go to heaven or hell. The body has often been seen as something between unimportant and evil. The passions have often been judged as wrong or bad. The belief in original sin carries the implication that there is a dangerous animal inside us that needs to be caged in. As far as I understand them, these are not the teachings of Christ, nor of some of the prophets, but interpretations of others that gained a momentum of their own. In the East, spiritual progression through many incarnations is sometimes seen as being at the expense of both the body and the mind which may both be looked down upon. Of course not all Hindus, Buddhists, Christians, Moslems, or Jews believe that the physical world is inferior. Many great spiritual masters have spoken of the body as the temple of the soul: "The kingdom of heaven is within you." Nevertheless, as a general force of belief in this world, the idea of the inferiority of the physical is immensely powerful and generalized.

For those who believe in their inner "badness," their thoughts, feelings, and actions must necessarily (and quite logically) be restricted. But there are many others who longer believe in original sin who nevertheless believe deep inside that they are not okay and that they therefore cannot trust themselves. I have seen many clients who have held this belief very strongly though they've had no overt religious upbringing—sometimes I have found that the belief can be traced back to a grandparent or great-grandparent who was religious: their offspring rejected the religion on the outside but never confronted (or perhaps even recognized) the belief "I am bad inside," which was then silently passed on from generation to generation.

It is actually extremely difficult to avoid this influence in Western culture. If you have not been directly or subtly influenced by a religious ancestor, it is almost impossible to avoid the influence of Freud, who himself was strongly (though perhaps unknowingly) influenced by Judeo-Christian traditions of original sin. Freud believed that the irrational desires of the inner self were fundamentally antisocial and that there would *always* be a conflict between the good of society and the expression of the inner self. The belief "the inner self is bad" or "I am bad inside" persisted in disguised psychological form.

The belief that the inner self is antisocial is so general and so strong that many assume it to be a fact, backed by much personal and circumstantial evidence. Unfortunately, the evidence is often real because of a fundamental self-fulfilling prophecy: If we believe the inner self is antisocial, we naturally repress our inner feelings. After months or years this repression twists our feelings until they become antisocial. For example, an inner feeling of self-assertion which, if expressed, might have corrected an unfair situation may, if repressed, lead to bitterness, spite, and hate.

Some ethologists have pointed out that we may have many socializing, creative, and indeed moral instincts, just as chimpanzees have. Be that as it may, it is still impossible to prove whether we are "good" or "bad" inside. Our belief in our fundamental "goodness" or "badness," however, has a tremendous impact on our lives.

LIFE IS HARD

This central belief is an umbrella for many related beliefs on avoiding pleasure. Life is seen as rather unpleasant; all resources seem scarce. Here are some examples:

Life is full of sorrow.
There isn't enough for everybody.
There is always more work to be done.
It is immoral to have when others have not.
Being poor is more spiritual.
Wealth is evil.
Food is nothing more than a biological necessity.
Pleasure is the temptation of the devil.
I have no time for sex/sport/exercise/eating.
It is not okay to have fun when others in the world are
    miserable.
I cannot enjoy myself.
If I am good, I should not be happy.
Pleasure is an indulgence.
This life is an unpleasant preparation for the next.
Suffering is worthy.
All great artists suffered greatly.
Pain is a virtue.

In recent times in the West the central belief that life is hard has been most commonly associated with the Protestant work ethic. You may find similar beliefs in the Hindu ascetic who may go to greater extremes of physical deprivation, though he may be much less judgmental of happiness.

The "hard life" central belief is really a large subset of "the physical world is inferior." Life on earth is seen as an unpleasant and tough test. Godliness is associated with self-control, and self-control is erroneously associated with suffering. Godliness and suffering are therefore seen as closely connected. Work and pleasure are seen as opposites.

Once again, people's inability to experience pleasure may be far removed from any direct religious teaching or any conscious awareness that pleasure is frowned upon.

ALL KNOWLEDGE IS MEDIATED THROUGH THE FIVE SENSES

This central belief is in materialism—that the only source of real knowledge is the perception of material reality through vision, hearing, taste, smell, and touch. A number of other beliefs are subsidiaries of this central belief.

Sensory perception is the only source of real knowledge.
Science is the only route to true understanding.
Scientific knowledge is the mark of civilization.
Science will eventually provide all the answers.
Life is a series of physical/chemical reactions.
I cannot trust my intuition.
I cannot trust my feelings.
Bad dreams are caused by indigestion.
You are what you eat.
Only a doctor can cure me.
ESP is nonsense.
The soul/spirit does not exist.
God does not exist.
Life is a series of random occurrences.
Life is meaningless.
The greatest objective is to understand more about physical reality.
The greatest objective is to increase the material wealth of yourself, others, or society.

Personal problems are caused by material unfairness in
society.
People would be happy if materials were distributed
equally.

In recent Western history, the two main pillars of materialism have been science (and empirial philosophy) and
Marxism. Scientific development and, to a lesser extent,
Marxism, were both influenced by the philosopher John
Locke (1632–1704) who propounded the empirical philosophy that the senses are the basic faculties that give us knowledge. This statement now seems obvious because our culture
is steeped in empirical philosophy and scientific observation,
so much so that many assume that science is the only source
of knowledge. This was the position taken by the philosophical school of Logical Positivists, who believed that knowledge that was not capable, at least in principle, of being
proved or disproved by observation, was meaningless. The
philosopher Karl Popper answered that that which cannot
be disproved by observation is simply "non-science." This
does not mean that it is untrue or meaningless, but simply
that its parameters cannot be simple or limited enough to
make it fit a controlled experiment.

For some, scientific observation is a useful source of knowledge which is applicable only to the material world or relatively simple situations. For others, observation is the *only*
source of knowledge, and "unobservable knowledge" is
meaningless. For the latter group, it is difficult to escape the
conclusion that a rather meaningless mechanical universe
inevitably deteriorates through the laws of entropy.

However, there are many caught between these two extremes who believe that mechanical explanations are not
enough and yet who cannot seem to stop themselves from
trying to explain everything in mechanical terms. Intellectually they know that science cannot explain all phenomena
and yet they experience a lack of inner hope through not
being able to believe in any other source of knowledge.

DESIRE IS MORE IMPORTANT THAN REASON

Here, the central belief is that the only thing that really matters is the stirring of the spirit, subjective experience, and unconscious desires or beliefs. Intuition and feelings are believed to be more important than outer reality and objective reasoning. Some examples are:

My creativity is deeply buried.
The most valuable insights are unconscious.
I cannot know the truth until I understand my unconscious.
Material reality is unimportant.
Feelings are more important than intellect.
Expressing feelings is liberating.
Intuition is more important than reason.
The spirit is more closely related to feeling than it is to the mind.

To some extent, these beliefs originated as a reaction to the materialism of science and to excessive attention to deductive reasoning. Many became eager to feel more and to express themselves more, which was encouraged by the growth movement of the nineteen-sixties. At that time, great emphasis was placed on "trusting your feelings" without the understanding that many feelings are manufactured from the limitations of the mind. What started as a redressing of balance became for some a form of invidious comparison: many who valued or explored their inner selves looked down on those who appeared to focus more on outer reality.

Limitations occur as soon as there is comparison. Anyone who considers thinking more important than feeling or anyone who considers feeling more important than thinking has to limit their experience to support their belief. While intellectually many will not put one above the other, most people have a preference and a judgment. The same is true of subjective and objective reality. It is only when one is put above the other that a limitation in personal capacity is created. "Comparison," a sage once said, "is the root of all suffering."

I'M A VICTIM OF THE PAST

Virtually everyone the world over tends to blame their past for something. The modern Western cultural flavor of this universal belief comes from psychology which fuels the focus on the past. A fundamental tenet of Freudian analysis was that incidents from the past or fixations in the past caused present neurosis. Much analysis involved searching out these incidents or fixations, and all problems, including the entire character structure, could be explained in terms of past events.

Psychology has lent much credence to an age-old belief in limitation from the past. It has also taught thousands to believe that they had an unhappy childhood (see introduction, pages 13–15), or at least to exaggerate the early difficulties of life.

I CANNOT ESCAPE MY CLASS

The most limiting class belief is to consider ourselves lower. This central belief usually comprises a cluster of subsidiary beliefs that can have an enormous effect on our lives (see pages 37 and 265).

WOMEN ARE FEMALE, MEN ARE MALE

We are raised with preconceptions about how men and women should be based on what we observed and absorbed in our own homes (see generalizations on gender behavior, page 39). The commonest gender beliefs in the West are:

Women are relatively powerless without a man.
Women are weaker than men.
Women are stronger than men.
Women are manipulative.
Women are not good at math.
Women have less aggression.
A woman's lot is hard.
Women are more intuitive.
Women look after the children.
Women are more tender.
Women are more sensitive.

Men do not cry.
Men are tough.
Men are unintuitive.
Men don't wear pink.
Men fix things in the house but don't do the washing
 up.
Men earn the money.
Men are better at driving backwards.
It is unmanly to admit a mistake.
It is unmanly to be tender.

All these beliefs may of course be true of some men and women: the question is, how much is any one person limited by unconsciously following these powerful preconceptions, even while he or she might intellectually disagree.

This chapter shows that there are common belief clusters based on the history of our society. Yet every individual is different. Each person has a unique make-up and personal history and therefore a unique matrix of beliefs. Chapter 8 gives some examples of these matrices.

▼

BELIEF MATRICES

SOME EXAMPLES OF HOW BELIEFS INTERACT

A woman of forty complained of seemingly irrational aggressive outbursts against her husband. She was afraid of losing her marriage. She also felt bad that she could not feel the same love for her son that she felt for her daughter. She was asked to make a few generalizations about men and women, even if they were irrational.

"A woman's lot is hard," she said, "and men treat you badly—and I'm not so sure that that's so irrational." She smiled and then added, "I guess that comes from my father." She said that she felt very close to her father until the age of about four, at which time her brother was born and "suddenly my father forgot that I existed." She was jealous of her brother, and so angry with her father that she just couldn't forgive him.

After being given some time for these feelings, she saw that her father was caught up in his own limited belief system that men and boys were more important. Gradually she realized how much her anger hid a deeper feeling of wanting more with her father, and as this happened, she began to feel warmth for him and to forgive him.

With forgiveness, the memories of the good times she had had with him came flooding back. Her *history* changed dramatically! Nevertheless, despite understanding that her ideas about men concerned her particular history with her father, and despite having forgiven him, she was still stuck with an old ingrained belief system that said "women have a bad time," and "men treat women badly."

When she was asked what the advantages of continuing this belief were, she was initially surprised, and then smiled to herself. "In some ways I'm proud of it," she said. "You know, I can take it, I am strong. I can suffer. Men are hurtful and insensitive; so I am better than them. I am also better than other women who are fooled by men, who actually think men are okay." She laughed.

She began to realize that so long as she kept in her familiar system of understanding, she felt safe. She saw that many life choices she had made in the past fit what she believed: Part of her job in social work had been to help women who had been mistreated by men. Her belief in being mistreated seemed to absolve her from personal responsibility because as long as she could see her husband as bad, she had an excuse not to respond to him.

She could also make accurate predictions about life: She knew that men would treat her badly, and of course they did. First of all she chose a series of men who, for their own reasons, had a tendency to treat women badly. Added to that, she was so abrasive to the men she chose that they naturally retaliated. As soon as this happened she would say, effectively: "That proves my case. He is rejecting me; he doesn't care about me. Men don't care about women. Men treat women badly." Her son, too, behaved aggressively and was "a difficult child," partly in response to her; and this completed the same self-fulfilling prophecy about males.

Her memory was very selective. She had remembered only how distant her father was, for example, and she remembered how difficult her husband had been, but she forgot the good times and the intimate moments. She kept on seeing the things that were wrong with her husband. She noticed when he was insensitive, but didn't notice or misinterpreted the times when he was genuinely warm to her. When he would give her something or be kind to her, she would rationalize: "He's only doing that because he wants something out of me." Sometimes she would even distort the expression she saw on his face so that he appeared mean or uncaring.

She was particularly struck by the realization that her beliefs created feelings. The strongest feeling that she manufactured was anger. Because other women had pointed it out, she knew that her outbursts of anger were not warranted or triggered only by what her husband had done. However, the anger, and especially the background feeling of injustice, made her think (because she basically trusted her feelings) that her belief in being mistreated was accurate and well-founded.

Her belief also affected her imagination. In the back of her mind, she would always think that the marriage was going to go sour, and that in the end she would be rejected. She kind of "knew" this would happen, so what was the point of really trying to change the relationship?

When she looked at her belief in this fashion, she could not escape the conclusion that not only had she created that reality for herself, but she had also spent a great deal of energy maintaining it. She was a little shocked at these understandings, but also felt a sense of liberation, because she now knew it must also be possible to create a different reality. Within two months, her outbursts against her husband stopped. This is not to say she didn't get angry with him— sometimes he deserved it. At the same time as her attitude changed, her son stopped his difficult behavior and became more affectionate.

This example is fairly simple in that only one basic belief is involved. Although it is usually important to try to focus on one belief for the sake of clarity and understanding, beliefs naturally impinge on each other, working together in one area and contradicting each other in another. The next example involves a mixture of "I'm not intelligent," "life is hard" and "I'm lower class," working together to make dreams seem impossible.

The son of a Dutch farmer started psychotherapy because he felt dissatisfied with life. He was a handsome young man with a good physique who had been raised with a very strict Protestant view of life. He was taught that it was wrong to question either God or his father: Rules were rules, and that was that.

From an early age he was encouraged to work on the farm where he was still working when he started psychotherapy. Though he was not very happy with this work, he couldn't imagine himself doing anything else, as he had no special training and didn't consider himself very intelligent. But his secret dream was to be a pilot.

Two years later, with a great deal of encouragement from his friends, he eventually decided to try to learn to be a pilot. He found the money by working hard at different jobs and by borrowing. He had little difficulty with the practical side of flying and studied at all hours to try to master the complicated theoretical details.

When the exams came, he was very nervous, and failed. It was then that he really began to examine his belief in his lack of intelligence. He saw that his nervousness about failure created a self-fulfilling prophecy because he simply could not think while he was scared.

As he went back over his life he began to see how his own natural intelligence had hardly ever been supported. The rigid rules of his home and village community had stifled any creative expression. He had not been able to believe that he could be anything but a dumb, hard-working farm boy.

When he saw that his "stupidity" was more a matter of belief than finality, his confidence grew and he passed the early theoretical exams. Eighteen months later, his final exams involved instrument flying at night. In the practical side of this exam, the windows of the two-engined plane were covered up so that he had to rely totally on instruments for his approach to landing. He got flustered and made mistakes which caused him to fail.

In a private therapy session, he examined his limiting beliefs in detail. Some of these were:

I cannot pass
I cannot be a pilot
I cannot do more than one thing at once
I'm not clever enough
I'm a farm boy

These beliefs were supported by his imagining himself failing: He would imagine himself getting flustered and making mistakes; he would imagine the moment of learning that he had failed, including all the feelings of disappointment, fear, and dread.

After understanding these limiting beliefs, he worked hard to practice the opposite, positive, and unlimiting beliefs. When he retook the exam, in his final approach to landing, another plane got too close which entailed a creative maneuver at a moment's notice. His examiner commended him on his quick and thoughtful action. He passed. He had not only become a pilot, he had transcended the huge, invisible obstacle of his limiting belief.

Quite often exploration of one belief leads to several others that can be explored later, if useful. One man from Washington came to see me because he realized he had "some strange belief about money, which stops me making it." He had always worked hard at his career in building, but had not been smart in organizing himself and his practice, so that he was always short of money or in debt.

I asked him to try out several wordings of what he thought the belief might be, with license to be as irrational as he wanted. He came up with:

Money's not important.
Using your mind is not work.
I'm not very smart.
Doing well doesn't matter.
I'm not going to succeed.

When I asked him about the advantages of these beliefs, he could not think of any. But when he was asked for his judgment on others who did not hold these beliefs, he said: "They're dishonest; they get their money through devious means." "They're suckers; all I have to do is to be cute and loveable and the people with money will take care of me. I weasel myself into their affections and they'll feel sorry for me, be responsible for me. They're fools."

From the first judgment ("They're dishonest"), he realized that his ego advantage was "I'm honest." From the second ("They're suckers"), the ego advantage was, "I'm shrewd." The two ego advantages pretty well contradicted each other, for his shrewdness was not far removed from dishonesty. The idea of being smart and shrewd also contradicted his initial belief: "I'm not very smart." Such contradictions are very common. Many beliefs held in the preconscious are logically incompatible. Somehow they are kept separate, and the contradictions are usually unnoticed.

His beliefs gave him a sense of safety because he had been living with them for more than thirty years—they were familiar. About work and responsibility, he said: "I don't have to use my mind; I don't have to worry about money. I can do whatever I want because it doesn't matter. In fact, whatever I do in this life is not very important—we are just a spot in the universe. Other people will look after me, do my work for me. People will feel sorry for me."

From the information so far, three belief systems are apparent:

1. THE LOWER CLASS BELIEF SYSTEM (PAGE 265)

I'm not going to succeed.
Using your mind is not work.
Those who are smart are devious and dishonest.
I'm not very smart.

2. THE DEPENDENT PERSONALITY HABIT (PAGE 65)

They will take care of me.
They will do my work for me.
Others will feel sorry for me.
(I'm smart to get away with this.)

3. "THE PHYSICAL WORLD IS INFERIOR" (PAGE 304)

Whatever I do in this life is not very important.
We're just a spot in the universe.

All three belief systems unite in one feature—*it's not worth bothering to do very much,* because: (1) I'm not going to succeed; (2) others will take care of me; and (3) what I do in this life is not very important anyway.

This man had several self-fulfilling prophecies:

• I don't care about money, therefore my financial arrangements get into a mess, which shows that I'm no good at dealing with money. As I'm no good with money, what's the point of bothering. I don't care about money.

• I'm going to fail in the end. Therefore I won't try to build a better life. Therefore I'm going to fail in the end.

• I'm not very clever about business. Therefore I'll concentrate on just working hard. Therefore my business does not do very well. Therefore I'm not very clever about business.

• I need someone else to take care of me. If someone else is going to take care of me, I do not need to develop myself. If I do not develop I need someone else to take care of me.

As we spoke of all these issues, he was visibly shocked at the understanding of what he had created. "Perhaps I will always be like this," he said with a tone of self-pity. What he was really saying was, "I'm not sure I want to make the effort to change this." Then he added, "It's hard to believe that the mind can have so much power." Here a fourth major belief system came in. Having had a great deal of psychological training in the importance of expressing feeling, he had come to believe that feelings were in some way primary or more important than thinking. However, when he looked back on this one session, his self-manipulation was irrefutable. He walked out shaken, shaken enough, perhaps, for him to wish to give up some of his comfortable limitations.

A single belief can have many possible roots in one person. "I am poor" for example can be part of any or all of the following:

I do not deserve to succeed.
The physical world is inferior (therefore material effort is not worthwhile).
I'm no good at business.
I am not intelligent.
I had a bad education.
My parents were limited.
I have no self-discipline.
I must remain loyal to the lower class.
I cannot have when others have not.
Life is hard.
The pure pursuit of knowledge is the only thing that matters.
My inner self is better than the outer (material welfare is unimportant).
All great artists suffer.

A single belief may have completely different origins and meanings in different people. One forty-year-old overweight woman who believed "I am not attractive" had a very low self-image combined with self-judgment and self-hatred. She believed that she was not good enough and that nobody liked her. These beliefs were generalized from experiences with her mother who found her a nuisance, continually criticized her, and called her fat. Despite feeling unattractive, she enjoyed and wanted sex. The opposite belief for her was "I respect and love myself" (see chapter 14, Unlimiting Beliefs).

Another woman who was fifty and also overweight apparently had the same belief: "I'm not attractive." But for her, self-dislike was not the main issue—it was primarily men and sex. Her belief was generalized from experiences with her father who was embarrassed at the sexual attractiveness of his daughter. He used to discuss philosophical issues with her but assiduously avoided physical or even eye contact. She repeated this pattern in her choice of partners, who were highly intelligent but did not really notice how she looked. "He told me he never saw that blouse," she said, "but I had had it a whole year!"

Her belief was complicated by two other beliefs: "The body is less important than the inner self" and "luxury is a waste." These were apparent when she was asked about how her belief in being unattractive boosted her ego. "I'm above bothering about the superficialities of appearance," she said. "Those who are concerned about how they look are superficial. They waste their time and money. They play silly games with the opposite sex. They make themselves nice on the outside to cover up what's inside. If they were nice inside, they wouldn't have to bother with appearances."

She felt safe because she could not be trapped in the seduction game. She did not have to bother about male/female battles or the complications and tensions of sexual relationships. She also didn't have to work at being attractive or looking after her body.

If men did notice her, she would minimize their attention, deny it or even tell them to stop it. "Actually I'm scared," she confided. At parties she would hope that men looked at her and she would hope that they did not.

The opposite belief for her was "I am a beautiful, sexual woman." She visualized her father saying "You look beautiful" (see chapter 13, History Revisited: Changing the Past). She imagined herself looking beautiful at her present age and allowed herself to feel how that felt within. "It's like a dream," she said. "I'm open, I'm soft—and I'm scared." Positive Action (page 191) for her involved taking care of her body and allowing herself to enjoy the reactions of men, rather than following her fear and running away or closing herself off. After three months, she had lost forty-five pounds and was dressed beautifully. Her tension had softened and her face glowed. "You look beautiful," her husband said to her, "you look fantastic, just beautiful."

"Oh, stop it," she said, glowing even brighter, and this time both of them knew that she didn't mean it.

Chapter 9

▼

CONTAGIOUS CASES

THE SPREAD OF LIMITING BELIEFS

*I*n 1898, Mr. J. H. Patterson joined the construction party of the trans-East African railway. Unexpectedly, the first major difficulty he encountered was the presence of two formidable man-eating lions in Tsavo. Over a period of nine months these two lions ate twenty-eight railway personnel as well as uncounted numbers of local people. Despite watches being set up every night, the lions, with the most extraordinary cunning, always managed to find an un-guarded spot. Although huge fences surrounded each camp, the lions climbed them or broke through them without mak-ing a sound—a feat that nobody could explain. With pro-digious strength they dragged their screaming victims through these barricades.

The animals were tracked and hunted, but escaped time after time. Only on one occasion was one of the lions com-pletely surrounded. As the lion broke from cover, Patterson had his first clear shot from close range. But his gun had a bent pin and did not fire. The workers began to believe that these were not lions but devils in disguise. The be-lief spread. One by one, more and more people were dragged out of their tents at night and eaten. The survivors could hear the bones of their companions being crunched in the darkness. As the terror escalated, all work on the railway was brought to a standstill. The lions, they believed, were invincible.

This generalized belief created the most extraordinary self-fulfilling prophecy. Patterson set to work building a lion trap that was made of two compartments, one for the bait and the other for the lion. The lion's compartment had a sliding trapdoor: the bait in the adjacent compartment was two men. The two compartments were separated by bars made of railway tracks only three inches apart embedded in railway ties so that the men would be safe. The whole contraption was enormously strong. One night the lion went for two workers whose turn it was to be in the trap. The trap door closed and the lion was totally encaged in steel. Just for extra safety, the two men who acted as bait were each armed with Martini rifles with plenty of ammunition. All they had to do was poke a rifle through the bars and shoot. But the "devil," crashing against the bars with rage, paralyzed them with fear. When they started shooting, they were in such a state of panic that they shot in all directions. Any other person in the camp could have walked up to the lion at leisure and shot it from point-blank range, but no one could get near the cage because bullets were flying in all directions. The two terrified men shot over twenty bullets, dislodged one of the bars of the door, and freed the lion, which escaped totally unscathed.

If the lion had seemed a lucky devil before, now it seemed immortal. Only Patterson still believed it was a mortal lion, and even his belief was tested to the limit.

He took as bait a donkey that the lions had already killed, erected a platform above it and waited for a shot at one of the lions. In the dark of the night he at last heard a lion and knew from the animal's sigh that it was hungry. But the lion was not interested in the donkey—stealthily, it stalked Patterson in the darkness. For five hours he held himself at readiness to shoot a silent silhouette, springing through the air towards him from any direction. Anticipation mounted.

Suddenly, at about midnight, he felt claws strike the back of his head. Such was his terror that he nearly fell off the platform. Perhaps if he had believed the lion was truly a devil, he would have fallen. As it was, he quickly regained his senses and realized that he had been hit by an owl that had mistaken him for a tree. The lion growled with the commotion and approached, ready to spring. Patterson took careful aim and fired. The lion gave a mighty roar and then was motionless. Nevertheless, he did not dare go near the body till dawn and even then, he found it hard to believe that the "devil" might not have escaped in some mysterious way. The lion was dead. The second lion, no longer held to be immortal, was killed soon after.

This true story illustrates how the spread of a belief converts a private reality into a public reality, making the self-fulfilling prophecies that much more powerful. In a less dramatic way, common beliefs spread through almost every institution, community, or group of friends. We may, for example, dislike somebody. Quite automatically our mind reaches out for everything that is wrong with that person. Tell a few others about our dislike, and their minds will start to do the same. In this way factions are created. Sometimes they begin in the most innocuous and trifling of ways.

One day Robert walked past his friend Sharon with a quiet "hello." Sharon did not hear him and was upset that he ignored her, so she didn't say hello back. Robert could not understand why he didn't get a reply to his greeting, and he too was silently offended.

Robert and Sharon then went their respective ways, each thinking "Why didn't she or he say hello?—What's wrong?" Before they knew it, their minds began to pick out all the instances in the recent past when the other might have been unfriendly. They searched for negative motives. The cases had begun.

Both of them were worried and talked to their friends. Robert said: "You know, I don't know why, but Sharon ignored me the other day." Without knowing it, Robert's friends began to think of the times when they too might have been ignored by Sharon.

"I wonder what's going on with Robert?" Sharon said to her friends. Her friends then began to question in their own minds what could be wrong with Robert. In this way two private cases, by the most subtle and undeliberate means, grew into opposing camps of people attracted by agreement to an unspoken thought. Robert's friends believed, "Sharon is unfriendly," and Sharon's friends believed, "Something is wrong with Robert." Vague suspicion was amplified by each friend's private speculations about hidden motives, and cemented by sincere gossip. In this way, a division was created which no one really wanted, and everyone felt bad.

These kinds of communal cases occur very often. Mountainous cases can be built on the tiniest molehills of misunderstanding. Once we build a case against somebody, we are almost guaranteed to get a case back against us. The process goes something like this:

Case-Building

1. MAKING ASSUMPTIONS.

A case often begins when we assume that unclear actions have negative intentions. This is a sure self-fulfilling prophecy, because once we make hostile assumptions about someone, we evoke defensive hostility.

2. I AM RIGHT, THEY ARE WRONG.

A case is bolstered with the further assumption: "*I* am right/ sincere/trustworthy/concerned (and not to blame)" . . . etc. "*They* are awful/insensitive/political/negative/disrespectful/ uncaring/greedy" . . . etc. This process of self-justification makes the case grow larger.

3. PROVING THE CASE.

Proving a case to ourselves is usually simple and automatic. We tend to select out all the times from the past when someone's behavior fitted our case. At the same time we carefully avoid any memory of the times our case was contradicted. Since we have the capacity to alter our perception according to our belief, the person we're building a case against can also be made to look more hostile, controlling, ugly, or anything else we want. This seems to provide further evidence for the seeming certainty of our case.

4. MAKING THE GENERALIZATION.

Once our case is proven, we can make our generalization (to ourselves or to others). Generalizations about other people— words like "always" ("She always . . .") or "never" ("he never . . .") or "Them" (not us), give us a greater sense of control. In fact almost any adjective about someone is a generalization. If we say someone is "controlling," for example, that very word takes on a power of its own. All actions can get interpreted in the light of this single word, and then it is easy to forget that this is just one aspect of a multifaceted and immensely complex being. Adjectives are dangerous. Praising or blaming someone is very often a subtle form of control.

5. MAKING THE FEELING TO MATCH.

Once the case is built, appropriate feelings are manufactured to support the case—usually indignant self-righteousness, leading on to hostility, anger, or even hate, perhaps with a little fear mixed in. We can make our feelings fit the preconceptions of our case. Trusting such feelings seems to validate our case still further.

6. CREATING DISTANCE.

If our feelings become too obviously hostile, we are likely to suppress them. This creates an uncomfortable feeling of distance. Building a case does not feel good. In fact it feels terrible. But, as a man said to me recently, "At least it makes them feel terrible too!"

7. GOSSIP.

One of the ways we try to feel better about our case is to talk about it, creating camps or factions. What starts between two people can easily spread through a whole community. All we need to say is: "So-and-so is not looking so good" and our listeners may start to hink: "Oh, perhaps so-and-so is not in a good state." Or we can say, with great concern, "I'm worried about so-and-so" and we may get the same reactions. The extent to which we get this reaction depends on the strength of our influence and on the others' willingness to fall into the convenience of our case. Even when people don't talk, they are unconsciously attracted to those who hold the same views.

8. WAR.

The camps will go to war without our having to do anything more—often it's a political or a cold war. Some may prefer to fight whereas others may be more comfortable with flight—lying low or getting out. Either way, the war continues as a battle of fixed attitudes.

This whole process unfolds very rapidly. You can get to stage 6 in about thirty seconds. The camps take a bit longer. Once the cold war has started, it can last for years, or even generations. Why do we do this?

One reason is that blaming somebody else, especially when others agree with us, seems to absolve us of our own responsibility. Blame is giving up our own authority. We cannot blame somebody else if we believe that we make our own reality, or even if we accept responsibility for our life. People who blame others are never happy because they do not feel in control of their own lives.

A second reason for creating communal divisions is the temptation to make ourselves seem better than others. As mentioned in chapter 3, all limiting beliefs contain an element of "I am right and you are wrong," and therefore tend to be divisive. Our egos are attached to our position and those who agree with us are seen as "good," whereas those who disagree are seen as "bad." This division is then cemented by selective attention, distorted perception, and all the other mechanisms discussed in chapters 3 and 4. Our position feels as though it is right, and our disappointment, anger, or bitterness with the other side feels completely justified.

As we meet others on our side who agree with us, our belief seems confirmed. As the other side reacts with bitterness, anger, or hate, our position is further vindicated. Anger on one side creates anger on the other, hate creates hate, and the negative feelings escalate by mutual provocation. Case-building, especially shared cases, creates a great amount of suffering.

Only the avoidance of gossip can prevent the spread of a case. But once a case has spread, it is very difficult to eradicate. There are many examples of an error in a textbook being duplicated over and over again until it just becomes an accepted part of the literature. For example, most books still credit Marconi with the invention of radio, yet over fifty years ago, on June 21, 1943, after many years of bitter dispute, the U.S. Supreme Court ruled that Nikola Tesla, an extraordinary electrical genius, anticipated all other contenders with his radio patents. Tesla, not Marconi, had invented radio. Marconi actually used Tesla's radio patent (filed in 1897) to make his famous cross-Atlantic transmission in 1901, while Tesla had publicly demonstrated radio communication as early as 1893.

In a close-knit community, once a person or group of people is seen as in some way "bad," the label tends to stick. Even if one person changes her mind about them, she has to contend with the disagreement of the rest of the group. If she persists in her good opinions about them, she may be viewed as "on their side" and therefore disloyal or even "bad." Family therapists have written extensively on the scapegoating that goes on in families. Once a scapegoat is found, the pattern becomes set for decades unless an outside force, such as an effective family therapist, intervenes and disrupts the lopsided balance.

Some beliefs naturally spread through larger communities and countries, and of course countries build cases against each other. Quite often the case starts with fear of another country. When the fear is disguised or not admitted, it manifests as hostile suspicion, which may easily create a self-fulfilling prophecy that goes something like this:

Disguised fear exaggerates suspicion.
Suspicion leads to self-protection.
Self-protection condones aggression.
Aggression provokes retaliation.
Retaliation justifies suspicion and fear.

The unchecked cycle can create war. A similar vicious circle occurs in racial or religious prejudice—the hatred appears to be justified by the retaliation it creates. What makes it especially hard to change is that everybody on a person's side agrees with him. So the communal case is doubly vindicated—he lives among those who share his belief; and the other side proves that his prejudice is justified by retaliating with hate, anger, or violence. Cases, whether public or private, almost inevitably arise from limited beliefs creating assumptions and divisions.

The Cure for Case-Building

It is said that if we are supremely connected to our own inner strength, we will have no need for cases, no need even to think badly of anyone. Meanwhile, there are many things we can do that greatly help to cure the unhappiness of case-building. Here are some suggestions:

1. Let yourself know something is wrong if it is. You may only be aware of distance between you and somebody else—but don't accept this state as okay.

2. If you think someone is hurting you, ask yourself: "Is this reality? Or am I being paranoid?"

3. Whatever the answer, assume the best possible motives from the other person. Even if you have a strong negative feeling, say to yourself: "I *could* be mistaken." Even if the other person has hurt you, assume that she acts from ignorance rather than nastiness. Even if she was being nasty, your good assumptions may change her heart.

4. Make personal contact. Paranoia tends to build up with distance. Sometimes a moment of human contact is enough to dispel all suspicion.

5. If personal contact is not enough, mention your own hurt, *without accusation*. Speaking of your own hurt, rather than what the other person has done to you, evaporates defensiveness. This requires the courage to be vulnerable, the curiosity to want to know what is happening with the other person, and the humility to admit that you don't really know.

6. See the other person as a person of unlimited potential rather than as a limited character. See the spirit, soul, or whatever aspect you can relate to of the "center" in another person. See whatever difficulties they may have as part of their learning process. Find the good in another. When you look at people in this way, judgments disappear.

7. Avoid gossip. Gossip converts cases into camps. If you have negative thoughts about somebody (whether you are right or wrong), keep it to yourself or speak to the person in

question. If you hear negative gossip about someone, stay objective or say, "I don't want to hear that." Don't believe what other people say: make up your own mind. Remember that even a seemingly innocuous remark about someone can create a separate camp of friends. The effect of gossip is divisive and destructive.

8. If your case is already built, it may seem very solid to you. But a case is actually a very unstable structure that depends on the opposing case to prop it up—like two playing cards leaning against each other. All you have to do is dismantle your case, and the one against you will probably fall. Don't attempt to dismantle the case against you—it will make both cases worse. If you give up your own completely, it will not even matter to you whether the case against you continues or not. When you drop your own case and all the emotion that goes with it, you *know* that the case against you is simply a misunderstanding of your true nature.

9. Sometimes an entrenched case becomes structured into society's legal powers. Some unresolved cases end up in court. Sometimes you need the discrimination to know when to fight. If you fight, ask yourself if it is *against* the other person, or *for* the most loving solution. The two motivations may create very different consequences.

10. Ask yourself why you hold your present views. If you believe in creating your own reality, no one can ever wrong you. You simply choose different teachers for life's different lessons. Ask yourself without self-judgment: "What am I learning from this?" Remember that every situation is a mirror of your own inner state.

11. Aspire to connect to your innermost self. At the deepest level, from the pleasure of your deepest self (see chapter 16, page 186), it is quite impossible to judge other people or build any cases at all.

Gandhi's Solution to Racial Case-Building

Once you live in a situation of division, whether it is in your family, community or country, it takes objectivity, courage, and respect not to take sides in anger, bitterness or hate. In 1908, General Jan Smuts, the Defense Minister of South Africa, promised Gandhi that if the Indians in South Africa registered voluntarily (which meant compulsorily carrying identity cards), he would repeal the Asiatic Act, a law that discriminated against Asian people. Although Gandhi agreed, his followers did not trust that Smuts would keep his promise. Some of them vowed publicly to kill Gandhi if he registered. Gandhi replied that it was right to trust in human nature and proceeded to register. As he was about to enter the registration office, he was beaten up by some of the followers who had threatened him and almost died. Nevertheless, as soon as he regained consciousness, he registered. Smuts then went back on his word and refused to repeal the Asiatic Act.

Not surprisingly, Gandhi was confronted by his followers with his apparent credulity. To their astonishment, he replied that he had been absolutely right to trust Smuts. By assuming the opponent's best intentions you give the opponent a chance to change his mind, he said. If he fails to do so, everyone can see who is in the wrong.

In 1914 Gandhi planned an Indian mass march in South Africa. It so happened that at the same time the South African railways went on strike. As soon as Gandhi knew of this concurrence he canceled his march. Once again some of his followers could not understand why he did not take this opportunity to humiliate the government. Gandhi replied that his tactics were not to hurt or humble his adversary, but to convince his opponent's brain and capture his heart. As Martin Luther King, Jr., was to do some decades later, he broke the self-fulfilling prophecy of hate creating hate, and sowed the seeds of consideration.

Smuts was in fact moved by Gandhi's generosity and it was soon after this that he granted Gandhi many of the concessions that the Indians sought. While in prison before-hand, Gandhi had fashioned some leather sandals, which he later gave to Smuts. In 1939, on Gandhi's seventieth birth-day, Smuts wrote to him: "I have worn these sandals for many a summer since then, even though I may feel that I am not worthy to stand in the shoes of so great a man." Gandhi had won his heart.

Chapter 10

WHAT DO YOU BELIEVE?

BELIEF DIAGNOSIS

*A*fter reading through chapter 7, you will probably have found a few beliefs that you connect with. Others will be more hidden. This chapter presents three further avenues for diagnosing your beliefs, based on three simple questions:

1. What stops you from having your heart's desire?
   Diagnosis from blocked ideals
2. What are your judgments?
   Diagnosis from disapproval
3. What influences have affected you in your past?
   Diagnosis from history

Diagnosis from Blocked Ideals

What keeps us from our heart's desire? One of the biggest barriers, of course, is our limiting beliefs. Some of these may pop into your head as you think about obstacles to achieving particular goals in your life. This is what to do: Get a notebook and sit in a relaxed position. It is important to answer the following two questions quickly and without censorship. Allow yourself to be irrational—allow yourself to write down things that you disapprove of or that you are not sure of. Making a mistake will cause no harm, but trying to avoid mistakes will stop you from discovering anything you don't know.

QUESTION 1

What are your goals in life? Write down each goal on a separate sheet of paper. They do not need to be realistic in terms of your present situation and they should not take into account anything that anybody else wants or needs from you. These are your dreams and your ideals. If you wish, you can consider goals under different headings, for instance: work, relationships, money, leisure, self-expression, and personal growth.

QUESTION 2

What is it that stops you from having these goals right now? For each goal write down all the things that seem to you to be in the way—aspects of yourself (your body, your feelings, your inner self, your mind, your characteristics), aspects of others, of society, the past, your age, time, loyalties, the inevitable way life is. Write fast. Don't think too much. Allow yourself to be unreasonable.

Go over these two questions a day or two later. Do not make any deletions but add on any other thoughts or feelings that come up. Do not be concerned if there are contradictions. You will find that your answers provide a rich supply of beliefs and self-imposed limits. Underline the phrases or sentences that suggest a belief. Compare these beliefs with those in the Belief Manual (page 199) or in chapter 7.

Diagnosis by Disapproval

Disapproval is, surprisingly, the most reliable indication of a hidden belief system. Quite often the only way disguised beliefs show themselves is through moments of emotional judgment or disapproval. A man may, for example, think that in this modern day, it is perfectly okay for a man to cry; but if, when he sees a man cry, he finds a hint of disapproval in himself, then he may suspect an underlying belief: "Men should not really cry—at least not too much." Paradoxically, if he believes that men should not cry, he might also disapprove of a man being hard, for the hardness may remind him of his own self-imposed limitation.

Let's say that a woman walks into someone's house and disapproves of their rich decor. Instantly she can know that she is suffering from a limiting belief: it could be that "being poor is more spiritual" or it could be "life should be self-denying and suffering." It could even be "I must keep a low profile" or "people are only out for what they can get." A particular disapproval may relate to different limited beliefs in different people. What is certain, though, is that disapproval *guarantees* a hidden limiting belief system of some kind.

Why, someone asked me, is it limiting to disapprove of cruelty or genocide? To answer this question means making a distinction between "understanding that something is wrong" and having an "emotional aversion." By disapproval I mean emotional aversion. Understanding that cruelty is wrong does not imply a limitation at all. But if we have an emotional aversion to cruelty, it points to a limitation within us (for example, our own cruelty or else old reactions to cruelty experienced in the past. Or it could be that we believe "the world is a terrible place" or "people are bad" or "men are brutes"). It is the reverberation with an inner limiting belief that creates the emotion. Understanding contains compassion, whereas emotional aversion contains the seeds of hate. The same distinction applies to judgment and judgmentalism.

JUDGMENT AND JUDGMENTALISM

The word *judgment* as used here is unemotive and often essential to making useful choices. *Judmentalism,* however, is

emotive disapproval which usually makes both the judger
and the judged feel bad. Judgmentalism is the process of
putting down and putting up, making ourselves higher or
lower, or seeing in terms of right or wrong.

Most often we are not aware of such assumptions: All we
are aware of is the feeling of disapproval. *Disapproval* can be
defined as: (1) The unpleasantly superior feeling that arises
when we witness something that does not fit our limited
beliefs; or (2) the unpleasant sense of repugnance that arises
when we witness a limitation that reminds us, uncomfortably,
of our own similar limits.

Awareness of our disapproval can be a great asset—for
we can use it as a signpost of a lurking limited belief that
could use some expansion. Here's what to do: Carry a notebook. Every time you notice a feeling of disapproval in yourself, write down what you disapprove of. Your own
disapproval may itself be disguised. You may feel discomfort,
irritation, tension, or a desire to get out fast. Consider these
as possible signs of disapproval and ask yourself if there is
any possibility that you do disapprove. When you have time,
look at what you have written on your disapproval list. Sometimes the belief will be quite obvious. For example, a man
tells a woman of a "meaningful coincidence" which he as-
cribes to ESP. Her judgment says "It could have been explained in another way," but her judgmentalism says "He's
stupid." Her judgment may be quite correct, but her judgmentalism informs her that she has a limiting belief system—
such as "life is random," or "all knowledge is transmitted
via the five senses," or "men are dumb."

On other occasions, the limiting belief is less immediately
obvious, and it is necessary to question ourselves further. Ask
yourself these questions:

QUESTION 1

"What do I disapprove of?" Write down your thoughts and
allow yourself to be privately judgmental and irrational. This

may suggest a belief system. If it does, try to make the suggestion into a definitive statement, even if it sounds dogmatic and off the walls. Remember that this is a process of exploration which eventually aims to go beyond the limiting belief. The first step is to have the personal honesty and courage to see what the limiting belief might be. Usually when you hit on one of your central beliefs, you have a feeling of "Ah— that's it." (An example of this process follows after question 5.)

QUESTION 2

"What do the people or things that I disapprove of have in common?" List both the assets and the liabilities that they share. Again allow yourself the freedom to be privately judgmental and as irrational as you want.

QUESTION 3

"So what does that make me?" or "How am I different?" or "How am I similar?" The answers will either be the opposite to the characteristics of those you judge or the same. This leads to the "ego advantage" (page 205) or the "self judgment" (page 206) of your belief system, from which you may be able to deduce your central belief. If you feel different from those you disapprove of and you still cannot make sense of it, go on to question 4.

QUESTION 4

Irrationally speaking, "what is more important than what?" To be more specific, "*which item* is it in this belief about myself (question 3) that is more important than *which item* I disapprove of in others?" Write down your thoughts freely without deliberation, and later, compare them to some of the belief systems in the Belief Manual or chapter 7. If you are still unclear, go on to question 5.

QUESTION 5

Sit down quietly and close your eyes. Relax and focus on your breathing. Assume there is a wiser intuitive knowledge within you and ask this intuitive part of yourself: "I do not understand the connection—please give me any clue which helps me understand the belief behind my disapproval." Then, as you focus quietly on your breathing, wait and see what comes up—it may be a thought, an image, some words, even a feeling, which provides an indication of a belief or a direction of explanation. If you find that you cannot remain objective, imagine that your consciousness is standing outside yourself, looking at yourself both objectively and compassionately.

Example
John found himself disapproving of another man. He did not know why. In the privacy of his notebook he allowed himself to be openly judgmental (question 1): "The guy's an oaf— a big stupid blundering idiot." A little surprised at the strength of his criticism, he became more aware of his disapproval in similar situations. What did those situations or people have in common (question 2)? Again he allowed himself irrational freedom in his private notebook: "They are big idiots—they are all brawn, no brain—they are insensitive, clumsy, and not very bright." As he thought of four people he saw as similar, he realized they were all men and they were all big, but none of them was in fact stupid. His irrational belief was "large men are stupid."

"So what does that make me (question 3)?" he asked himself, and the answer of course was, "intelligent—smaller men like me are intelligent." But why the connection of intelligence and size? "*Which item* is it in this belief about myself that is more important than *which item* I disapprove of in others (question 4)?"

The answer is clear: "intelligence is more important than size"—not as objective judgment but as emotive judgmentalism. If he had read chapter 7, he probably would have made a connection to one of the belief systems under "The Physical World Is Inferior." As it was, he went on to question 5.

He sat down in a relaxed position, closed his eyes, and asked the intuitive part of himself the question: "I do not understand the connection—please give me any clue which helps me understand the belief behind my disapproval (Q.5)." An image came up of some hearty big men laughing, eating with enjoyment, speaking loudly. Some of the men got up and wrestled for fun. He immediately saw that he disapproved of all these physical activities. Putting this understanding into statements, he later wrote: "the physical side of life is lower," "animal impulses should be controlled," "the body is inferior."

He was quite surprised by this realization because on an intellectual level, he disagreed. But as he looked back on his life, he saw how much difficulty he had had in enjoying the physical side of life. He had put all his energy into his intellect and then supported this limitation of himself with his ego, which said, "I'm right—they are wrong (and stupid)." Awareness of emotive disapproval had pointed to the ego. The comparisons of the ego had pointed to the underlying belief system.

Diagnosis from blocked ideals and diagnosis from disapproval show us the disguised beliefs that are most important to us. Diagnosis from disapproval, especially, shows the beliefs that have most emotive impact and which tend to affect us most deeply. Diagnosis from history is a less reliable approach, but may nevertheless point to some beliefs that were missed by the other methods.

If it interests you to do this, fine, or if the other methods do not work for you, okay. **But it is not necessary to try to analyze every belief we have.** First of all it could take us more than a lifetime. Secondly *it is only useful to look at the beliefs that prevent us from living a fulfilled life.*

Diagnosis from History

Clearly we are affected by the beliefs that surround us. When we were very young, adults appeared to us as great models of perfection and we learned by copying them. So by looking at the beliefs of those who surrounded us, especially in our early years, we can get some idea of our *likely or possible beliefs.* Ask yourself these questions:

1. WHAT WERE OR ARE MY PARENTS' BELIEF SYSTEMS?

As discussed earlier, it is almost impossible not to be affected by the beliefs of our parents. For every strong belief they had or have (you can find these by checking through chapter 7), ask yourself if there is *any* evidence that you have the same belief. Sometimes the evidence comes from our holding the opposite belief very strongly. So long as we are in rebellion against our parents' limiting beliefs, we are still being affected and molded by these beliefs. If your parents' belief is not clear to you, remember what they approved of and disapproved of.

2. WHAT GENERALIZATIONS ABOUT LIFE DID I LEARN FROM:

My country?	(page 36)
My culture?	(page 36)
My class?	(page 37)
My education?	(page 40)
My color?	(page 119)
My religion?	(page 94—97)

Many of our beliefs are molded, without our being aware
of it, by these powerful influences. You can diagnose a whole
stack of beliefs just by asking yourself these questions. One
small warning, though: It is easy to say to yourself, "Oh yes,
they believed that, but of course *I* don't." Again ask yourself if there is *any* evidence that you hold the beliefs you
were taught, even if they are in disguised form. The most
common and easily detectable evidence of such disguised
beliefs are:

1. Disapproval of others who do not share the belief you
   were taught, who were brought up in a different way
   (Diagnosis by Disapproval).
2. Disapproval of others who *do* share the belief you were
   taught and who act as uncomfortable reminders of your
   limitation (Diagnosis by Disapproval).
3. Creating a reality that does not fit what you think you
   believe (Diagnosis from Blocked Ideals). For example if
   a boy was beaten up at school by bigger children, he
   might have learned the fixed belief "I am small and
   afraid." Now at the height of 6 foot 4 he naturally does
   not think he has this belief, but he might suspect it if he
   finds he cringes whenever he meets an irritated dwarf. A
   woman who was taught that success was not for her type
   might well disbelieve it on rational grounds; but if she
   has consistently failed despite superb opportunity and
   promise, she might suspect that the old irrational belief
   could be operant.

Although history is the most commonly used psychological
method of diagnosis, it can be quite unreliable, for the fact
is we attach ourselves to some beliefs that surround us but

not to others. History gives us an indication of which beliefs we *could* be attached to, but no indication of which beliefs we *are* attached to. A therapist may recognize whether or not we are attached by emotive or body language signs that the self-diagnoser may miss. However, in similar fashion, you may experience the "Aha" feeling when a historical belief accords with your present belief.

These methods of diagnosis will reveal most of your important belief systems. Some other limiting beliefs may appear as you tackle the belief manual and as you start to take positive action to change some of your limitations.

Naming a Belief

Some people find that it is helpful to name the old limiting belief to help disempower it. A particular client had several beliefs which clustered around the issue of authority. Though he was forty, he sometimes felt like an adolescent rebeling against authorites which, in his thinking, seemed to victimize him arbitrarily, just like his father had done. These beliefs kept interfering with his work and relationships. After diagnosing them, he came up with a name for his belief cluster, "R.A.V.A.D."—the Rebellious Adolescent Victim of an Arbitrary Dictator. The name would make him laugh. When he caught himself thinking in the old limiting way, he would say to himself, "Ah, RAVAD again," and smile.

It may seem that this contradicts what was said about the dangers of labeling. Labeling has a negative effect when we use it to put ourselves down or when we identify ourselves with the label. Naming is positive when:

1. It is used to control the limitation, not the person.
2. The name is only for the belief, not the person.
3. We do not identify with the label. We identify with the far greater inner self of unlimited capacity.
4. We do not use it to put ourselves down.

5. We use it with great respect for ourselves. Respecting ourselves *as we are now* means respecting even the limitation (though not abiding by it). Limitations get stronger when we try to fight them—it is better to treat them with kindness and humor.

The only limiting beliefs worth knowing about are those that interfere with our leading a fulfilled life. So long as we do not judge ourselves, the discovery of these beliefs is a fascinating journey. Discovering the limitation is the first step towards changing it and unlocking the potential hidden beneath constricting ideas.

Part 2

Belief TRANSFORMA-TION

If one advances confidently in the direction of his dreams, and endeavors to live the life which he has imagined, he will meet with a success unexpected in common hours. He will put something behind, will pass an invisible boundary; new, universal, and more liberal laws will begin to establish themselves around and within him, or the old laws will be expanded and interpreted in his favor in a more liberal sense; and he will live with the license of a higher order of beings.

—Thoreau

Chapter 11

▼

CHANGE YOUR MIND
CHANGE YOUR WORLD

*O*nce you have diagnosed one of your limiting beliefs, it is an eye-opening experience to understand why and how it was maintained with so much secret dedication.

If you study a belief in this way the difference between your belief and reality becomes clearer; you are freed from thinking that reality is as narrow as your belief. So it is useful to examine your beliefs in some detail.

Then, once you have dislodged your belief from what you used to think was realilty, you are free to create a better belief. Such a simple statement may seem hard to accept at first. Many people have tried positive thinking techniques, only to find them unreal or too good to be true. A limiting belief is, by nature, cynical. When faced with the unlimited, it projects a screen of disbelief: "Come on, you've got to be kidding," it says. Somehow the old limiting belief is so firmly ingrained in the mind as reality, that the new positive thinking is simply unbelievable. The question, then, is how can we *ingrain* the new belief. This is answered in chapters 14 to 19. Armed with this knowledge and a willingness to work, it really is possible to practice an unlimiting belief, until it becomes your new reality.

The rest of this book shows you how.

A belief is a thought that has been reinforced by feeling and imagination. In ingraining a new *positive* belief or affirmation, we start with a simple idea of what we would like to believe, based on the belief opposite to our limiting belief (chapter 14). This thought is then deliberately strengthened with feeling and imagination (chapters 15 and 16) until it becomes a "possible reality." After practicing the new belief in imagination, we then take positive action (chapter 17), using the "possible reality" as if it were absolutely true. In this way we begin to create a positive self-fulfilling prophecy. In time, the accumulated positive self-fulfilling prophecies give us a reflection of our belief in reality, and we know we have truly changed.

First it is necessary to practice our new unlimited belief in the imagination, and for this it is useful to be able to slow down the rhythm of our brain to alpha frequency. This is the subject of the next chapter.

Chapter 12

▼

ALPHA

THE FREQUENCY OF CHANGE

In the 1989 Oscar-winning film *Rainman,* Dustin Hoffman gave a clinically accurate portrayal of an idiot savant, a highly limited autistic adult with isolated pockets of sheer genius. He could not add three and three and yet could remember every card played in six packs in a game of blackjack. In real life, people with similar powers exist. Leslie Lemke is blind, severely mentally retarded, and has cerebral palsy. He cannot hold a knife and fork and can only repeat what is said to him in a monotone. Yet, at the age of fourteen, on hearing Tchaikovsky's piano concerto No. 1 for the first time, to the astonishment of his foster mother, he played it on the piano immediately and accurately. Though he has had no formal musical training, he can play back any piece he hears in its entirety and without mistake, no matter how long or complicated. A famous pair of twins can tell you the day of the week of any date you care to mention within the last (or next) 40,000 years. Such feats of computation cannot be deduced logically at such speed and must require an intuitive "leap," or else a prodigious memory.

Several theories have been advanced about the origin of these strange geniuses with IQ's of less than 25. One is that savants have left-brain damage associated with poor logical functioning, and that the right brain compensates by becoming more predominant. The right brain is associated with creativity, intuition, and the nonverbal arts while the left brain is associated with language and logical reasoning. What is interesting about these conditions is that they show that the brain may have extraordinary capacities which are often untapped. Under hypnosis, some people can remember minute details of experiences long before their conscious memory. Similar effects have been achieved by sticking tiny electrodes in people's brains: sometimes memories are released with extraordinary vividness and detail—such as seeing the color of every car on a street you walked down twenty years ago. It seems that the brain records, somewhere, everything that ever happened to us.

It is frequently quoted in psychology that we only use 10 percent of our brains. If this is so, the interesting question is how can we develop the other 90 percent? One method of reaching the right brain resources of creativity, intuition, and sensitivity is by slowing down the frequency of brain waves, as measured by an electrical recording machine called an electro-encephalogram. In the waking state the electrical discharges of the brain oscillate at a frequency of 14–20 cycles per second. This speed is associated with logical or linear left-brained thinking and is called *beta rhythm*. In the sleeping state the brain waves oscillate much more slowly, at about 4 cycles per second. In this state there is little logical thought and, at times, much seemingly undirected creativity (as, for instance, in dreams). Between these two states—between sleep and conscious awareness—at about 10 cycles per second, it is possible for left and right brain functions to occur simultaneously. Intuitive and creative faculties can be combined with logical direction to make mental faculties more incisive. This slower rhythm of between 8–13 cycles per second is called *alpha rhythm*.

Techniques for reaching slower brain rhythms to augment mental abilities have been used for thousands of years in many different cultures. Meditation, self-hypnosis, and various trance induction techniques are examples. Most of these methods have had a mixed reception in Western society—meditation because of its association with religion and the

East, hypnosis because of its association with embarrassing stage shows, and trance because of its association with magic and mediums. Alpha rhythm techniques, however, are in themselves completely neutral. They are a method of reaching a natural state in which imagination and creativity are enhanced. These facilities can be used for many different purposes.

Alpha rhythm occurs spontaneously at times of going to sleep and waking up. Most people have experienced seemingly unsolvable difficulties to which a solution "arrives" when they wake up in the morning. Unfortunately this does not happen very often because the sleep and dream processes cannot easily be directed. Alpha rhythm also occurs naturally during daydreaming. Although we can be highly creative and imaginative at such times, the process is usually undirected or else directed towards empty fantasy.

To be able to direct ourselves in our imaginations requires a balance of cognitive and imaginative faculties. Deeper hypnotism or meditational states can enhance creativity, sensitivity, and ESP but usually at the loss of intellectual capacity. These states are associated with an EEG brain wave pattern of around 4–8 cycles per second (c.p.s.). Alpha rhythm (8–13 cycles per second) is the meeting point of intellect and imagination, of right and left brain and of inner and outer orientation.

The Basic Brain-Wave Patterns

1–4 c.p.s.	delta waves	Predominant in sleep
4–8 c.p.s.	theta waves	Predominant in deep hypnosis or deep meditation. Associated with greatly augmented facilities for creativity, imagination, sensitivity, and ESP. Associated with inward focus.

8–13 c.p.s.   alpha waves   Predominant in light medita-
                              tion, light hypnosis, "alpha
                              techniques," or in daydream-
                              ing. Associated with height-
                              ened creativity, imagination,
                              and sensitivity in combination
                              with cognitive faculties. In-
                              ward and outward focus
                              maintained simultaneously.
14–22 c.p.s.   beta waves   Predominant in most people
                              during physical work, think-
                              ing, and using the eyes. Asso-
                              ciated with focusing on the
                              outside world.

The Uses of Alpha

There are three main benefits from using alpha rhythm: relaxation, imagination, and reprogramming of beliefs. All
three effects are useful in the process of ingraining a new
unlimiting belief.

1. RELAXATION

It is almost impossible to go into alpha without considerable
muscular relaxation, the effects of which can last throughout
the day. When we are relaxed, spontaneity, clear thinking,
and the capacity for pleasure are all increased. Undue muscular tension, on the other hand, is associated with more
rigid thinking, anxiety, incapacity for enjoyment and poorer
communicating skills. Tension over large periods is associated with greater morbidity. A study of Dr. David Orme-
Johnson published in the *American Journal of Psychosomatic Medicine* compared meditators with an equivalent group of nonmeditators. He found that the meditators spent 87 percent

less on cardio-vascular treatment than the nonmeditators, and that in seventeen out of eighteen specialties, the meditators spent less on hospital treatment. (The eighteenth specialty was obstetrics: they had more babies.) Even without the effects on imagination and belief transformation, alpha techniques can be worthwhile for relaxation alone.

2. IMAGINATION

Alpha rhythm can also be used for creative problem solving through visual imagination. For example, visualizing a good performance beforehand can improve our results. This concept has been used in self-healing techniques, in sports, and before business meetings. Many creative solutions occur in alpha or slower brain rhythms. Bernard Crick found the answer to the structure of DNA—the elegant double helix— in a dream. Anton Bruckner heard the Scherzo of his seventh symphony in a dream. One of Albert Einstein's concepts of relativity derived from imagining (in alpha) angels traveling down a light beam.

The word "inspiration" has two main meanings: the inhalation of the breath, and the exalted state of creativity. For thousands of years people in both Eastern and Western traditions have focused their minds on the breath in order to attain the exalted and creative states of the slower brain rhythms. Alpha rhythm and increased imagination go hand in hand, and imagination is the first essential step in any change.

3. REPROGRAMMING

Alpha can be used for reprogramming from limiting to unlimiting beliefs. Limiting beliefs are like computer programs—once programmed, the computer's responses are fixed. New information that does not fit the program is either discarded or else altered until it fits. These beliefs are held at a conscious or preconscious level and, as we have seen, have an extraordinarily powerful effect on our lives.

Under alpha rhythm, however, the hold of limiting beliefs is loosened. Intuition and creativity become more available, as the beliefs of the mind are temporarily suspended. Under alpha, our imagination of our new unlimiting belief has a chance to live without being strangled by limiting thoughts. The tinted lenses of our usual beliefs no longer dominate our vision, because we are looking inwards as well as outwards.

In alpha rhythm, as in hypnosis, we are more suggestible. This does not mean that we will accept a nonsensical suggestion—our connection to rational thinking remains intact. But, a creative new belief can more easily be assimilated.

Going into Alpha Naturally

Everyone goes into alpha rhythm every day, in daydreams, imaginings, and before and after sleep. Read the following passage, then close your eyes and imagine it in as much sensual detail as possible; or, get someone else to read it to you slowly.

> Imagine a lemon. See the lemon skin with all the little pores. Now imagine cutting the lemon in half. Hear the sound of the knife cutting through the skin. Feel the lemon with your hands. Feel the cool wetness of the cut. Be aware of the smell of the lemon. Then cut it again so that it's in quarters. Now pick up a quarter and take a large bite.

Chances are, your mouth will water. Salivation is an example of an automatic process that can be affected by imagination but not by will-power alone. Also, you will almost certainly have been in alpha rhythm, because successful visualization requires higher proportions of alpha waves. All you have to do is to focus more inwardly in your imagination, rather than outward on the world, and you are in alpha.

Visualization

When you last saw an elephant, which way was it facing? To answer that question requires some kind of visualization. Some people think they cannot visualize. In fact, everybody can, but the process appears to be different in different people. Some can close their eyes and visualize in fine detail a realistic looking picture. Others do not make a picture so much as have an idea of a picture. The picture may not be "seen" or may be seen as once-removed, or "kind of behind a curtain" as one client put it. When I have asked people in seminars and lectures about their experiences of visualization, I find that about 50 percent visualize a real-looking picture, while about 50 percent have more of an idea of a picture, but I have never met anyone who cannot visualize. For some it is easier to imagine hearing, touch, smell, or taste. In fact imagination of any of the five sensual modalities takes you to alpha rhythm. We speak more of visualization because vision is our predominant sense, but we can "auditorize," "tactilize," "gustatorize," or "olfactorize" if we want to. The more richly and sensually a scene is imagined, the more effective it is in changing a belief. Imagination of any sensual modality gets easier with practice.

When you visualized the elephant you were remembering an old picture. This process has been termed *remembered visualization*. Now picture an ostrich walking along a ladder suspended between two zebras. This is less likely to be a memory. Constructing a picture that you have not seen before is termed *constructive visualization*. *Remembered visualization* is a useful tool in changing the past. *Constructive visualization* is important in changing beliefs and the future.

Going into Alpha at Will

You can train yourself to tune into the alpha range in order to reach qualities of relaxation and imagination as well as to exercise belief transformation. With practice this can be done in the space of a few seconds. The graded exercises that follow will enable you to do this. They combine selection of the best methods of alpha induction that I have come across in the fields of hypnosis, meditation, and deep relaxation techniques. All the methods depend on using your imagination fully. If you believe that you have little imagination, do not worry, it will develop with consistent practice. Just as you salivate by imagining food rather than through your will alone, so you relax by imagining looseness, relaxation, or heaviness, (rather than by willing yourself to relax—which makes you tense). The power of your imagination is formidable and this power can be developed and harnessed with practice and effort.

Unfortunately it is difficult to read and stay in alpha at the same time, since focusing your eyes tends to put you straight back into beta rhythm. It is possible, though difficult at first, to remember an exercise and repeat it to yourself with your eyes closed. Alternatively you can make your own tape recording of the words, adapting the reading to your own style and speed. In this case the words should be spoken in a different tone from your normal voice, softer, deeper, relaxed, slow and with many pauses. If you find alpha rhythm induction easier with somebody else's voice, try to get someone else to record the words.

POSTURE

There are two important things about posture in alpha rhythm. The first is that you should be comfortable, so that you can relax. You can lie on your back or sit down. For most people I recommend sitting because that makes it harder to fall asleep. (Using alpha lying down can, in fact, be a very effective means of going to sleep.)

The second important thing is to keep your back comfortably straight. If you are sitting down, place the feet firmly on the floor. Your back should be kept away from the back rest, or else supported by a fairly straight back rest, preferably one that supports the small of your back.

If your chair is so low that your knees stick up and your thighs are not supported, cross your lower legs (not your thighs or knees) so that your thighs are horizontal and supported.

TIME

The whole exercise takes only ten to fifteen minutes each day. The hardest part is having the discipline to start, especially when your day is already full from countless demands. It is so easy to lose faith that all this can really accomplish anything—it takes time to develop the belief that changing something within can *really* change your outer life. It does not matter how much evidence is presented in this book, it is the experience that will convince you. In the meantime, relying only on the fact that it makes intellectual sense to try, the only answer is to practice regularly. The easiest way to develop this discipline is to do the exercise at the same time each day, so that it becomes as routine as brushing your teeth. Once it becomes routine, it takes far less effort, and even becomes something to look forward to.

For most people, the best time is the early morning, at the very start of the day and before eating. But some prefer the evening. If you have children, find a time when they are out of the house or asleep. Many parents find the best time is the early morning, before the children get up.

If you have used alpha techniques before or are familiar with meditation or self-hypnosis, it is probably best to keep with the method you know. If not, the following exercise can be used. At first it will take a few minutes, but gradually the process will become faster, with fewer and fewer words necessary, until you can go into alpha at will, in the space of a few seconds.

THE WORDS TO ALPHA

Close your eyes. Get comfortable in your chair, feel secure in your position with your back comfortably straight. **Imagine a screen in front of you. Imagine on this screen the words being written "body relax." As you look at the words take a deep breath in. And then as you breathe out say to yourself the words "body relax", and feel your body relax.**

Focus your attention on your legs. Feel the weight of your legs on the floor, as they relax. *Be aware of your feet on the floor. Feel the relaxed weight of your legs supported by the floor.*

Feel the weight of your body on the chair. *Be aware of where your body touches the chair. As you become aware of the places where your body touches the chair, your body can relax more deeply and your breathing becomes easy and regular.* With each breath out, your shoulders relax and drop. This relaxation spreads down your arms, making them feel relaxed and comfortable.

Now *be aware of your head and neck.* As your neck relaxes, *feel your head getting lighter,* so that it seems to be lifting up and you feel more at ease. *Let your face relax.* Feel your forehead relax. Your eyes relax. Cheeks relax. Lips relax. Jaw relax. As your jaw relaxes, your tongue relaxes, drops down, falls to the base of your mouth. And *as your tongue relaxes, your whole body becomes looser.* Feel the support of the chair and the ground under you. As you feel this support you can relax still further.

Now **Imagine the screen again. Imagine the words being written: "mind calm." As you look at the words take a deep breath in. And then as you breathe out say to yourself the words "mind calm," and feel your mind relax.**

Focus your attention on the very center of your head in the middle of your brain. Imagine an area of warmth in this center; concentrate your thoughts and your imagination to make this sense of warmth stronger. Gradually, the warmth from this center spreads outward to your whole brain, relaxing all the tensions of the mind. Let it move forwards to your eyes, spreading into your eyes gently, allowing your eyes to relax. Now feel the warmth spreading downward from your brain, through your neck, and down to the center of your chest. *Imagine that your thoughts are dropping down, falling gently, dropping down towards your heart. As you feel the sense of falling, know that your mind will be calm and secure.*

Feel yourself balanced in your body, calm in your mind and know that you are now in a state of alpha rhythm. In alpha rhythm your memory, creativity, and intuition are enhanced, focused and alert. You are now in a state of alpha rhythm where old beliefs can be questioned with greater understanding. You are now in a state of alpha rhythm where new beliefs can be practiced and entertained as possible realities. *As your body stays relaxed, your mind is alert, focussed inwards, creative, and ready to begin the exercise.*

COMING OUT OF ALPHA

In chapters 13 to 16 there are exercises that are best done under alpha rhythm. To come back to beta after an exercise, tell yourself the following:

You will feel alert and good and you will be able to take the benefits of the exercise with you to your everyday life. Stretch your fingers, your toes, and then the rest of your body. Open your eyes.

SPEEDING UP THE TRANSITION TO ALPHA

1. Do the whole exercise, using all the words, every day for at least two weeks or for up to two months, or more if you wish. It is not important how long it takes you. What is important is that the repetition begins to build a kind of conditioned reflex. The words "**body relax**" become connected to your body physically relaxing, which is con-

nected to the sequence of legs, body, breathing, shoulders, arms, head, and tongue becoming looser or heavier. Eventually only "**body relax**" will be necessary. The same applies to "**mind calm**."

2. After some weeks, use only the words in boldface and italics. The rest of the sequence should take place automatically. If it does not, go back to 1 until the sequence becomes more ingrained. If you made a tape of all the "words to alpha," you can make a second tape of just the words in boldface and italics.

3. After a few more weeks, use only the words in boldface. Imagine the rest of the sequence taking place. If you cannot, go back to stage 2 without self-judgment, then try 3 again when you feel ready.

4. Eventually, you need only say to yourself on two consecutive long out-breaths:

"**Body relax**" (as you feel your body relax).

"**Mind calm**" (as you feel your thoughts "drop".)

You will be able to go into alpha in the space of two breaths. The time it takes you to reach this point is not so important since the exercises can be done just as effectively whatever your speed in reaching alpha. The main reason for getting to alpha faster is that it can eventually be used as a tool which is readily available at any time of day. You can learn to switch almost immediately to more creative, intuitive resources. The best judge of when to move up a speed is you, but in general, don't push it, and if you are in doubt, wait until the conditioning of the sequence is well consolidated. Everybody can benefit from the qualities we tap into in alpha. A few people can go into alpha automatically with no training. But for the great majority, it is necessary to find the switch from beta to alpha, which requires practice. Sooner or later it will become a conditioned reflex, available on command. In the meantime, even on the first time you use the alpha technique, you can still benefit from the exercises in belief transformation.

Questions and Answers

Everybody is different and responds differently to visual, auditory, and tactile messages. For this reason, the exercise given here contains several different interwoven techniques, some of which will be more amenable and effective for you than others. In time you will automatically focus more on the parts that are more useful for you. In teaching these techniques to people in seminars, I have often been asked the following questions. One or two of these may be relevant to you:

Q. How do I know I'm in alpha?
A. At first you may not. There is no dramatic difference from the beta state. You may be aware of greater relaxation. In general, if you are focused on an imagined scene or any inner sensation, you are in alpha. If you are focused on logical thinking, analysis, or on what is happening outside you, you are in beta. Another clue is that being in alpha is nearly always pleasurable. In time and with practice the difference between alpha and beta becomes more palpable.

Q. I found it hard to focus on the right words. Other images kept appearing. Can I learn better control of my images?
A. Yes, as you practice, your ability to visualize what you want to see improves.

Q. What if I can't see any words at all? Should I leave them out or keep trying?
A. Do not bother to try to visualize the words at first. Focus on the sound of the words and on your own sensations within the muscles of your body. Hear the words and feel the relaxation in your body. For some people (especially those who are highly visually oriented in beta), visualization is a less effective method of reaching alpha. Later, as your capacity to visualize improves, you may find you are able to "see" the words—but it is not important.

Q. I find it hard to see things on a TV or movie screen. Should I visualize something else?

A. You can visualize the words being written on anything. You can see them written in chalk on a blackboard or, if you wish, in lights in the sky.

Q. When I close my eyes I see various lights and patterns. Are these different from visualization?

A. Probably. Such patterns are often caused by some light travelling through your eyelids. These patterns are sometimes interpreted or transformed by the brain into images. Such images are less likely to occur when the room is dark. Some people put a folded cloth lightly over their eyes to create more darkness—this is a matter of personal preference. Even in total darkness, if your eyes have just been in the light, after-images appear for a few minutes as a physiological effect in the receptor cells of the retina of the eye. With practice, you will not notice any of these patterns or images as your focus becomes more successfully directed to your object of visualization.

Q. How do you stop yourself from falling asleep?

A. If you sit upright (without a backrest if you can do so comfortably), you are less likely to fall asleep. As you drift into the alpha state you have an increasingly high percentage of alpha waves. If you continue to drift down, the proportion of theta waves and then delta waves increase until you lose consciousness. It's a continuous process with no distinct dividing lines. With practice, it becomes easier to know where you are and to stay in alpha.

Q. I keep going in and out of alpha. How do I stop this?

A. Don't try too hard to stop it and don't worry about it. Bring your mind gently back to the image or the exercise. Your capacity to concentrate and stay at one level will gradually increase.

Q. How do I stop being distracted by my own thoughts?

A. It is the natural tendency of the mind to wander. Do not judge yourself for losing focus. Simply bring your attention back to the exercise you are doing. Using a tape recording helps stop the mind wandering too far or for too long.

Q. How do I stop myself from being distracted by noises or discomforts?

A. They need not interrupt you if you incorporate them. Simply say to yourself, for example: "the itch on my calf is relaxing me further," or, "the sound of that car relaxes me further." Virtually anything can be used as a signal for deeper relaxation and slower brain rhythms.

Q. What happens if something occurs in your environment that you need to attend to?

A. There are some exceptions to *anything* being able to relax you further. "The sound of that nuclear explosion relaxes me further" is unlikely to work. If there is anything you really need to attend to, you will find yourself alert and ready for beta-action immediately.

Q. When I try to imagine a warmth at the center of my brain, I cannot feel anything, but I can imagine blood vessels dilating. Does it matter what you imagine?

A. No. Some people prefer coolness, liquidity, energy, dilation of blood vessels, lightness, heaviness, etc. All that matters is that it is acceptable to you, reasonably easy to imagine, and relaxing.

Q. As I go into alpha, I sometimes start to get nervous or even tense. I don't know why. What can I do about this?

A. Some people, when they first start, feel a resistance or fear of a relaxed state. Sometimes it is a fear of the unknown and sometimes it is connected with a sense of greater vulnerability. As you practice, these fears will pass and alpha rhythm will be a state you begin to enjoy. Sometimes when you relax into alpha, feelings that were previously blocked come to the surface. In this case, the fear is of experiencing the possible pain of these feelings. Letting yourself be aware of such feelings is nearly always a relief and dispels the fear.

Q. When in alpha, sometimes I notice some movements in my muscles that I can hardly control. Is this normal?

A. It's common. Sometimes when you are going to sleep, your body jerks suddenly. This is known as a *myoclonic jerk*. In the same way when you go into alpha or slower brain rhythms your muscles relax and you sometimes get an impulse of spontaneous movement. The best thing is to let it happen without resistance or worry.

Q. I find time is very hard to judge when in alpha. How do you know when to come out?

A. Use an alarm clock. This creates a time limit which gives an incentive to focus on the exercises. It also stops you worrying about the time or worrying about missing an appointment through falling asleep.

Q. I feel very warm *or* I feel very cold when in alpha. Is this to be expected?

A. Changes in body temperature are common. If you feel very warm, don't worry about it. If you tend to get cold, dress very warmly—this is important because coldness creates muscle tension which interferes with the relaxed alpha state.

Q. Sometimes I get scared I won't be able to get back to beta. Can this ever really be a problem?

A. No. You will always get back to beta. All you have to do is open your eyes. The only thing that will stop you getting back to beta is falling asleep, in which case you will wake naturally.

Q. What can I do about a slightly groggy, lethargic feeling after going into alpha?

A. Most people feel rejuvenated after some time in alpha. A few people feel lethargic for a few minutes afterwards, especially if they go deeper than alpha. When you come out of alpha it is a good idea to do something physical and mundane, such as walk, stretch, or have a cup of coffee.

Q. Is there any danger of alpha techniques making you spaced out?

A. Only if you overuse alpha (for hours each day!) and if you use it to escape from the world rather than to deal with the world more creatively. I do not recommend either of these approaches. Alpha rhythm, used once or twice per day for short periods makes our bodies more relaxed and our minds clearer. Focusing our imagination with direction and purpose increases our capacity to handle ourselves and the world around us with creativity and grace.

▼

Chapter 13

HISTORY REVISITED

CHANGING THE PAST

*I*n some senses, the past does not exist. If you watch six people discuss a past event, especially on emotional issues, you will hear six different perceptions and six different interpretations, creating six versions of "reality." When two people argue about the past, it is sometimes difficult to believe they could be talking about one event. You find the same thing if you look at history books published in different countries.

In any one "event," there are as many observed events as there are observers. There is no such thing as *objective reality* about the past because no recording instruments (human or otherwise) are perfect or can see from every angle. But there certainly is a *subjective reality*. We are affected by our memories of the past, and because these memories seem to *be* reality, we can feel trapped, changed, or even damaged by what we believe happened. And some of us are caught in restricted patterns of behavior which we never even realize we are copying from selected moments of the past.

You are not bound by your past—
But you are if you think you are.

This statement is incredibly liberating if we can believe it. It challenges the psychological model that past trauma causes present difficulty. What happened to us in the past only affects us now if we are willing to accept that it does (whether consciously or unconsciously). Yet there seems to be so much evidence that suggests that past trauma *is* damaging. Some of the evidence is undeniable. The question is how much of this damage is created by focus on the past, by the belief that the past is damaging, and by the fear of changing an old rut of behavior?

Many people, especially those that have undergone some form of psychotherapy, see themselves as being in some way damaged by their past. As both client and psychotherapist, I used to think this way. I remember visiting a hypnotist in England called Denys Kelsey. I had found a book he had written forty years before and was pleased to find him still alive in his eighties. He said to me, "You know, people think they have a right to be loved as babies and as children, but we are born with no rights at all. Who said we have a right to be loved?" What a fresh approach, I thought; when people give up believing they have this right, then there is nothing to complain about any more. It is not that one should be unsympathetic to people who have had a rough childhood. The pain of not being loved is all too real. It is simply counterproductive to focus on what we missed. Focusing on what we did not get concentrates our mind on what is assumed to be lacking in us and, as we shall see, our belief in our lack will inevitably prophesy the reality we manufacture.

Understanding the past can sometimes be useful to help us see the origins of our generalizations. But the danger in psychotherapy is that it is so easy to use it to foster the belief: "there's something in my past which makes me wrong now." All experience can be seen through the darkening screen of "what is wrong with me?" Searching deeper and deeper in the past inadvertently bolsters this belief "there's something wrong with me. . . . and now there's something else wrong with me."

There's nothing wrong with us at all, other than our stubborn belief in our limitations. We use the past as evidence for our little beliefs, which then act as magnets for similar future events. In fact only a few pieces of the past get used to maintain our belief systems—for our memory of the past is highly selective and intricately molded to fit our present beliefs and our future expectations.

Looking at it numerically, let's say you've had a hundred thousand pieces of experience. Somewhere our brain probably records everything that ever happened to us yet we select out two or three events that support a particular point of view. There may be an equal or larger number of events that contradict that point of view, but we remember what we are most emotionally attached to. In fact we are forced to be selective because we cannot take into account all hundred thousand experiences. Even to try to do so would mean living eternally in the past (which admittedly some do attempt). When we have found two or three past experiences that fit our belief, our mind then reverses the process and tells us that those experiences *created* our belief.

One of the main functions of "revisiting history" is to alter our selection of events, to select out the more positive experiences. These may not be any more "real" than the negative experiences, but knowing we can change our perception of the past gives us a freedom from the seeming restrictive power of past limitations.

An hour before seeing one client, I was reading about a particular Neuro-Linguistic Programing technique used with great success on phobias. During the psychotherapy session that followed I happened to mention the word "fence" in a figurative way. To my surprise my client got very angry.

He was man in his early fifties. During the Second World War, at the age of three, he had been imprisoned in a Japanese concentration camp. Although he and his family survived, he was left with terrible memories of his three years in prison. Whenever the word or the image of a fence appeared in his mind, it reminded him of the fence around the camp, which was inextricably associated with horror—he could smell the very sweat of the Japanese soldiers. His whole life had been affected by such memories and he saw himself as a victim of this terrible experience. Every year he met other victims of the Japanese concentration camps, all of whom saw themselves as permanently damaged in various ways.

Following the instructions that I had just read, I asked him to imagine himself in the projection booth of a movie theater watching himself in the audience watching a film of the concentration camp scene with the fence. This is a means of *distancing* or *disassociation* from the emotional reverberations. Then I asked him to be ready to play the film that he had just seen, backwards and very fast. Before he did this, he was asked to jump into the film (i.e., fully identified or "associated" with the little boy in the camp). As he imagined this, his body shuddered and then a few seconds later he smiled a little as he completed the speeded up reverse-motion movie. I asked him to repeat this exercise three times. By the third time there was no emotional reaction and the word *fence* had no effect on him at all. He had disassociated from the horror of the memory and had reassociated with the ludicrous memory of the camp in fast reverse motion. I was amazed at the speed with which history had been altered. Though the physical memory remained the same, the unpleasant emotional association had disappeared.

Although this changed his view of himself as a "concentration camp victim," it did not immediately affect his general identification of himself as a victim. Since he had seen himself as a victim (preconsciously) for most of his life, he had formed many interrelated beliefs in his incapacity to govern his own life. These beliefs manifested as habits of complaining and blaming others. Sometimes these habits made others get angry with him which would make him feel victimized, thus completing a self-fulfilling prophecy. In one sense, he really was a victim of a powerful, though understandable, belief system. But any belief system can be changed.

One way of changing the past is to disassociate from bad memories. The degree to which we identify or associate with our bad memories is actually a matter of personal choice. It makes sense to dissociate from bad memories and associate with good memories, and people who do this are generally happier. Disassociation does not mean that we forget what happened—it means that we are not emotionally attached to what happened. It implies a distance between you and the event so that the event no longer has control over your feelings or actions.

The following are clues that you are over-attached to the past:

• When you look back at an event, you experience anger or resentment. See Exercise 1.
• You keep replaying an unpleasant event in your mind. See Exercise 2.
• You feel bad or guilty about something you did or didn't do in the past. Whenever something reminds you of this incident, the bad feeling or the guilt surfaces. See Exercise 3.
• You believe your past was miserable or you cannot remember anything good or pleasurable that happened. See Exercise 4.
• You follow rules or dictates from the past—unwittingly you behave in the same manner as your parents/peers/ profession/class/age group, etc. See chapter 10, and the Belief Manual to diagnose and analyze your belief systems.
• One or more of your belief systems is supported by seemingly strong "causative" evidence from the past. See Exercise 5.

The following exercises should only be done if the past seems to be in the way of your developing an unlimiting belief or leading a fulfilled life. Unlike all the other exercises on alpha rhythm and changing belief systems, (chapters 14 to 17) the exercises on the past need only be done once or twice. The first three exercises are based on Neuro-Linguistic Programming techniques (see Reading List, page 321).

DISASSOCIATION FROM YOUR OWN POINT OF VIEW:
EXERCISE 1.

The following exercise is useful if you are involved in an argument with somebody and cannot detach yourself from your fixed point of view. Self-righteousness never actually feels good to the person who thinks he or she is right, but sometimes it's hard to see another angle. The exercise can be used for any argument in the past which still bothers you, no matter how long ago it happened:

1. Go into alpha.
2. For about thirty seconds, imagine yourself arguing your point of view. Be aware of the feelings associated with your point of view.
3. Now, jump out of your body, so to speak, and stand behind the person you were arguing with. Look over his or her shoulder at yourself arguing. Be aware of how you look and what it feels like to listen to you.
4. Come back to beta rhythm.

In this exercise you manipulate yourself literally into a different point of view. In the space of two minutes, your view of the past can be dramatically altered. One client said: "When I was in myself, I thought I was absolutely right. I didn't think it, I knew it! I could not understand how she could not agree. When I looked over her shoulder, I saw myself standing there and I didn't want to listen. No one would have wanted to listen to a person talking like I was! Now my judgments about her seem to have gone."

REASSOCIATION WITH GOOD MEMORIES: EXERCISE 2

This exercise can be used for a recurrent bad memory which gives you an unpleasant feeling:

1. Go into alpha.
2. Imagine the scene of the memory, only this time play it through with loud circus music.
3. Go back to beta rhythm.

Some people will start to laugh when they do this—they are literally putting their memory into a different feeling context. Others will be appalled that such a serious subject can be treated so flippantly. Seriousness is sometimes a sign of the ego's strong attachment to a memory or belief. Others will say: "but this is trickery—it's manipulation—it's just unreal." Yes, it is sheer manipulative trickery. The treatment matches the dis-ease: for it is internal trickery and manipulation in the first place which keeps us haunted and fixed on a particular memory associated with a particular feeling.

This technique will probably not work so well if you had the childhood experience of being mauled by a lion during a circus or if you were bitten by a clown. The circus music is just an example of a different feeling context within which you can place your previously fixed memory.

GOING BACK TO THE PAST WITH DIFFERENT RESOURCES: EXERCISE 3

Russian psychologists have carried out some interesting research on artificial reincarnation. Subjects under hypnosis were "given" past lives in which they were told they had exceptional talents in certain areas. On testing these subjects in these same areas, after their artificial past life experiences, they were found to score much higher than before hypnosis. For example, if you believe you're no good at music, and a hypnotist tells you that you were Bach in a previous incarnation, your musical ability will probably improve (even if you never were Bach). What this really illustrates is the power of visualization in changing an old belief. It shows that we can take an imagined resource and apply it to the past—which will then affect our present capacity.

The following exercise is useful if you have had a bad or guilty feeling about something you did or did not do in the past. Perhaps similar situations remind you of this past lack and make you feel bad.

1. Imagine the past experience as if you are seeing it on black and white film (in other words dissociated).
2. Think of an internal resource that you did not possess at the time, but which would have changed the situation if you had possessed it. Examples of internal resources are confidence, trust, assertiveness, caring, love, understanding. It may be an internal resource that you now possess to some extent, or it may be an internal resource that you have seen in someone else, or read about, or seen at the movies.
3. Go into alpha.
4. Go back into the past experience taking your resource with you. Imagine what happens as you use this resource. Imagine this in as much sensual detail as possible (i.e., fully associated). Feel what it is like. See the response in the other people involved and notice the effect this has on you.
5. Go back to beta rhythm.

In a way, this is an exercise in self-forgiveness. When you see how the situation would have been different if you had had that asset, you see that you simply lacked a particular resource at that time. The guilt evaporates. You are not a bad person. You are also rewriting your history positively, and freeing yourself from the restriction of past bad feeling.

REFINDING A GOOD MEMORY FROM THE PAST: EXERCISE 4

The following exercise is useful if you hold the belief that you have no good memories, that your past was miserable, and that your past is the cause of your present difficulties:

1. Search in your memory for at least one pleasant event or feeling, no matter how small and how transient.
2. Go into alpha.
3. Relive the experience as if you are there right now. See the scene in bright color, close up, and in as much sensual detail as possible: see it; hear it; feel it; "smell" the atmosphere. Be aware of how it feels inside to have that experience.
4. Go back to beta rhythm.

This exercise deliberately changes your focus from negative past to positive past. Remember that either way of seeing the past is a matter of personal choice. So, since you cannot help being selective, you might as well select out the best. It feels better. It is not that you will forget the things in the past that you did not like, but your attachment to these bad memories or resentments will dwindle. After you have remembered one positive event, the memories of others will sooner or later be jogged into consciousness.

THE POSITIVE PAST: EXERCISE 5

This exercise is useful when your belief system seems supported by so much evidence from the past, or such a strong incident from the past that it's hard not to believe that it's true. The exercise only needs to be done once or twice for each belief system that seems over-rooted in the past.

1. Identify your belief system.
2. Identify the opposite belief (chapter 14 and Belief Manual).
3. Remember one time in the past when this opposite belief was manifest, even if only partially. If you cannot find an actual memory, make up a past event that contradicts the old limited belief. If you think your mother never loved you, for example, imagine a scene in which you can feel how much she loves you. Often you will find that the

imagination of a positive happening will remind you of a positive memory sooner or later. Even if it doesn't, the imagining of the positive past gives you an alternative history. Since the past is only in your mind anyway, your mind can make this alternative history just as powerful and effective as what you think is your "real history."

4. Go into alpha.
5. Relive the memory/imagining of this moment of positive feeling. Live it as if you are actually there right now. See it; hear it; feel it; "smell" the atmosphere. See the scene around you in bright color and close up. Picture every detail and be aware of how it feels inside.
6. Go back to beta rhythm.

This exercise involves a deliberate reselection of past events. Previously your past was selected and interpreted to fit your limited belief system. Now you are consciously selecting events that fit your new unlimited belief. This can be a surprising and liberating experience. From doing this exercise (and any of the others in this chapter that are appropriate to you) you begin to experience that you really are not at the mercy of your past and that you can select any history you wish. When you realize this, your history loses its power over you. When we know it's a matter of our personal selection, assortment, abridgment and censorship—when we know the past is our choice, we become free from its expectations and restrictions.

Chapter 14

UNLIMITING
BELIEFS
CHANGING THE PRESENT

*O*nce you have diagnosed your belief and shown yourself how you make that belief seem to be true, you have at least an intellectual awareness that your belief and reality are different things. This chink in the old intellectual armour gives you a chance to take the next step, which is to affirm the opposite unlimiting belief while in alpha rhythm.

Postive affirmations were first brought to notice in the Western medical world by Emile Coue, a French pharmacist, born in 1857, who was famous for his saying "Everyday, and in every way, I am getting better and better." Coue noticed that several of his patients improved when they focused on positive health rather than the negative fears and imaginings of illness.

Since then, affirmations have been used increasingly in hypnotherapy and by a proportion of psychotherapists. They have been used, with visualization, to enhance sports performances and in several self-healing methods. They are the basis of positive thinking techniques.

However, affirmations may be really difficult to believe, which is why positive thinking techniques are sometimes restricted in effect. There are three main reasons for this: The first is that the affirmations in beta rhythm cannot deal with the preconscious doubts. It is of little use for the intellect to insist "I am calm" when you are scared as hell inside.

Affirmations are more effective in alpha rhythm when the preconscious, as well as the intellect, is open to change.

The second reason for the limited effectiveness of positive thinking is that negative thinking is often avoided or not dealt with. In psychotherapy as a whole there tends to be an over-focus on the origins of negative or limited thinking which, as we have seen, can have the effect of accentuating the belief in limitation. In many positive thinking techniques, on the other hand, an exclusive focus on the positive can result in a sense of unreality. For example, if you have a strong inner belief that you are ugly and that the world is a bad place, telling yourself that you and the world are beautiful is not going to work even under the best alpha conditions. It is often necessary to recognize and challenge the negative before the positive can be effective. If you do not, you end up in a state where positive suggestions ("I am beautiful") and negative suggestions ("I am ugly") play themselves out, swinging you one way then another. Unfortunately the old limiting suggestions tend to be the ones that win in the end, simply because these beliefs have been ingrained into your life over many years. This is why it is important to substitute the opposite belief only after the limiting "certainties" of the old belief have been loosened by belief analysis. The old belief can then be exchanged for the new.

The third problem about affirmations is this: How do we attain the wisdom to know what is good for us? I believe that many self-help books go wrong in advocating affirmations to get what we think we *want* rather than what we *need* to make us happy. For example, let's say you have a limiting belief that you will always be poor. Your opposite belief is that you are rich and through practicing in imagination and believing in yourself, you become richer financially. But everyone knows that money can't buy you love or even happiness.

This is a limit that this book cannot take you across. I can only offer an observation, made by many writers, which is that grasping for more creates unhappiness in the grasper.

If we use an affirmation to get more for ourselves in a grabbing kind of way, it is unlikely to fulfill us, because, psychologically, selfishness is based on a limiting belief in lack of abundance: "I have to get what I can because there is a limited amount available." Greed is always related to an inner belief in limitation, and all limiting beliefs are connected with tension and lack of joy (see Chapter 17).

Trying to get more for ourselves in a selfish way may give us a welcome relief from our fear of lack, or our fear of the future, but it will not create any deep pleasure and it is associated with an inner lack of self-respect (even if our success is seen by millions). Thousands of outwardly successful old people will testify to this. Conversely, giving is the natural state that comes from a sense of inner abundance and is associated with pleasure. Going back to the limiting belief, "I am poor", we can use the opposite belief, "I am rich" in a very different sense. If "rich" refers to our inner state (i.e., we are rich in spirit or inner essence) then that sense of richness will be associated with self-respect or self-love. This feeling of inner abundance may in time attract us outward riches, depending on other factors. Whether it does or not becomes less important for it is the inner state that relates to happiness. People who get rich through grasping for more and more are rarely happy, whereas people whose riches reflect their inner state may be very happy indeed.

In short, affirmations should be designed to change our inner state, not outward reality. Outward reality will of course be influenced by our inner states (see chapters 1–9), but according to its "will," not ours.

However, imagining a change in outward reality can change our inner state, so long as the basic motivation is to change inwardly! For example, one woman who had a limiting belief that she could never earn enough money, used the affirmation "I can earn all the money I need" and imagined herself being able to pay for furnishing her house. This imagining began to change her inner belief. What was important was that her *motivation* was to change her inner state.

She was searching for a feeling of abundance as opposed to being greedy to acquire more.

Requirements for Affirmations to Be Maximally Effective

1. Understanding and accepting that the old belief is not reality.
2. Genuine desire to change.
3. Alpha rhythm.
4. Substitution of the old belief by the new affirmation.
5. Combination of affirmation with vivid imagination (chapter 15).
6. Combination of affirmation with inner feeling and desire (chapter 16).
7. Combination of affirmation with positive action (chapter 17).
8. Vigilance to notice when the old habitual limiting belief is creeping back, so that the new affirmation can be substituted immediately (see page 212).

Affirmation under alpha rhythm is really a form of positive brainwashing. We have been brainwashing ourselves for years with limiting beliefs such as, "I'm a bad person." When you substitute an opposite unlimiting belief such as, "I love myself," you are deliberately washing your brain with what seems at first to be an artificial construct but which you hope to be able to believe.

The artificiality of affirmations may be a problem at first. For example:

It is my natural state to be happy
I am free from my past
I am filled with love

can all sound pretty ridiculous if you're feeling unhappy and angry about something that's happened in the past. The trick is to play with the new belief *as if* it were true. Our minds cannot yet accept a belief that contradicts the old limits— but it can accept a kind of imaginary game in which we play with the new belief as if it were reality. It is through the play and the practice that the new belief gradually becomes more believable.

Constructing an Affirming Opposite Belief

Affirmations need to be over the top. Make them as strong and positive as possible. For example, if your limiting belief is "I cannot love" the opposite belief is "I can love," but this wording portrays a vague possibility which is not as strong as "I love" or "I am a loving person."

If your old belief is "I'm no good at being a woman" (and you are a woman) the opposite belief could be "I am good at being a woman" but this is not as strong as "I am a beautiful and unique expression of womankind." It doesn't matter if you can't believe it—you are just playing with this new possibility. However, if you find you really cannot stomach the "over-the-top" affirmation after trying it in alpha, then it is fine to choose an intermediate affirmation as a stepping-stone along the way. The Belief Manual offers many different gradations of affirmation to choose from.

Sometimes the opposite belief may still be limiting. For example, the opposite of "I'm a bad person" is "I'm a good person," but for some this wording will imply all kinds of hidden rules and restrictions about being "good." A more expanded wording could be, simply "I love myself" or "I respect myself."

Your personal wording of your unlimited belief will be unique to you, but the following guidelines are useful:

1. Write down your limiting belief.
2. Write down the exact opposite. This is a purely intellec-

tual exercise requiring no feeling or belief. Do not worry if the opposite seems ridiculous.

3. Convert the opposite into a stronger and more positive statement. If the opposite belief is still limiting, try to find an unlimiting equivalent.
4. If the affirmation is about yourself, make sure it contains love and respect for yourself. If the affirmation is about another, make sure it contains love and respect for the other.
5. Make sure the affirmation is based on a belief in abundance, not on grasping for more.
6. Make sure the affirmation is in the present tense. It is happening now, not at an unspecified time in the future.
7. Make sure the affirmation contains no "can"s or any sense of "perhaps." The affirmation is spoken as a certainty.

One person who believed she was too old to get a job wrote as her opposite belief: "I will be able to get a job not withstanding my age." This construction has three drawbacks— the future tense (it will happen sometime in the future), the being "able" (it could happen, but it might not), and the "not withstanding my age" which is negative and reminds the person of the limit. A better affirmation would be simply "I have a new job." This of course appears to be untrue since she does not actually have a job at this moment. However the affirmation is the practice of a new reality in the imagination. We are more likely to be moved by our new belief if we play as if it were real, certain, and happening now. We are deliberately and consciously creating our own faith through playing the game with all our heart.

But playing in our imagination does not mean that we can manipulate reality. She may not get a job for various other reasons. The affirmation is simply opening us to wider possibilities. Many unemployed people lose confidence in their ability to find work; their depressed attitude then ensures that no employer takes them on. Changing their inner belief will improve their attitude at a job interview; it may attract better "coincidences" or help them notice more subtle opportunities; almost certainly it will make them feel better about themselves. But it does not *guarantee* them anything on the outside. It takes some humility to be open to change without demanding change. And it takes some humility to accept that change often does not occur in the way we expect it. And yet our life *will* change, in its own way, and in its own time, in response to our inner transition.

So what happens then if our limited belief is about other people? A woman, for example, was having a rough time with her husband and blamed him for his insensitivity. Her opposite belief was "he is kind and sensitive" and she imagined him noticing what she needed—for example noticing that she was upset and then holding her. After this imagining, she found herself expecting him to react differently and was then resentful when he seemed as insensitive as ever. Her resentment made him defend himself by becoming more distant and that made her more resentful. Her mistake had been to try to change him, and not herself.

She went back to imagining him "kind and sensitive" but this time *without expectation*. What happened then was that she softened, she felt love in response to his imagined kindness. For months he did not change but she did not mind because she was feeling her own love for him. She realized then that this feeling of her own love was a thousand times more valuable, and pleasurable, than any love she could "get" from outside.

The key to healing a limited belief or judgment about another is to view only their potential, to see them with love and respect. The key to healing a limited belief or judgment about ourselves is to view only our own potential, to see ourselves with love and respect. Affirmations are means of delivering this. Any affirmation that is demanding, selfish, or lacking in love or respect should be discarded, for it will create unhappiness in the end.

In chapter 7 we saw that every limited belief contains an "I'm not good enough" component, which can be translated as, "I do not accept, respect or love myself." Every limited belief either puts us down or diminishes others, the world, and life. The converse of this is that every unlimited belief contains acceptance, love, and respect for ourselves and others. We see the best and believe the best. This does not mean that we lose discrimination. It means that we choose to focus on the highest. In this way the best is encouraged and both perception and reality are gradually altered in accordance.

Theoretically, if we could say, "I love and respect myself and others" and completely believe it, we would have no need for further affirmations. If we always acted on this belief, we would be happy in virtually any circumstance. All the other affirmations are means of reaching this greater affirmation. For this reason, it is often useful to add this affirmation to a particular opposite belief. The wording of this should not give the impression of some distant future possible scenario, it should refer to us as we are right now. Here are some suggested wordings:

> I accept myself as I am now
> I respect myself as I am now
> I love myself as I am now

When we truly accept, respect and love ourselves, we find that that attitude extends to others.

SOME AFFIRMATIONS CONSTRUCTED FROM LIMITS

Limiting Belief	Example of Unlimiting Belief
I'm not good enough	I love myself as I am now
I am a victim of . . .	I am fully in charge of my own life. I respect myself.
I am loyal to the lower class.	My deepest loyalty it to my own inner authority. I respect my inner self.
Life is a burden.	Life is full of joy.

I am ugly.	I love my body.
They know more than I do.	There is no higher authority than my deepest self. I respect myself as I am now.
I can't help it.	I create my own reality. I respect myself.
I am too old for . . .	I am the perfect age for what I have to do. I accept myself as I am now. I love myself as I am now.
I cannot make . . .	I have infinite creative power. I respect myself. I love myself as I am now.

For further and more specific examples of affirmations see the "unlimiting beliefs" of each of the beliefs in the Belief Manual. Though these wordings may not be the ones you would choose they give you an idea of some possibilities.

Once you have created the unlimited belief and you are satisfied with the wording, you need to learn the sentence or sentences before going into alpha. Under alpha rhythm, you then repeat the affirmation to yourself while you imagine a scene in which the affirmation is played out (see next chapter, "Imagination: Changing the Future"), at the same time as fostering the inner feeling which such a situation would create (see chapter 16, "Better Within: Changing the Inner Feeling").

Affirmation, imagination, and feeling together create a full picture of the new possibility, and this picture needs to be practiced for a short time (only five to ten minutes) each day. With practice in imagination, the new belief gradually begins to be accepted as a possible reality. With confirming positive actions (see chapter 17, "Better Without: Taking Positive Action") the inner reality gradually merges into outer reality.

Chapter 15

IMAGINATION

CHANGING THE FUTURE

What is now proved was once only imagined
—William Blake

*O*ur imagination has immense power over our lives. It is the key to changing both our past and our future, and it is the key to changing our inner feelings about life.

Imagination is like an instant mental template which can gradually be formed into physical reality. It is the plan of action. Alone it is no more than a daydream, but when combined with direction, desire, and will for action, it is a powerful tool for change. Imagining a negative outcome goes a long way to creating that negative outcome (chapter 4). In the same way, imagining a positive outcome is a potent ingredient in positive change.

One of the most obvious and visible results of practiced imagination is in the field of sports. Eastern European athletes regularly trained to imagine the details of success, and this was a significant factor in their winning performances. Thousands of athletes have practiced success as an exercise of the mind.

Billie Jean King, women's champion of tennis in the seventies, used to prepare for important matches by visualizing them the night before. She would imagine each serve or stroke of her opponent and then she would imagine her best reactions to these shots. During the match the next day, she would find that she automatically reached for shots that she had practiced in imagination.

Jack Nicklaus, golf champion, said that he prepared himself mentally before swinging his club. He would imagine the ball flying down the fairway and landing exactly where he wanted it to land. He attributed much of his success to this practice in imagination.

Healing Techniques

Imagination of health or disease also has a powerful effect on the body. There is considerable evidence that visualization of health promotes health, and visualization techniques are being used increasingly in healing centers. Most of the techniques involve going into alpha rhythm and then imagining a healing agent cleaning or clearing the disease from the body. The image needs to be acceptable to the imaginer. A scientifically oriented person may choose to visualize white blood corpuscles eating up germs or cancer cells. Others may imagine little men sweeping out dust and dirt with mops and brooms. You can imagine a screen being passed through your body sieving out all impurities. Or you can imagine your body being filled with white light which transforms all impediments.

Helping "terminal" cancer patients to use such techniques, the Simontons found that predicted survival times were, on average, doubled, while a significant percentage of patients completely recovered from their disease. It seems that the imagination can reach places that the intellect cannot touch. This is true of both automatic body processes and the preconscious mind.

The Preconscious Mind

Trying to change a belief by willpower alone usually does not work. The belief seems to be rooted in a place we cannot affect. With our intellect we may be able to prune some of the actions which result from the belief, but digging out the belief itself seems impossible. In fact trying to stop a belief through willpower is usually counterproductive because it focuses our attention on the limitation. Imagining the opposite belief, on the other hand, focuses our attention on the unlimited and the positive. For example, the intellect might say, quite reasonably, "I should stop believing that I'm going to fail." But this focuses the mind on failure. It creates fear of failure rather than expectation of success. It could be better if the intellect says "I'm going to succeed!" but even with this positive statement, the preconscious old belief in failure usually will not accept success as a possible reality. It is only when a successful scene is imagined that it begins to have enough emotional impact to challenge the old limitation. It is the emotional impact that has an affect on the automatic body processes, which normally remain completely untouched by willpower or intellect.

Automatic Body Processes

If you will yourself to cry, salivate, or get sexually excited, you are unlikely to have much success unless you use your imagination to visualize a sad or succulent scene. With our imagination we can recreate any feeling or sensation and all the connected bodily responses. We can even affect the rates of secretion of many of our hormones. We have only to imagine a scene of fear, for example, to increase our output of adrenalin into the bloodstream, and this will then affect every cell of our bodies.

Our imagination automatically affects the intricate patterns of muscular tension within our bodies. Imagine anger and your jaw will tense. Imagine fear and your shoulders will tense. Such patterns of tension are nearly always unconscious unless they cause us pain. But these patterns have an enormous effect on how we feel, on what we communicate to others through body language, on our available body energy, and on our coordination. These effects are often the mediators between a belief and a self-fulfilling prophecy.

Of course it is no use gritting your teeth and saying to yourself: "I must not tense my jaw." It is more profitable to imagine yourself within a relaxing environment and to imagine your muscles loose and relaxed. When we imagine positive outcomes and positive beliefs, our automatic body processes, including patterns of muscular tension, will adapt themselves. This creates a powerful physical reinforcement of the "reality" of our new positive imagined outcome. For example, if you imagine yourself as calm, your muscles will tend to relax and this relaxation will then give you a physical feeling of calmness.

Changing Our Belief

For us to believe our new beliefs, they must have an impact on us. We are selling ourselves a new deal which is likely to go against the old grain. Creative writers are taught that they will make more impact if they convey the picture rather than the technicalities. Books on good conversation technique tell us that we will be more interesting company if we describe a scene in sensual detail, as if we were there, rather than describing abstract generalities. Great story tellers fill in the important details that create presence or atmosphere. Courses on selling emphasize the need for "picture power": salespeople are more likely to make a sale if they can create a picture in the mind of their client than if they present facts or technicalities. In the same way we "sell" our new unlimited belief to ourselves by creating a picture. Imagination moves us where reason is impotent.

Constructing Positive Imagination

After you have identified a limiting belief imagine a scene that matches it. Then imagine the opposite. If your belief was in shyness, for example, you might initially imagine a scene of awkward conversation; the opposite scene might be of friendly, expansive and enjoyable conversation. If you can't find the limiting picture or you cannot think of its opposite, you can find a picture that fits in with your affirmation or unlimited belief. One of the opposite beliefs of "shyness," for example, could be "I am confident." You might then imagine yourself making a decision with confidence and self-trust.

It is important for your new picture to be sensual, using all five sensual modalities if possible and appropriate. This gives impact. The new picture must also be totally positive. We cannot really imagine not doing something without also imagining doing it. Try, for example, not to think of the color green. Obviously, even to comprehend that sentence, you have to access in your own mind the color green. In the same way you cannot imagine "not smoking," "not being shy," or "not feeling like a failure" without also imagining cigarettes, shyness, and failure. Such pictures can be highly counter productive. Sometimes parents say to a child, "Don't spill the milk!" The child then sees in his or her imagination a glass of milk spilling. Unwittingly the parents have planted in the child's imagination, "spill milk." So sometimes children, not through rebelliousness but because they have been exposed to such a picture, will do something which seems to be the opposite of what the parents want. While the intellect can comprehend a negative, the imagination cannot.

Sometimes, people worry that they do not have imagination. Everybody does. Think of the letter M and then think of an upside-down M. In your mind's eye, put the upside-down M on top of the right-way around M. This will create an enclosed space in the middle. What shape is that space? If you can think of the shape of this space without using a pen or pencil, then you have imagination—enough imagination for any exercise in this book.

How you create your picture of your unlimited belief will be unique to you, but the following guidelines may be useful:

1. Find the limited imagination of the limited belief. (This is detailed in the Belief Manual—"Justification by Imagination of Future Results").
2. Make the opposite imagination or make a picture in your mind of yourself acting out your new unlimited belief. At this point, it is a purely intellectual exercise, requiring no feeling or belief. Do not worry if the picture seems ridiculous to your present belief systems.
3. Make sure that the picture is completely positive and is loving and respectful of yourself and others.
4. Add sensual detail, as if you are actually there. See the essential aspects close up and in bright color. Hear the words or the background sounds or even the silence. Feel any object you are touching and be aware of your own inner feeling. Smell the atmosphere. Make the scene as vivid as you can.
5. Play the scene as if it is true, certain, and happening now.

For example, a man's limited belief had been "people are only out for what they can get" and he imagined negative results from other people's selfishness. The opposite and liberating imagination was genuine kindness and care from these people. He imagined them giving him something out of true generosity with no strings attached.

This did not mean it would happen in reality in the way he expected. Nor did it mean that he should be blind to other's possible selfishness. But if just 3 percent of their action was genuine kindness and he was open to it, he would begin to encourage a different form of communication.

The purpose of practicing positive imagination is not to change reality by some kind of magic. It's not that we can force the outward world to change. It is more that, through imagination, we can be open to seeing and experiencing the positive side of ourselves and others. As we practice this focus, we encourage both ourselves and others to change. But of course another person always has a free choice in whether to be open to our lines of encouragement or not.

If you used to imagine anger leading to damage of property or person, your liberating image might be of your own positive assertiveness creating a positive change. You might, for instance, imagine speaking your mind and being listened to. You might imagine someone who had previously intimidated you hearing what you have to say. Again, your practice in imagination will not guarantee any result in others, but it will create a different attitude in you—less fear and more confidence. Eventually this may attract to you different realities and, in the meantime, it makes you better at dealing with adversity.

It is necessary to construct our imagination with love and respect to both ourself and the other. If we try to use our imaginations to beat somebody or win, we will lose in happiness. This is because the need to beat the other person is based on a limited belief of *"Either . . . Or . . ."*—*"Either* him *Or* me." This implies there is limited room, limited resources, or limited love. A belief in limitation is always associated with an inner sense of constriction and limited capacity for pleasure (see chapter 16, page 186). Conversely, the greater our feeling of connection to unlimiting beliefs, the less our bodies need to defend themselves, the more our bodies can relax, and the more pleasure we can feel in life.

Your imagination can be more poetic than specific if you want. Let your imagination go. For example, a woman who had the limited belief, "I have to keep fighting—life is a battle," created the affirmation, "I trust life." She then imagined herself going down a river in a canoe, having to trust the direction of the stream, and found to her surprise, that she enjoyed the freedom. Her opposite belief to "I'm no good" was "My inner self is perfect", and she imagined a golden light within her shining through all her ideas of limitation. As this inner light shone on the limiting thoughts, they sparkled like jewels, unique and beautiful.

The human mind has a tendency to say, "Ah yes, but that was reality and this is just imagination. The past was real, but what I want is just illusion." However, if you play the game seriously, you come to realize that what you consider to be present "reality" was originally created from your imagination and prejudiced selection, and that what is now an exercise in imagination can truly become reality.

The liberating imagination is the practice of a new reality. Play it as if it were true, certain, and happening now. Let it move you. Once again, you are deliberately and consciously creating your own faith, and eventually your own reality, through playing the game with all your heart. When this is combined with your affirmation and your full and involved feeling (see next chapter) you create a powerful force for change.

▼

Chapter 16

BETTER WITHIN

CHANGING THE INNER FEELING

*M*ost circumstances do not affect us unless we choose to focus our minds and feelings on those circumstances. For example, you can be anxious about all the things you have to do. Then in the middle of your tension, you remember a joke, you laugh to yourself, and for a short while your anxiety has gone. The circumstances of what needs to be done have not changed. You have simply changed your focus.

Most unpleasant feelings are caused by focusing our minds on what we judge to be unpleasant circumstances. We can train ourselves to change this focus—and that can truly change how our lives feel. We always have the choice of whether to focus on our limits or to focus on the unlimited. For this, it is essential to be able to control the runaway mind, or it will control us. The exercises later in this chapter are designed to improve our ability to focus on what we *choose* to focus on. All limiting beliefs tend to make us seem smaller than we are. They proclaim in subtle ways: "I cannot—I am small—I must defend what little I have." The more we think of ourselves as small, the more we tend to think of the possibilities of life as small. It seems there is only so much to go around. And from here it is a small step to feeling we need to grab what we can, to believing that competition is an inevitable necessity of survival in a grasping world. The feeling of smallness and defensiveness (I'll hold on to what I have) is commonly associated with a degree of protective muscle tension. Both the muscle tension and the inner sense of limitation tend to feel unpleasant.

Unpleasant Feelings

Feelings are manufactured as byproducts of our limited belief systems. If you believe "People are only out for what they can get" you will likely feel suspicion. If you believe that showing anger is wrong you may bristle with feelings of disapproval. If you believe you are helpless you will probably feel hopelessness. If you believe "The best part of my life is now over" you will sense the insidious crabs of cynicism. Whether it is suspicion, disapproval, anger, resentment, hate, outrage, hopelessness, emptiness, inadequacy, awkwardness, weakness, anxiety, or any other feeling that comes from limitation, there is one factor common to all of them—**lack of joy.** All the unlimited beliefs, on the other hand, create a feeling of pleasure.

Muscle Tension

Because limited beliefs make us feel small, we have a tendency to protect ourselves; this is automatically reflected in increased muscle tension. The muscle tension itself has a negative effect on our experience: it literally limits our freedom of movement, and slowly strangles our natural grace. It stops us from breathing fully. It affects our blood circulation. It also feels physically unpleasant and deadens our ability to feel fully. As soon as the muscles are relaxed, the ability to feel the movement of energy within the body and the ability to feel pleasure are increased.

Feeling and Memory

Feeling is secondary to our interpretation of events. If a rope is lying in the middle of a road and you believe it is a snake, you may feel anxiety. If, however, you believe it is a rope, you will feel something different. Of these two possible events within your mind, you are much more likely to remember the snake version because it has more emotional impact.

Although it may be true that our brains store everything that ever happened to us, the bits that stick in our accessible memories are the events that create feeling or drama. Whereas all events may be lightly printed in some inaccessible library of the mind, emotive events are engraved in red. It is these engravings that determine our belief systems.

It is for this reason that the light print of the intellect, however scintillating or brilliant, can never cover the deep engraving of a major belief. It is only when we imagine a scene with feeling that it can have enough emotive effect to be re-engraved, and even then it requires repeated practice.

Making the New Scenario Vivid

The last chapter emphasized developing sensual presence—experiencing an instance of your new unlimiting belief as if you are there, right now, seeing, hearing, touching, smelling, and tasting it. Immersing yourself in all five senses of the new belief creates greater impact. But as well as this, it is also useful to be aware of the *inner* feeling that the new belief creates in you. So as you imagine the new scene with vivid sensual impact, be aware of the feeling inside.

For example, a man found that his opposite belief for "People are only out for what they can get" was "she really does care for me." He imagined the sensations of being cared for, for example, seeing her eyes of love, hearing her tenderness of voice and even hearing concern in her anger. Within him, this created a feeling of warmth. It was as if he could relax for a while, as he gave up defending himself against all those people who were "out for what they could get." As his physical resistance melted he felt a warm melting sensation within which was both a relief and a pleasure.

Once again, the motivation for such exercises must be to change oneself, not another. In this exercise you deliberately imagine, and feel, the best from somebody in order to change your own limited understanding.

If you believed "The best part of my life is now over," the supporting feeling would likely have been one of cynicism, low energy, unworthiness, or lack of hope. Your opposite belief might be: "My life is a continuous process of growth." As you affirm this new belief and you imagine yourself carrying out a future venture with active energy, you feel differently within. You may feel a sense of worthiness. You may feel a pleasant sense of anticipation. You may feel energy flowing through your body.

Relaxing to Innermost Pleasure

In the alpha rhythm exercise, much attention is given to physical relaxation. Whereas tension is associated with defensive and limiting beliefs, relaxation is associated with emotional openness and greater capacity for pleasure.

When you are in the relaxed alpha state and you imagine the results of your new unlimited belief in sensual detail, you may find the inner feeling is there quite naturally. This inner feeling, associated with an unlimited belief, usually has some of the following qualities:

Warmth, melting, pleasure
Energy coursing through the body
A sense of inner strength
A sense of inner meaning
A sense of connectedness to all things
Self respect, a feeling of worthiness

Love

Laughter

Underlying all these qualities is joy. It is so much more fun to believe the unlimited—and since this belief will be as much a self-fulfilling prophecy as a limited belief—it makes sense too.

Sometimes it is difficult to be open enough to this good inner feeling. For this reason, the following exercises are useful to add to your basic alpha rhythm relaxation. These exercises also help teach control of the runaway mind—the mind that determines what we think about—which determines how we feel.

Exercises

The exercises depend on the strongest possible use of your imagination. Imagine every suggestion taking physical effect on your body. This takes a lot of concentration which you may find hard work at first. But it gets easier with practice and the results are worthwhile.

Exercise 1

You are already in alpha with your body relaxed. Be aware of your breathing. With each breath in, feel the expansion of your chest. Know that the air you take in is deeply nourishing. Imagine that each breath warms you inside. Feel that warmth in the center of your chest with each breath in. Focus your attention on the center of your chest just behind the breastbone. Imagine the warmth, no matter how small. Feel a spark of warmth ignited by your breath.

As you continue to focus on your breath and the center of your chest, feel the warmth gradually spreading outward from the center just behind your breastbone. With each breath in, feel the sense of warmth gradually expanding.

Now feel the warmth slowly moving upwards through your neck and up to the center of your head. Feel the warmth expanding through your brain, melting all resistances with pleasure. Feel the warmth spreading forward, bathing your eyes, relaxing your eyes. Feel the warmth spreading upward from your eyes through your forehead, and then back through your scalp, relaxing your forehead and scalp. From your scalp let the warmth spread downward through your face, relaxing all the muscles of your face. And then, feel the warmth from your face spreading down through your jaw, relaxing your jaw and moving down to warm and relax your neck.

Now be aware of the warmth spreading down from your neck. Feel it moving down and outwards through your shoulders and arms. Feel that warmth gradually spreading downward through your arms. Feel it deep within your arms as if the very cores of your arms are being eased and melted. Feel that warmth spreading right down through your forearms, down through your hands, melting the very bones of your hands. Feel the warmth pouring out through your fingers. Be aware of that warmth where your fingers touch your thighs.

Now feel the warmth pouring back up through your arms and then flowing down your chest. With each in-breath, feel the warmth being drawn down through your lungs. With each in-breath, feel the warmth increasing till your lungs feel hot.

Now feel the warmth spreading downward through your belly. Imagine your inner organs being warmed. Feel the warmth radiating downward through your pelvis relaxing all the structures within your pelvis. And now feel the warmth spreading downwards through your legs, relaxing your thighs. Feel the warmth spreading downward from your thighs, through your knees, down through your lower legs, and further down to your feet. Feel the warmth of your feet spreading downward into the ground.

Feel your whole body warm and alive. Be aware of this warmth. Be aware of the energy present within your body.

This exercise involves concentrated use of your imagination. You may find that "warmth" is not the right word for you. It may be easier for you to imagine breath or energy or liquid or light or even blood moving through your body. The exercise gets easier with practice. You are likely to find that some places in the body are much easier to imagine warm (or flowing) than others. Don't let this bother you. Simply move on to the next area without judgment or concern. If you prefer, or in addition, you can use Exercise 2.

Exercise 2

You are already in alpha with your body relaxed. As you breathe, be very aware of the breath moving through your nose and down through your throat to your lungs. Be aware of that breath as air or energy or light, whichever is preferable and easier. As you continue to breathe, change your focus to the center of your chest. Imagine now that you are breathing as if through a hole in the center of your chest. With each breath in, imagine energy pouring through the center of your chest, and with each breath out imagine energy moving out through the center of your chest. Do this until your chest feels more open.

Then move your focus upward to the crown of your head. Imagine each breath moving in and out through the top of your head. Feel as though the top of your head is open. Feel the energy of each in-breath moving down through the top of your head to your lungs, and then each out breath moving up from your lungs through the top of your head.

Now move your focus downward to your belly. Feel each breath moving in and out through the front of your belly till the area of your belly feels more open.

Then shift your attention once more to the very base of your spine. Imagine each breath pouring in from the base of your spine to the center of your chest and out from the center of your chest through the base of your spine.

Now imagine breathing in and out through different points of your body. Imagine yourself breathing in through the top of your head and breathing out through the center of your chest. Imagine yourself breathing in through the top of your head and breathing out through your belly. Imagine yourself breathing in through your heart and out through the base of your spine. Imagine yourself breathing in through the base of your spine and out through the top of your head. Do this several times.

Imagine that with each breath in, your body is full of energy. This energy feels good.

This second exercise also involves concentrated use of imagination. You are imagining greater flow within your body by focusing on an actual physical event: the breath. In reality the breath does move to every part of the body, in the form of dissolved oxygen in the blood, energizing every cell. We do not usually feel it like this. This exercise deliberately focuses on the movement of energy within the body—a sense of aliveness, which we could experience if we were not restricted by our limiting beliefs and their associated muscle tensions. In moments of great relaxation and pleasure you may have noticed this movement of energy within the body.

After either of these exercises you will find yourself more amenable to connecting to the inner pleasure of your new belief. The exercise should be done after working out (in beta) your opposite belief with its liberating imagination. Do the exercise immediately after going into alpha and just before using the affirmation and imagining the new belief in action.

With consistent practice, you will find that a new positive energy and feeling becomes more and more available to you. This good inner feeling feeds your new positive belief and vice versa. But much more than that, the good inner feeling makes life feel worth living. Many great sages have said that this inner joy *is* the true reality. Whether you agree with this or not, it is certainly a reality that is worth creating within. It will change your perception and experience of outer reality and eventually that will influence outward reality itself.

Chapter 17

BETTER
WITHOUT
TAKING POSITIVE ACTION

*A*fter imagining your belief and living it to the full within, it is time to practice it on the outside world. Putting the inner belief into outward action confirms and strengthens the new belief. In fact, if we do not convert our practice in imagination to practice in the world of action, the inner exercises remain unreal and waste our time.

The action we take need not be very grand. The smallest endeavors in line with our new unlimiting beliefs help to stabilize them. For example, let's say you had a limiting belief that you were shy. You work on your unlimiting belief in your imagination, seeing yourself conversing easily with others. You sort of half-believe this is possible. Your positive action involves making the move to talk to somebody, behaving as if you believe it will work out fine. In other words you create a good act. After the act, the very fact that you did it feeds your belief: "Hey, it really is possible."

What you are really doing is acting on faith. You hope that your new belief can be reality and so you act *as if* it is reality. At first you do this in such a very small way that it is not too dangerous. It has to be a step that you know is possible.

The first step takes courage. When the lion in *The Wizard of Oz* asks the wizard for courage, the wizard's response is to send him on a very dangerous journey. The lion is terrified of the dangers but forces himself to go through with them. In this way, though shaking with every step, he finds he has courage. In fact, we do not either "have courage" or "not have courage." The belief that we have no courage is an excuse for non-action. Courage is simply taking the action that we fear.

These first steps of putting our new belief into practice are a good time for not following our immediate feelings. Apprehension and fear can be expected as common accompaniments to any new step. Accept them but do not follow them. Follow instead your decision to practice a more expansive view of life.

At first, this practice in reality is done in the smallest of ways, setting easily obtainable goals. You deliberately make the goals so small that you guarantee success. Each tiny success strengthens the new belief. In the example of shyness, your first goal could be simply to start talking to somebody. A later goal could be maintaining a conversation for a minute.

If you used to believe that "change is dangerous," positive action might involve changing some of your life routines. At first, these could be in fairly nonthreatening parts of your daily schedule and habits. For example, you could try spicing your food differently, changing your diet, or changing the times and the places you eat. You could try changing your sleeping hours, and changing the timing of some of the routine events of the day. You could try giving people different answers from the ones you normally give.

If you believed "the best part of my life is now over," you could take up a new activity that challenges this belief. At first, it could be something very small, practiced for a short time each week. You could take up calligraphy, tennis, walking, piano playing, or any number of activities. Somewhere, there is something for everybody that is challenging, interesting and enlivening. Often the most important aspect of our new activities is that it brings out a less developed part of us. If you have been more inwardly oriented, for example, you might want to develop your physical skills. If you have been mostly outwardly oriented, you might want to explore more within, for instance, with some form of meditation. Whatever your new development, it supports your new belief that life is a continuous process of growth.

If you believed in "original sin" or that you're somehow bad inside, positive action may involve expressing your inner feelings, even seemingly negative ones, in a creative and positive way. A common example of a seemingly negative situation is when we are angry with somebody. Anger is usually created by something happening or someone doing something that does not fit in with our concepts. Sometimes anger disappears when we realize this. Anger can also be a defense to avoid another feeling, especially fear; it is nearly always associated with some degree of insecurity. It is, after all, an animal reaction to threat. Fear and anger have virtually identical hormonal and physiological pathways and are inextricably interwoven in the fight or flight reaction. If we let ourselves feel the fear or the insecurity, once again the anger often evaporates. Sometimes anger can be a useful means of reaching another person, but even when this is so, it is not necessary to be so involved with our anger that our blood pressure rises. If your children heedlessly cross the road, you can shout at them with a loving smile in your heart. Because your children take your anger seriously does not mean that you have to. But while these things may be true, we still face the question of what to do with old anger that is already there. If we cannot transmute it through deeper understanding, it seems that we are left with the alternatives of repression or expression. If we repress it, it builds inside and confirms our worst beliefs about being bad inside. If we express it so that it hurts others, it also confirms our beliefs about our own destructiveness. So it is useful to learn to express it harmlessly, sublimating the energy in a creative way.

A woman I know was visited by three friends who, enjoying the comfort of their stay, gradually decided to prolong their visit from three days to two weeks. She began to feel resentful of their intrusion but the more resentful she felt, the more she feared a "disaster" if she expressed herself. And if she didn't say anything she felt like a repressed mouse. Finally

she practiced a few shouts in the car driving home, just to
free her energy, and then she said to her friends with firmness,
lightness, and a touch of humour: "Okay, you guys, you need
to decide what you are going to do, because on Sunday I'm
throwing you out. . . . I want to have next week alone with
my family." Despite her great fears of the result, no disaster
occurred and she succeeded in expressing herself while maintaining a good feeling both about herself and the others.
Success in terms of our own good feelings, depends on maintaining love or respect for both ourself and others. Any anger
that puts the other person down also belittles the aggressor
who suffers from the limited belief in *"Either* (them) *Or* (me)".

Another common example of a seemingly negative feeling
is jealousy. If we cannot transmute the feeling through our
own deeper understanding, it is not helpful to repress it but
neither do we need to express it in any hurtful way. We can
use the jealous energy to express ourselves with good feeling
and give a compliment instead. For example, one could say
with both lightness and sincerity, "What you have is wonderful. I wish I had it. I just think it's great." Once again,
the goal is to find a means of genuine expression that main-
tains our good feeling both about ourselves and the other
person.

If you believe that you're weak or that you get sick easily
or that the physical body is inferior, you can take positive
action by caring for and strengthening your body. Exercising
your body, building your body strength, enjoying your body
movement all feed the new belief in your own strength, health
and agility.

Sometimes our limited beliefs involve expectations of other
people. If your limited belief is about others, ask yourself
what it is that *you* do to create, maintain, or contribute to
the situation. Looking at the self-fulfilling prophecy may help
you with this. Once you have found your part in what makes
the other limited or negative, do the opposite. For example,
if a man believes "they are against me," it is no use for him
to try to make *them* take positive action to be nicer to him.
It's more profitable for him to look at his own self-fulfilling

prophecy, which shows that his own suspicion and negativity push them to be against him. Then he can take positive action to treat them so well that the self-fulfilling prophecy is broken. This positive action involves actively assuming that they are coming from the best motives and welcoming them accordingly. This action will fit his new belief that people can be good or caring and that he is worthy of being liked. He is inviting a different response, and more likely than not, he'll get one.

In the same way, the belief that "people are only out for what they can get" or "they don't care" is counteracted by the positive action of taking care of somebody. A woman did just this to break the following self-fulfilling prophecy: because it seemed people were only out for what they could get, she tended to keep her distance from them; so their natural reaction was to keep their distance from her; therefore they appeared not to care and it seemed they were only out for what they could get. As soon as she was caring, she invited a different response. But even before she got one, she felt much better from her own improved state of mind.

Similarly, the self-fulfilling prophecy "men are brutes" is counteracted by the positive action of treating a man with tenderness. The self-fulfilling prophecy, "women are not to be trusted" can be counteracted by the positive action of treating a woman with love and with the assumption that she is a good person. In these ways we correct what is our part in the negative interaction.

Sometimes there seems to be no doubt that a negative action was initiated by somebody else, but even so, our reaction may greatly affect the outcome: Early one January, a woman I know received an anonymous phone call from a man who threatened her, demanding money. He told her that he had been watching her house for days and proceeded to describe details of her family and even her dogs.

This woman was not one to be easily intimidated. Her first reaction was anger that her privacy was invaded and she spoke to him assertively. But the more assertive she became, the more aggressive he became. In desperation, knowing the situation was getting worse and worse, she prayed for inspiration. She remembered the words of a meditation master, Swami Chidvilasananda: "Love is your greatest protection. Without love a friend becomes an enemy, and with love an enemy becomes a friend."

Changing tack completely, she said to the man: "You know, it makes me very sad that a good person like you is involved with something as horrible as this. This is not worthy of you. You are good. So you should do something good."

There was a pause at the other end of the phone while the man tried to digest this extraordinary change. After a while he said, "You know, you're right, but I have to make a living."

"I know," she said, "but this is not the way. Because you thought this was the way, you stopped looking. Keep looking till you find a good way."

"You know, you're a very good person," he replied.

"We are all good," she said, "but since we do not always know it, we do not behave as if we are."

After a few minutes of this conversation, the man was friendly and polite. "It certainly has been a pleasure talking with you," he said, "and Happy New Year to you."

"Thank you," she answered, "and the same to you." As she said these words, she realized that she meant them!

A few weeks later the man called again. He told her that he had been thinking about what she had said. He wanted her to know that if she was ever in trouble, she could call him day or night, and he gave her his phone number.

Thinking the best of somebody and acting on that thought often creates positive changes in both ourselves and the other person. Naturally, intelligent discrimination is required to know when it's necessary to protect ourselves or to fight. But even when we are protecting ourselves, it is not necessary to have a bad feeling about somebody. After all, *we* are the ones that would feel bad—why give someone else that power over us?

If some of the steps suggested in this chapter seem rather large, it is possible to start with very small ones. Taking care of somebody, for example, can involve one small act of kindness in the way that we speak. It could involve asking someone a question which showed concern. Even if we do not really feel any concern, asking the question *is* an act of concern. Quite often the feeling comes later.

Giving something is a positive action which counteracts the limited belief "I have nothing to give" or "no one ever gives me anything." We are deliberately challenging the old part of us that demands gifts or energy from another (which results in our receiving less and less). However, when you first give, do not expect to feel great generosity. Perhaps you give some flowers with no feeling whatsoever, purely as an idea of mind in order to help change your old belief. Nevertheless it is still a gift and an act of faith. Sometimes the pleasure comes afterwards from seeing the response of the receiver. And sometimes it takes time to learn the pleasure of giving.

Each belief system in the Belief Manual ends with a section on positive action. You can choose one of these or, alternatively, an idea for action may come up as you imagine your unlimiting belief. A woman who felt "unwomanly," for example, imagined herself walking elegantly down the street wearing a hat. The next day she wore a large brimmed hat through the streets of Amsterdam: She felt like a million dollars.

It is said that knowledge without application is nothing more than a burden. Each little action that we take, confirms our new belief: "This is not just a possibility—it really can be true for me." Each step we take shows that we have courage and that change really does occur. We begin to see that we really have choices in our own reality. What confidence that gives!

Part 3

The Belief Manual

Common Limiting Beliefs and Their Opposite Affirmations: The Process of Belief Analysis And Believe Transformation

BELIEF MANUAL—CONTENTS

▼

Chapter 18

USING THE BELIEF MANUAL

The Belief Manual demonstrates the process of Belief Analysis for thirty-seven common beliefs. Through recognizing our hidden biases, we can obtain greater clarity and more freedom from the restrictions of our beliefs. Most especially we see that we are different from our beliefs, and we see that reality is different from our beliefs. Through belief analysis, the belief is deliberately detached and *disempowered:* It loses its hold on us. In its place, we are free to develop a belief in the unlimited, and this will create equally powerful self-fulfilling prophecies. These are the steps:

1. After diagnosing your belief, see if it connects with one of the beliefs in chapter 7. Reading about the belief may give it a useful context or will remind you of similar or related beliefs.
2. Check the Belief Manual index (page 201) where you will find thirty-seven common listed beliefs. There are, of course, thousands upon thousands of beliefs. But you will find that many beliefs relate to at least one of these common ones. If your belief does not appear to fit, check the subtitle "similar beliefs" under the belief that's nearest yours. Or else check the subtitle: Judgment of Others. If you still cannot find one that fits, analyze your own belief

by going through the steps of belief analysis described on
the next pages.

3. Next, go through all the subtitles under the belief. Check
   through the advantages and maintenance mechanisms,
   noticing which describe you and asking yourself what
   other maintenance techniques you use to hold on to your
   belief. If you go through this process thoroughly, it will
   almost surely shake the certainty of your limiting belief.

Most of the text under each subheading of the beliefs comes
from actual examples. Do not expect the wording to fit your
situation exactly—it may, or it may provide more of an indication of which direction to look. The following explains
the subheadings for each belief in the Belief Manual:

Similar Beliefs

The belief may be worded in a way that you do not connect
to, or that does not fit with your experience. "Similar beliefs"
lists a number of alternative experiences of the same essential
belief. For instance, you may have no experience that "consistency is essential," which is listed as a belief, but you may
consider that "life is limited" or that "I cannot afford to
make a mistake," both of which may be closely associated
beliefs. With each belief it is useful to read through the list
of similar beliefs to find the wording that most accurately
fits your experience. Alternatively, use the whole list to provide you with a sense of the direction of the belief, and form
your own wording.

Possible Related Beliefs

Many beliefs tend to link up in belief clusters. This section
in the Belief Manual points to other beliefs you may have
which may or may not have been dianosed in Belief Diag-

nosis. Check these related believs to see if they are also relevant to you. Most, if not all, limiting beliefs are connected
to the belief: "I'm not worthy" or "I'm not good enough,"
and all limiting beliefs are associated with more or less "helplessness" (page 222).

Life Choices

This section of the Belief Manual gives some indication in
very general terms of the kinds of choices you are more likely
to take when you hold a particular belief. However, there
may be many other beliefs, some of them contradictory, pull-
ing you in other directions. For this reason this section will
probably be the least consistent. What it does provide is a
challenge to consider if and how your own life choices have
been affected by your belief.

Ego Advantage

The "ego advantage" is our way of converting a limitation
into a seeming quality that we are proud of, so that we seem
special. The sense of specialness is one of the temptations
that keep us hooked to the belief. As far as I know, there is
always an ego advantage, though sometimes it is difficult to
see. If you cannot find yours in the Belief Manual or through
self-questioning, ask youself what is your judgment on people
who do not share your belief—the opposite of that judgment
will be your superior attitude. The trick is to leave aside your
ideas of what a "correct" answer should be and say the first
thing that comes into your head, however silly it seems.

A second way of finding a hidden ego-advantage is to look
at how you judge yourself or put yourself down, then assume
the opposite. An attitude of superiority is always connected to
a corresponding attitude of inferiority. Usually only one is
conscious, while the other is preconscious. If, for example, like

the man in chapter 3, you believe, "I am unintelligent—therefore I am inferior" you may assume the existence of the opposite: "I am unintelligent—therefore I am superior." The same applies to any judgment or feeling of "I'm not good enough."

Judgment of Others

Insofar as we are "special" because of our limited belief, others are to an equal and opposite extent ordinary or inferior. This division is usually given great energy because it is our means of feeling separate and individual. Finding out our judgments of others can be a particularly useful exercise since the judgments are often more easily recognized than the belief system itself (see "Diagnosis by Disapproval," page 125). You may find that some of the judgments listed in the Belief Manual fit your own. If not, answer the question "how do I judge others who do not hold this belief?" with as much honesty as you can.

Judgment of Self

Each belief in limitation carries with it an "I'm not good enough" phrase. This is the other side, the inferior side, of the ego advantage. Usually the judgment of self is conscious rather than preconscious. It is the aspect of our belief that creates an excuse for never changing—"I'm not good enough, therefore I can't" (see chapter 7). Notice how your own judgment of self provides a reason for staying the same.

The Illusion of Safety

All limited beliefs are well-worn containers of comfort and familiarity. Keeping to our belief saves us from taking risks into the unknown. For instance, the "I'm not attractive" believer may not have to risk the drama, tension, and complications of a sexual relationship. When we acknowledge our own safety factors (which may be found in the Belief Manual or through self questioning) it gives us further understanding of why we stick to a belief.

You might question why the *illusion* of safety. If you believe assertiveness is dangerous, for example, you can avoid battles, and that does not appear to be an illusion. But the limitation always costs us something. Suppressing your natural assertiveness might, for instance, eventually lead to physical ailments which might be much less safe than asserting yourself.

Less Work, Less Responsibility

It is easier to hold to an old belief because we can react and live automatically in familiar ruts and predictable patterns. We don't really have to think for ourselves. The limited beliefs give us an excuse not to work at thoughts or activities which are expansive or new and appear to absolve us from wider responsibilities. You may connect with some of the patterns listed in the Belief Manual. If not, consider how your belief saves you from work and responsibility.

Generalizations from the Past

The usefulness of finding the event(s) which we generalized into our beliefs is that it helps us see that the beliefs are not actually so general. Either it is not really our belief at all, but our parent's or some other influential person's, or else we realize that our belief is both out of date and out of proportion. The Belief Manual gives some examples of possible generalizations from past events, but your experience may well be different. For further explanation, refer to chapter 2, "False Convictions: How We Create Limiting Beliefs."

Selective Evidence from the Present

Selective evidence is noticing what fits our beliefs and ignoring what doesn't. Being aware of this is one more step towards seeing that our beliefs and reality are different, or that what we think is reality is simply our belief. Apart from the suggestions listed under this heading, ask yourself if there are any other ways you select life to fit your belief. See chapter 4 "Adapting the World: Belief Maintenance."

Distortion of Perception and Interpretation

Our perceptions and how we interpret our perceptions can be altered drastically to fit our beliefs. It is questionable if there is any such thing as an objective perception. Seeing that our perceptions depend on our beliefs is, initially, a daunting observation. You may be able to relate your experience to some of the distortions mentioned in the Belief Manual. If not, ask yourself in what ways you distort your perception and interpretation of events to support your belief.

Rationalization of Contradictory Evidence

Inconvenient evidence can always be explained away. Some typical examples are given in this section of the Belief Manual, but you may have different examples. Either way, seeing these rationalizations is a challenge to our ingrained systems of thinking.

Justification by Imagination of Future Results

A limiting belief creates a limited image of the future. The limited image of the future acts like a hypnotic suggestion which confirms our beliefs. If the image mentioned in the Belief Manual does not fit for you, close your eyes and imagine the future in accordance with your belief.

The Manufacture of Supporting Feeling

Our belief creates feelings. It is so easy to assume that the feelings are primary and that the belief follows, but often the feelings are a dramatized reflection of limited thinking. Think of the feeling that your belief creates and see how that feeling makes you think the belief must be true.

The Self-Fulfilling Prophecy

As with all the sections of the Belief Manual, only one or a few examples are given. These may or may not connect with you. If not, make up your own self-fulfilling prophecy and discover how you form reality to fit your beliefs. Most prophecies have three basic stages:

Belief creates action
Action creates result
Result confirms belief

For more information, see chapter 5, I Told You So: The Self-Fulfilling Prophecy.

In all sections of each belief, the material comes from real-life examples. Within a single belief that you know you have, you will probably connect to some of the advantages and mechanisms but not to others. You may be blocking out the bits that you do not connect to because they are difficult to admit; on the other hand, they may genuinely not relate to your process. Even within a single simple belief held by millions, the process for each person is different. I have given examples of some of the common ways beliefs are maintained. Some of these examples will fit you and others will not. But either way, you can use your understanding of the general direction of a subtitle to discover your own personal mechanisms and biases.

If one of your beliefs does not fit the Belief Manual at all, the examples from the Manual will help you analyze your belief yourself. Simply go through each step questioning how you perform each maneuvre of belief maintenance, following the suggestions in this chapter. Assume that you have at least one mechanism under each heading. If you cannot think of one, go on to the next heading. The important mechanisms you missed will probably surface later.

After going through this comprehensive belief analysis, it is almost impossible to avoid the conclusion that your limited belief and reality are different things. The belief has been detached from you and is therefore disempowered. You can now substitute the opposite unlimiting belief, through the following steps.

Steps to Ingrain the New Unlimiting Belief.

1. *The Opposite Belief/Unlimiting Affirmation*
   After looking at the self-fulfilling prophecies of your belief in the Belief Manual, go on to the "opposite belief". This is the contrary of the limiting belief, reworded to make it as unlimiting as possible. You are not expected to believe it immediately—it is an affirmation of what you need. Don't be concerned if at first it seems unreal, even ridiculous—it is unreal to your present belief systems. How to use affirmations constructively is discussed in chapter

14. The unlimited beliefs listed in the Belief Manual may or may not feel right for you. Find the one that fits most for you or else make your own wording according to the guidelines on pages 170–171.

2. *Liberating Imagination*

Your limited belief was justified and supported by imagining limited future results. You can find the opposite image by looking in the Belief Manual, or you can find your own. For example, if the image of the old belief is idleness, imagine yourself busy and happy. Make sure that the picture is specific, positive, and as vivid as possible. This is discussed in detail in chapter 15, Imagination: Changing the Future.

3. *Liberating Inner Feeling*

Your limited belief was bolstered by a *feeling* of limitation. This section in the Belief Manual suggests some opposite feelings appropriate to the unlimiting belief. Consider, intellectually, which feelings are opposite to the unpleasant or restricted feeling of your limitation. See chapter 16, Better Within: Changing the Inner Feeling.

4. *Alpha Rhythm*

The next step is to go into alpha rhythm, which involves deliberately slowing down your brainwaves to about ten cycles per second. At this brain rhythm, your fixed beliefs are loosened and you are more able to hear and imagine your new belief. Learning how to go into alpha is explained in chapter 12, Alpha: The Frequency of Change.

5. *Inner Feeling under Alpha*

Limiting beliefs are associated with lack of pleasure and muscular tension, while unlimiting beliefs are associated with relaxation and pleasure. As your body relaxes under alpha, you are better able to experience the pleasure of your unlimiting belief. Unfortunately, however, the body itself tends to be more or less used to a feeling of restriction and this habit persists in the form of deep muscular tension. For this reason, it is worthwhile exercising the capacity of your body to relax and to be open to the pleasure of your new unlimited belief. Use one of the exercises described in chapter 16 (page 187–190) after going into alpha and before practicing the unlimited belief under alpha.

6. *Unlimited Belief under Alpha*

    While in alpha repeat your new affirmation, the opposite belief that you have already carefully worded (step 1). Under alpha you are more suggestible and more able to accept the new belief as a possible reality.

7. *Liberating Imagination under Alpha*

    While repeating your affirmation, imagine the liberating image (which you have already created in step 2) as vividly as possible. See it, hear it, feel it. At the same time be as open as possible to the inner feeling (which you have already thought about in step 3) that this positive scene creates. Practice this exercise for two or three minutes, once a day.

8. *Positive Action*

    After imagining your belief and living it to the full within, it is time to practice it on the outside world. Putting the new inner belief into outward action confirms and strengthens the belief. In fact, without the action, the exercises in imagination remain unreal and ultimately a waste of time. The Belief Manual suggests some positive actions and the idea is explained further in chapter 17, Better Without: Taking Positive Action

9. *The Positive Past*

    This is an optional exercise which is only appropriate if the past seems to be getting in the way of your changing your belief. Either, remember a scene from the past which contradicts your old limited belief; or else, rewrite history to give yourself a deliberately engineered different experience which challenges your fixed generalizations about life. The relevant exercises are detailed in chapter 13, History Revisited: Changing the Past.

10. *Vigilance*

    There is one more thing that has hardly been mentioned before, and it is important. The old way of limiting thinking has been ingrained in our minds for years, usually decades. Habitual thinking has a tendency to creep back on us unawares, especially during times of stress when we reach out for anything familiar. Therefore it's important to recognize the old limiting belief system before its had an effect on our actions, and this requires vigilance.

Once you notice the old belief system, simply have your opposite unlimiting belief ready and substitute this affirmation, saying it to yourself several times. Your affirmation, which you can use at any time, will act like a protection from these old limiting tendencies.

These steps may seem quite daunting on reading them for the first time. But they are like the instructions for a board game or a game of cards: The reading is much more complicated than the playing. Once you start to practice, you will find that these steps flow quite easily. All you have to do is find your affirmation, think of the picture and feeling that go with it, and then, in the alpha state, repeat the affirmation with imagination and feeling. When feeling and imagination are added to a thought, it becomes a belief. These exercises are a deliberate process for converting a positive thought into a firm belief. When the new positive belief begins to be practiced in action and reflected in reality, the old limitation becomes an irrelevant memory. It's an exciting process of discovery. Good luck!

▼

THE BELIEFS AND THEIR OPPOSITE AFFIRMATIONS

► ## Being Assertive Is Dangerous

Similar beliefs
Showing anger is weak or bad or dangerous.
Aggression is only to beat another person down and is always violent. There is a dangerous animal inside me that must be held in.

Possible related beliefs
We are tainted with original sin. I'm weak. I must keep a low profile. Men are brutes. I am boring.

Life choices
Attracted to people who express little assertiveness, or, less often, to people who express aggression in a harmful or negative fashion.

Ego advantage
I am in control of myself. I am above such animal aggression. I do not need to resort to such an uncultured approach. I am polite. I do not impinge on others.

Judgment of others
Those who show aggression are limited/animal/unrefined/dangerous.

Judgment of self
I am a coward.

The illusion of safety
I can avoid arguments and battles.

Less responsibility/work

I can avoid the responsibility of communicating some of my thoughts and feelings. I can avoid helping other people learn. I can avoid protecting those who need protection. It's not my fault that everything's taken away from me.

Generalization from the past

1. Home atmosphere in which little or no assertiveness was expressed, or
2. Home atmosphere in which anger was expressed very negatively, for example, by a drunken parent.

Selective evidence from the present

Assertiveness creating negative effects noticed. Moments of useful/protective/loving/effective/creative assertiveness not noticed or minimized.

Distortion of perception and interpretation

Facial expression of assertive person seen as hurtful. Facial expression of "victim" seen as deeply hurt.

Rationalization of contradictory evidence

Although it may look as though it had a positive effect, that expression of anger was really an expression of dislike/competitiveness/violence/hatred.

Justification by imagination of future results

Images of aggression or anger leading to damaged property, physical injury, and/or death.

The manufacture of supporting feeling

Disapproval.

The self-fulfilling prophecy

1. Assertiveness is dangerous. Therefore I won't express it for as long as possible. Therefore it builds up inside. Therefore when I do express it, it is extreme and has a negative effect. Therefore assertiveness is dangerous.
2. Assertiveness is dangerous. Therefore, when someone is assertive/angry with me, I get cold or distant in an at-

tempt to protect myself. That makes them more angry, even violent. Therefore assertiveness is dangerous.

Opposite Belief

Assertiveness can be creative. It can be an expression of love. It can be used to protect what is right, without malice. It can be used to get through to another person. It can be a harmless release of tension. Even when I'm angry, I am basically a good person. I love myself. I respect myself as I am now. I have the right to express myself.

The positive past
Remember a time when an expression of assertiveness led to a good and positive result.

Liberating imagination
Images of being assertive, standing up for what is believed to be right. Images of assertion creating positive change.

Liberating inner feeling
Warm, pleasurable sense of strength and self-respect.

Positive action
Practice positive assertion (see the section on assertion in chapter 17, pages 193–194).

▶ Consistency Is Essential

Similar beliefs
Change is hurtful/dangerous/frivolous. I should not make any changes. I cannot afford to make a mistake. I'm scared of change. I have a rigid personality habit. Life is limited.

Everything has its place in my order. I know what's best for me.

Possible related beliefs
I am not good enough. I can't help it. I am boring. I must keep a low profile.

Life choices
Secure relationships and secure working situations, whether or not they create fulfillment or happiness.

Ego advantage
The things that I know, I know and do well. I know what's best for me. I know better than life (which does not seem to know what it's doing). I know the best formulas for survival.

Judgment of others
Those who don't follow advice or proven methods are fools. Those who change their minds are stupid—they should keep to one view. Changing your mind shows weakness—shows that you must either have been wrong before or are wrong now.

Judgment of self
I may be missing the most important parts of life. I'll never know what I'm missing. Being fixed in one way limits me. My lack of flexibility is a sign of weakness and lack of inner strength.

The illusion of safety
I do not have to face the threat of anything new.

Less responsibility/work
What I know is easy to continue. Change involves hard work—I don't have to invest that energy or take on the responsibility of more.

Generalization from the past
Remember changes in the past which caused turmoil or anxiety. Parents or other important figures may have been intolerant or frightened of change.

Selective evidence from the present
Select out the changes in others and yourself that seem to go wrong: "Aha—look what happened when she tried to change. . . ."

Distortion of perception and interpretation
Excitement in others misperceived as fear. The body signs of excitement in yourself are reinterpreted as unpleasant anxiety.

Rationalization of contradictory evidence
When change seems to go well in others, you say to yourself: "You wait; it will go wrong in the end."

Justification by imagination of future results
Images of possible changes creating negative results.

The manufacture of supporting feeling
Feel yourself as small, unable to cope. Feel fear or perhaps embarrassment. These feelings make it very hard to feel good about change.

The self-fulfilling prophecy
1. Change is usually negative. Since I have this idea, I shall be looking for the negative things that will result from change. Therefore my attitude will not be positive and I will not see positive opportunities. Hence I am unlikely to benefit from change and therefore change is usually negative.
2. Life is limited. Since life is so limited I don't think I'll get too involved. Therefore I don't have many exciting experiences and life, in my world, is limited.

Opposite Belief

Change is exciting. Mistakes are the best teachers. Whatever comes up, life will handle it. Change makes me feel more alive. I trust my intuition. I trust my inner self. I have the inner resources to handle what life brings. I celebrate variety. I respect my own capacity. I am flexible. I am flexibly strong. I have the right to express myself. I have the right to change. I respect myself as I am now.

The positive past
Remember one time in your life when change was positive. Picture the scene and remember the feeling vividly.

Liberating imagination
Imagine something changing in your life, while you manage everything with confidence.

Liberating inner feeling
Feel yourself as confident, with energy and ability to cope with anything that arises.

Positive action
Deliberately make some changes to your life routines (See chapter 17, page 192).

Feelings Are More Important

Similar beliefs
Desire is more important than reason. Expressing feeling is liberating. Intuition is more important than intellect. The spirit is more closely related to feeling than it is to the mind.

Possible related beliefs
The inner world is more important than the outer world. I am not very intelligent. I can't help having a bad temper.

Life choices
Relationships and occupations conducive to emotional drama.

Ego advantage
I'm a feeling person. I'm sensitive. I have heart. I am above those dry intellectuals.

Judgment of others
Their ideas are unreal, impractical, and empty. They are colorless, weak, and wishy-washy.

Judgment of self
I am not very good at equanimity. I get over-attached, so I, and those I'm attached to, can't be free. I am weak to be so attached. I am over-emotional. I'm trapped by my feelings.

The illusion of safety
I know the ins and outs of feelings so well, it's easy. I do not have to face the threat of deeper understanding.

Less responsibility/work
I don't have to work at developing my understanding. I don't have to take responsibility for my thoughtless reactions.

Generalization from the past
Memories of emotional times. Memories of getting what's wanted through emotional outbursts. Memories of the intellect being put down by parents or other influential figures.

Selective evidence from the present
Notice the pleasure of the adrenalin from the flow of feeling. Forget the pain and complications caused by the over-attachment to feeling.

Distortion of perception and interpretation
Calmness in others misperceived as coldness.

Rationalization of contradictory evidence
Intellectual success is rationalized by the explanation that others listen to intellectual talk because they are dry and devoid of feeling.

Justification by imagination of future results
Imagine intense feelings and dramatic interactions.

The manufacture of supporting feeling
Exaggerate smaller feelings into larger ones.

The self-fulfilling prophecy
1. Feelings are more important. So I will convey my feelings to others. They will therefore react back with feeling. Therefore feelings are more important.
2. Feelings are more important. Therefore I will not deliberate on what to do. Therefore I am over-hasty in making decisions. Therefore I create drama. The drama I've created proves that feelings are more important.

Opposite Belief

I have the right to value and honor all aspects of myself. I have the right to value and honor my mind. I have the right to greater depth. I have the right to calmness, peace and joy. I respect myself as I am now.

The positive past
Remember a time of joyful equanimity.

Liberating imagination
Imagine a time of joyful equanimity.

Liberating inner feeling
Go deep inside to feel the joy beyond feeling.

Positive action
1. Do the exercises in chapter 16 on "relaxing to the inner-most pleasure." These exercises are calming and help create more equanimity.
2. Practice reading, understanding and contemplation.
3. Practice thinking before acting. Consider, intellectually, all the consequences of the act you have a feeling for.

I Can't Help It

Similar beliefs
I am a victim of circumstance. I have no control of what happens to me. I am at the mercy of unconscious drives. I nearly always have bad luck. I cannot change my life because my basic character was formed in infancy. I am a victim of my parents/my marriage/him/her/the institution where I work. I cannot change my life because it is necessary for me to experience karma—I am dependent on events from past lives. I can't help what I feel/think. My life is directed by a God who seems capricious or even vengeful/by chance conglomerations of genes and chemicals/by environmental accident/by fate.

Possible related beliefs
(All limiting beliefs involve a degree of helplessness.)

Life choices
Risks are avoided. Doing the unexpected is avoided. Change is avoided.

Ego advantage
At least *I* have the wisdom to see how life really is. I see reality.

Judgment of others
Those who believe they are in charge of their own lives are fools. They think they have more hope, but it is illusory. They'll find out one day.

Judgment of self
I'm (more or less) helpless. I have little real power or capacity.

The illusion of safety
Since I'm more or less helpless, I cannot change my familiar path.

Less responsibility/work
It's not my fault. I'm not responsible. There's no point in working at changing things since there are so many influences that control my life.

Generalization from the past
Memories of having little choice. Teaching from a parent or other important adult that life is such-and-such a way and that there is nothing that anybody can do about it. Believing generalized life philosophies on human helplessness that have been heard or read.

Selective evidence from the present
Pay special attention to the times when trying to change circumstances fails.

Distortion of perception and interpretation
Misinterpretation of events, feelings, facial expressions, etc. to fit the belief.

Rationalization of contradictory evidence
Success at changing circumstances written off as luck or due to other circumstances.

Justification by imagination of future results
What has happened before will happen again. Imagine present limitations continuing indefinitely.

The manufacture of supporting feeling
Vague sense of lack of hope and purpose. A sense of being imprisoned. A lack of hope that it is even possible to feel free.

The self-fulfilling prophecy
1. I cannot really change my life. Therefore I will not waste my energy trying. I will accept life as it is given to me. Therefore I have little experience of attempting to change my life. Since I believe what I experience, it is evident to me that I cannot really change my life.
2. I am at the mercy of negative experiences in my past. When similar situations arise in the present I know my limitations and take avoiding action. Therefore I am at the mercy of negative experiences in my past.
3. I cannot do what I want so there is no point in trying. Therefore I cannot do what I want.
4. I am at the mercy of unconscious drives. Therefore I will control them. They will then get stronger or more distorted so that when they do come out, they are more destructive. Therefore I am at the mercy of unconscious drives.
5. I nearly always have bad luck. Therefore I will limit my enthusiasm and my eagerness to react. Therefore I will miss opportunities and people will respond less positively to me. In other words, my environment will consistently give me less than the "good luck" people get. I nearly always have bad luck.

Opposite Belief

I have far more capacity than I have been aware of. I create my own reality. I am in charge of my own life. I have great creative resources. I respect myself as I am now.

The positive past
Remember a time in your life when you felt good about changing outward circumstances through your own action. Picture the details and remember the feeling.

Liberating imagination
Imagine yourself succeeding at something you want (but had not felt able to reach). Imagine seemingly fixed circumstances changing for the better.

Liberating inner feeling
Feel the inner strength of being in charge of your life. Imagine the feeling of succeeding at something you want. Imagine the feeling of liberation when seemingly fixed circumstances change through your actions and desire.

Positive action
Start saying *no* to something you've always said *yes* to *or* start saying *yes* to something you've always said *no* to. Make some small moves to taking greater charge of your life. Try talking to somebody or taking other action to change a present limiting circumstance. Take a risk. Make a small change that you *know* you can do, and that will challenge the old restricting belief.

I Am Boring

Similar beliefs
I am dull. I am unexciting. People fall asleep when they listen to me. I have no interests.

Possible related beliefs
I'm not good enough. Consistency is essential. I can't help it. I must keep a low profile.

Life choices
Unexciting and slow-paced jobs and relationships.

Ego advantage
I am steady. I am sensible. I am solid. I have my feet on the ground.

Judgment of others
They are unreliable/untrustworthy/over-sexed.

Judgment of self
I am of little value.

The illusion of safety
Do not have to risk self-exposure.

Less responsibility/work
Do not have to work at communicating, being interesting, or feeling more alive. Can avoid the responsibility of communicating happiness.

Generalization from the past
As a child I was told several times that I was boring/unexciting. Other children were not interested in me. My parents found my brother/sister more interesting.

Selective evidence from the present
Pay special attention to when people do not respond. Screen out the times when they do.

Distortion of perception and interpretation
Perception of your image in a mirror seen as dull and uninteresting.

Rationalization of contradictory evidence
They are only interested out of kindness/pity.

Justification by imagination of future results
Imagine little response from others.

The manufacture of supporting feeling
Limitation of energy. Dull feeling within.

The self-fulfilling prophecy
1. I'm boring. Therefore I might as well stay in the background/hide myself. Therefore people don't respond to me. So I'm boring.
2. I'm boring. So I try to be interesting by talking a lot, but because I'm nervous about being boring, I talk too fast and without depth. Therefore I'm boring.
3. I'm uninteresting. Therefore I try to talk about myself so that I can show I am more interesting. As I talk about myself, people get bored. Therefore I'm uninteresting.

Opposite Belief

I am an interesting person. I am full of energy. I love myself as I am now. I am a unique expression of humankind. I have the right to express myself. I have the right to variety and enjoyment. I respect myself as I am now.

The positive past
Remember a time when you were full of excitement and others shared and responded to your excitement.

Liberating imagination
Imaging a scene of lively interaction with others.

Liberating inner feeling
Full of energy within.

Positive action
1. Be curious about somebody else—for example, ask them what made them choose the choices they made. Showing interest in another person makes you interesting.

2. Take up a new interest or hobby, even if you have to push yourself to start.
3. Exercise every morning till you feel the energy moving through your body.
4. Practice the meditation on relaxing to the innermost pleasure (chapter 16, page 186) which opens the flow of energy within the body.

I Am Lazy

Similar beliefs
I can't be bothered. I don't have much energy. It's too hard for me.

Possible related beliefs
I'm not good enough. I'm boring. I'm unhappy. Pessimism.

Life choices
Chocies involving the minimum of work.

Ego Advantage
I'm clever to get away with doing so little work.

Judgment of others
They're stupid to work so hard.

Judgment of self
I lack energy. I lack initiative. I have a negative attitude to life.

The illusion of safety
Since I don't really try at anything, I don't have to risk the insecurity of failure.

Less responsibility/work
I do not have to work at all. And it's not my fault. I don't have to risk the responsibility of success.

Generalization from the past
I've got what I want without work before.

Selective evidence from the present
Notice the times of lassitude. Screen out the times of activity
and the positive results of activity.

Distortion of perception and interpretation
Misinterpret the feeling of lassitude *caused* by inactivity to *be
the cause* of inactivity.

Rationalization of contradictory evidence
I acted energetically only because I was under extreme pressure.

Justification by imagination of future results
Daydreams of success without work.

The manufacture of supporting feeling
Indolence. Arrogance—I don't need to work.

The self-fulfilling prophecy
I am lazy. Therefore I don't work and I don't move. Therefore I feel lassitude. Therefore I'm lazy.

Opposite Belief

I am active. I have the right to work with energy and pleasure. I deserve to use my body and my mind. I respect myself.
I love myself as I am now.

The positive past
Remember a time of activity and the good feeling that that
created.

Liberating imagination
Imagine working hard at something which is satisfying.
Imagine the satisfaction of having worked really hard.

Liberating inner feeling
Energy. Warmth

Positive action
1. Excercise every day with some sport/activity that is enjoyable.
2. Clean your area, room, or house.
3. Get working—start by setting a reasonable timetable with breaks of rewarding activity to look forward to.

I Am Not Very Intelligent

Similar beliefs
I am dumb. Intelligence is judged (correctly) by society or exams. Basic intelligence cannot change. I can never succeed in mental work. I will never pass my exams.

Possible related beliefs
I cannot escape my class. The rational mind is best. I am boring. I'm not good enough. I will never be respected.

Life choices
Manual work. Repetitive mental work requiring little creativity or initiative.

Ego advantage
I am better because I am down to earth. I am strong. I am practical.

Judgment of others
Intellectuals and so-called "intelligent" people waste their time thinking rather than doing. They are impractical/weak/impotent.

Judgment of self
I'm stupid and it will never change.

The illusion of safety
I know my role.

Less responsibility/work
I don't have to use my mind. I don't have to bother to learn.

Generalization from the past
The memory as a child of being told by your parent or other important adult that you are stupid or "you'll never understand." The memory of being insulted when you did not understand something as a child. The memory of your family and culture supporting rote learning rather than curiosity. The memory of your family/culture supporting physical activity but looking down on reading or intellectual questioning.

Selective evidence from the present
Selective focus on moments of misunderstanding, failure, and the embarrassment of feeling dumb. Moments of clarity and understanding screen out.

Distortion of perception and interpretation
Information that is initially understood gets misinterpreted to uphold the belief.

Rationalization of contradictory evidence
Moments of creative success are explained away: "I was lucky that time"; "I only succeeded because I studied and studied and studied."

Justification by imagination of future results
Imagine making silly mistakes or failing at a mental task.

The manufacture of supporting feeling
The feeling of embarrassment from not knowing or from making mistakes. The dread or fear of failure.

The self-fulfilling prophecy
I'm dumb. Therefore I cannot do the job. Because I fear embarrassment and/or failure, I get increasingly nervous.

When I'm nervous I do not think very well. Therefore I make silly mistakes and do not do the job properly. Therefore I'm dumb.

Opposite Belief

I have an intelligent creative mind. I respect myself as I am now.

The positive past
Remember one time in your life when you were clear and bright and when this was noticed by somebody else. Picture every detail and remember how it felt.

Liberating imagination
See yourself succeeding in the task you envisage. See yourself calculating effectively and planning strategically. See yourself reacting quickly and cleverly.

Liberating inner feeling
Feel the pleasure and self-assurance of knowing and of succeeding.

Positive action
Develop your mind. Find a mental activity that you take pleasure in and practice it. Use your mind, and that will challenge the old restricting belief.

▶ I Am Poor

Similar beliefs
Money is wrong. I do not deserve to be well-off or rich. I never have enough money.

Possible related beliefs
I'm unhappy. I'm weak. I can't help it. I'm unintelligent. Life is accidental. My product will not sell. Pessimism. I'm lower class. Life is hard. I'm lazy. I'm dependent on others. They are against me. The physical world is inferior. I'm not good enough.

Life choices
Choices of job, partners, and investments which ensure continuing poverty.

Ego advantage
I'm more spiritual. I'm not greedy. I am above money. I am above competition. Blessed are the poor for they shall inherit the earth.

Judgment of others
Rich people are materialistic and shallow. They are greedy, competitive, and grasping. They do not care about other people (like me). They are not spiritual. It is easier for a camel to go through the eye of a needle than it is for a rich man to enter the kingdom of heaven. Money is the root of all evil.

Judgment of self
I am not good enough to earn well. I do not deserve success.

The illusion of safety
I know this state well. I do not have the discomfort of fighting for more. I do not have to undergo the fear of moving to town or moving to the country to find better employment. I do not need to suffer the insecurity of changing my work to a job that is more needed.

Less responsibility/work
I do not have to work at changing my work/my situation/ my living area. I do not have to work so hard at my present

job/I do not have to make the creative effort to find ways of earning more.

Generalization from the past
My parents were poor and could never change—they always struggled. My parents were well-off but miserable. I remember times when money and power were greatly misused. We had many possessions but our inner life was terribly empty.

Selective evidence from the present
Notice unhappiness/emptiness in rich people. Screen out opportunities for financial reward.

Distortion of perception and interpretation
Facial expression of the rich distorted to look greedy. Facial expression of the poor distorted to look pathetic.

Rationalization of contradictory evidence
Those rich people may seem to be happy, but it's a cover-up for their underlying emptiness. My recent success was luck.

Justification by imagination of future results
I will always be poor. Imagine scenes of struggle ahead. Or else daydream of opulent scenes, which contrast bitterly with present reality and diminish hope.

The manufacture of supporting feeling
Low feeling. Resentment. Anger. Resignation. Lack of interest.

The self-fulfilling prophecy
1. I'm poor. I'll always be poor so it's not worth working hard to change it. Therefore I'm poor.
2. I'm poor. Therefore I'm despondent. When I try to change my situation it takes a great deal of energy and possibly years of work. I'm too despondent and have too

little hope to maintain this initiative for such a long time. Therefore I stay poor.
3. I'm poor. It's the fault of the rich, whom I resent. Because I resent them they don't trust me and don't want to employ me or promote me. Therefore I stay poor.

Opposite Belief

I am rich. I am rich in spirit. I have money to spend on the things I need. I have enough to be able to give to others. I am earning well. I am worthy of happiness. I respect myself as I am now. I love myself as I am now.

The positive past
Remember the feeling when you had earned enough to buy an item or moment of luxury, however small.

Liberating imagination
Imagine the house, possessions, etc. you would enjoy having—not as an empty or unrealistic dream, but as a concrete scene experienced with all the senses. Imagine being able to give something to someone you love.

Liberating inner feeling
Inner feeling of energy and abundance.

Positive action
Consider whether you are poor by other people's standards or your own. If it is the former, see "I'm not good enough" (page 254). There are, of course, many people with little money whose lives are immensely rich.

If you are poor by your own standards, consider the following:

Spend a little more, even a few cents, on an item of luxury or on something that gives you pleasure that you would not normally choose to afford. This is an act of prayer and belief in your capacity for abundance.

Look at what you spend that does not give you pleasure or enhance your life.

Do work, or study for work, that gives you pleasure as well as financial reward.

I Am Trapped by My Past

Similar beliefs
I am what I am because of my parents/my ancestors/the Church/my country/the way I was brought up. I am what I am because of my past lives/karma. I cannot change because I cannot change my genes.

Possible related beliefs
I can't help it. I'm dependent on others. I'm not good enough. The spirit does not exist. Pessimism.

Life choices
Similar to your ancestors'. Limited by your conception of what you can be, based on what you learned from others.

Ego advantage
I understand myself. I am wise. I know why people are as they are.

Judgment of others
Those who think they are free of their pasts are fools. They haven't gone deep enough. They are superficial. They've repressed their unconscious.

Judgment of self
I do not have the strength or capacity to transcend the influences from my past.

The illusion of safety
I don't have to face the threat of change.

Less responsibility/work
I don't have to work at really improving my life. My responsibility in what I will give is limited by what I was given. Its not my fault. Although I may believe in the concept of personal responsibility, I can't really help how I am.

Generalization from the past
Underwent psychotherapeutic training in the concept of damage from the past, whether as client/therapist/psychologist or reader of psychology books. Selectively notice incidents in the past that relate to present behavior. Generalize the past as unhappy or damaging.

Selective evidence from the present
Selectively notice behavior in the present that relates to past incidents.

Distortion of perception and interpretation
When life is seen as moving in a particular direction determined by past influences, any data that do not fit this scenario are misperceived or reinterpreted. Then one can say: "See, it's happening again!"

Rationalization of contradictory evidence
That moment of freedom was not really me. They are only so different from their parents out of rebellion—and they only need to rebel if they are subconsciously trapped.

Justification by imagination of future results
I will always be like this basically, even if I make some superficial changes.

The manufacture of supporting feeling
Resignation.

The self-fulfilling prophecy
1. I'm trapped by my past. Therefore it's no use trying to change. Therefore I'm trapped by my past.

2. I'm trapped by my past. Therefore I'll do everything I can to be different. But when I try to be different I'm still being affected by what I'm trying to be different from. Therefore I'm still trapped by my past.
3. I am at the mercy of negative experiences in my past. When similar situations arise in the present I know my limitations and take sensible avoiding action. Therefore I am at the mercy of negative experiences in my past.

Opposite Belief

Although I have certain habits of thinking and action that relate to my past, my inner self is completely free. When I give up expectations of what I think I should have been given, I have no more anger and nothing to rebel against. When I accept and respect myself as I am now, I am free to make changes out of love. I have the freedom to develop any aspects of myself that I choose. I accept myself as I am now. I respect myself as I am now. I love myself as I am now.

The positive past
Remember incidents from your past that do not fit your beliefs about yourself. If you cannot remember any, make one up and imagine it in vivid detail (see chapter 13).

Liberating imagination
Imagine yourself acting differently with positive results.

Liberating inner feeling
Energy. Excitement. Freedom.

Positive action
When you catch yourself in a behavior trap, stop, take a breath, make absolutely no self-judgment, and change your behavior. For example, a man found himself shouting at his children with the same violent energy with which his father

had shouted at him. He stopped, took a deep breath, and then spoke to them firmly but without violence.

The more you practice this, the earlier you notice and change the behavior. After a while you begin to notice the feeling that arises before the behavior and you are able to circumvent the behavior altogether. This way you break the self-fulfilling prophecy.

▶ I Get Sick Easily

Similar beliefs
I am going to get cancer, a heart attack, etc. My body is weak. My resistance is low. I always get colds/flu/hayfever.

Possible related beliefs
The physical world is inferior. I can't help it. I'm a panicky person. I'm weak. The body is inferior.

Life choices
Avoid situations which tax, stress, or exercise the body.

Ego advantage
I am sensitive/finely tuned/open.

Judgment of others
Those who are more resilient are more insensitive.

Judgment of self
There's something wrong with me. I'm weak.

The illusion of safety
The familiarity of feeling sorry for myself or others feeling sorry for me.

Less responsibility/work
I can get a rest/be looked after. I don't have to go to work. I won't be able to take on so much.

Generalization from the past
Ailments from the past, in yourself, or in others who were influential.

Selective evidence from the present
Symptoms focused on and exaggerated. Feelings of health, resilience, and energy screened out.

Distortion of perception and interpretation
Body signs reinterpreted as symptoms of the feared ailment. For example, slightly runny nose due to emotional state interpreted as the first symptoms of another cold.

Rationalization of contradictory evidence
I'm feeling good now, but it won't last long.

Justification by imagination of future results
The symptoms of the ailment you fear. Severe illness, incapacity, even death.

The manufacture of supporting feeling
A feeling of malaise, weakness or the beginnings of specific symptoms.

The self-fulfilling prophecy
I get sick easily. Therefore I believe I have little resistance. Since resistance to illness is very much connected to belief, this means I actually have less resistance. Therefore I get sick easily.

Opposite Belief

I have a healthy body. My body has its own wisdom. I respect my body. I like myself. I love myself.

The positive past
Remember one time in your past when you were healthy and vibrant. Picture yourself and remember the feeling.

Liberating imagination
Body visualised as radiantly healthy.

Liberating inner feeling
Body felt as full of energy, radiating health.

Positive action
Get a medical check-up to see what areas need changing or improving. Balance your diet. Exercise your body. Build your strength and change your body image by using weights. Begin to enjoy the movement of your body and to feel its strength. Do the visualizations on making your body healthy (see page 176).

I'll Grab What I Can

Similar beliefs
There is only so much to go around. I have to get it before you do. One cannot afford to give away too much. I'm mean. I'm tight-fisted. I must defend what little I have. It's a dog eat dog world. I have to take care of number one.

Possible related beliefs
Life is hard. I am poor. The end justifies the means. The physical world is inferior. Life is random and material.

Life choices
Material security is put above happiness.

Ego advantage
I'm careful. I'm shrewd. I know what this world's about. I'm thrifty. I'm sensible. I handle money well.

Judgment of others
Those who give too much will regret it in times of need. They only give so that they get noticed anyway. They're spend-thrifts, licentious, unthinking, unintelligent.

Judgment of self
I am small-minded and ungiving. I lack generosity of spirit.

The illusion of safety
Grabbing what I can seems to make me secure. If I don't give I have more.

Less responsibility/work
I don't have to work at learning to trust life or others. I can avoid the responsibility of giving what I have been given. I can avoid the work of taking care of others. It's unnecessary to work at expanding productivity and earning power; it's easier to limit giving and spending.

Generalization from the past
My family was like this. I've seen times when people who gave were used. I've seen times of poverty.

Selective evidence from the present
Notice the times when giving goes wrong.

Distortion of perception and interpretation
Misinterpret other's interest for covetousness.

Rationalization of contradictory evidence
He only gave that to look good—and it will be misused.

Justification by imagination of future results
Grabbing what I can will make me rich.

The manufacture of supporting feeling
A sense of personal threat. Feelings of weariness. Contraction of mind and muscle—the body tends to be held tense in self-protection.

The self-fulfilling prophecy
1. I'll grab what I can and give only what I don't need. Therefore they will do the same to me. Therefore I need to grab what I can before they do.

2. There isn't much to go around. Therefore I'll keep what I can. Therefore there isn't much to go around.

Opposite Belief

Life is abundant. The greatest pleasure is in giving freely. The more I give, the richer I feel. Life's resources are infinite. I deserve to feel rich within. My inner wealth is infinite. I respect myself. I accept myself as I am now.

The positive past
Remember a time of giving with pleasure.

Liberating imagination
Imagine giving with pleasure.

Liberating inner feeling
An inner feeling of abundance and joy.

Positive action
Practice giving some (small) thing each day. Offer to somebody else what you would normally have taken first.

I'm A Nervous Person

Similar beliefs
I can't get myself together. I'm not calm. I'm disturbed by silly things. I get distressed easily. I'm hysterical.

Possible related beliefs
Helplessness. I'm not good enough. I'm weak.

Life choices
Interruptions to smooth flow, for example, leaving a secure job or relationship for something with more drama and uncertainty, *or*, avoiding even small risks for fear of fear.

Ego advantage
I'm important because I'm feeling so much at the center of
a drama. Look what's happening to me.

Judgment of others
They are dull, unexciting. They're cold and they don't care.

Judgment of self
I'm being silly. I'm not capable of intimacy. I'm not good
at thinking. I'm no good at deeper feelings.

The illusion of safety
I know this way of being. When I get so upset about minor
issues, I do not have to face more serious issues. I do not
have to face my deeper feelings.

Less responsibility/work
I can't help what I feel. It gets me attention from other people
who take care of me. I don't have to think so much. I'm too
scared to take charge of my life.

Generalization from the past
Panic or emotional state gained attention in the past, sometimes when all else failed.

Selective evidence from the present
Focus on times of panic or of not coping. Screen out the times
of coping well.

Distortion of perception and interpretation
Perception of emotive events heightened, and interpretation
exaggerated, to create greater dramatic effect.

Rationalization of contradictory evidence
Well, I managed it that time because I slept well/had a drink/
was in an unusual mood—any reason which does not contradict the belief.

Justification by imagination of future results
See events going wrong through nervousness or panic.

The manufacture of supporting feeling
Imagination of the results of panic creates the feeling of panic.

The self-fulfilling prophecy
I'm a nervous person. Therefore I will not be able to handle the situation well. This scares me and makes me nervous. I'm a nervous person.

Opposite Belief

I'm a calm person. I handle this situation with confidence and ability. I think clearly. I accept myself as I am now. I respect myself.

The positive past
Remember handling a difficult situation calmly.

Liberating imagination
Imagine yourself handling a situation with calmness and clarity.

Liberating inner feeling
Feel a sense of calmness within, a sense of certainty and confidence.

Positive action
Practice the exercises for connecting to an inner sense of relaxation and calm (page 186).

I'm Dependent on Others

Similar beliefs
I need to be looked after. Take care of me. Feed me. The world owes me a living. I should not have to work. I never got any love, so I need it now. I can't. I am in need. Nobody loves me. I'm always rejected. I have no energy. I don't know what to do.

Possible related beliefs
I'm not good enough. I'm weak. I can't help it. I'm dependent on drugs/alcohol/sugar, etc.

Life choices
Choose people and situations you can be dependent on.

Ego advantage
I'm too clever to have to work. I'm a deeply sensitive person.

Judgment of others
Those who work hard are stupid. Those I depend on are controlling and power-hungry, also gullible.

Judgment of self
I'm weak and needy.

The illusion of safety
I'm familiar with this dependent position. I do not have to suffer the anxiety of making my own choices.

Less responsibility/work
If they make the decisions, whatever happens is their fault. As a dependent, I have no responsibility. I do not even have to work at strengthening myself.

Generalization from the past
Focus on the times of not receiving love as a child—therefore it seems that love is still "owed" to you. Remember times of

your own strength/independence not being trusted (such as not being allowed to ride a bicycle in case you fell).

Selective evidence from the present
Heightened sensitivity to the tiniest innuendo of rejection.

Distortion of perception and interpretation
Perceive facial expression as rejecting. Interpret innocuous remarks as rejecting.

Rationalization of contradictory evidence
She/he is just being kind—she/he doesn't really love me.

Justification by imagination of future results
Imagine merging totally into the "stronger" person, or else imagine scenes of being rejected.

The manufacture of supporting feeling
Feel weak, physically and emotionally. Feelings of need. Lack of self-respect.

The self-fulfilling prophecy
1. Nobody loves me. When I find somebody who cares a little, I cling on. This drives them away. Therefore nobody loves me.
2. I'm dependent. I hate the person I'm dependent on. So he/she begins to reject me, which makes me feel more dependent.
3. I'm helpless, so there is no point in working hard. Therefore I work beneath my capacity or stay unemployed. Therefore I do not feel in charge of my own destiny. I'm helpless.
4. I can't. Therefore I won't try. Without practice, I can't.
5. I'm dependent. Therefore I have a dependent posture (limp muscles, caved in chest) and I breathe the minimum of air—therefore I feel little energy. Therefore I'm dependent.

Opposite Belief

I take care of myself. I make my own decisions. I already have the love within me. I have inner strength. I am strong and capable. I have resources and capacities I have not yet practiced. I respect myself. I love myself.

The positive past
Remember a moment of independent action.

Liberating imagination
See yourself in a situation where you are strong, decisive, and giving.

Liberating inner feeling
Strength and energy moving within.

Positive action
    Stand upright and bring your shoulders gently back.
    Breathe more deeply.
    Do physical work or physical exercise. Consciously strengthen your body.
    Work hard.
    Give to others, even if what you give is very small.

I'm Fat

Similar beliefs
I don't like my body. I'm too large.

Possible related beliefs
I'm not attractive. The body is inferior. I'm not good enough. Sex is an unfortunate necessity. Life is hard. I'm lazy. I can't help it.

Life choices
Avoidance of intimacy.

Ego advantage
I have weight. I am important. You have to notice me. You cannot ignore me or shove me out of the way.

Judgment of others
Other people are inferior because they are prejudiced against fat people like me. Others are smaller and less significant. Thin people have all the luck.

Judgment of self
I am unworthy. I don't like myself. I am lazy. I have no willpower.

The illusion of safety
I'm physically protected from other pepole. It's safer to travel alone because I'm bigger. I'm safe from closer relationships. I'm safe from sexual relationships and complications.

Less responsibility/work
I don't have to work at looking good or taking care of my body. I don't have to work at relationships.

Generalization from the past
Remember times when your body was disapproved of or when you were teased for your looks or your appetites. If you have been large in the past, the belief persist that it is your nature to be large. The times when weight is regained are remembered more than the times when weight is lost.

Selective evidence from the present
Notice critical expressions from others and ignore compliments. Notice especially the parts of the body that you consider too large.

Distortion of perception and interpretation
Body image seen as fat even after losing weight. Perception of the image in the mirror is actually distorted to fit the belief.

Rationalization of contradictory evidence
I only managed to lose weight through punishing myself or suffering from my willpower. My body only looks good/reasonable because it's covered up.

Justification by imagination of future results
Visualize body as fat. See others as being put off.

The manufacture of supporting feeling
Heavy feeling. Feeling of being slowed down or depressed.

The self-fulfilling prophecy
I'm fat. Therefore I do not look good and I don't like my body. Therefore it doesn't matter if I eat, and at least eating is comforting. Therefore I'm fat.

Opposite Belief

My body feels good. My body is beautiful. I have a fit and healthy body. I'm worthy of being loved. I love myself. I respect myself as I am now. I accept myself as I am now.

The positive past
Remember a time, no matter how long ago, when you felt lithe and fit. Picture doing an activity at that time in which you used your body fully, and remember how good it felt.

Liberating imagination
Picture yourself doing some movement you really enjoy. Picture your body as the weight you would like it to be. See yourself as beautiful and moving with grace.

Liberating inner feeling
Feeling lively. Liking yourself. Loving yourself.

Positive action
Take care of your body sensually. For example, do *enjoyable* exercise, take massages, take care of how you dress and look.

Do not diet in a self-punishing way. Diet only with the feeling of imagination of how you wish to enjoy your body. Take small mouthfuls and eat slowly, savoring the taste of each morsel of food.

I'm Not Attractive

Similar beliefs
Men never see me. Women never see me. Being attractive is not important. I'm unwomanly. I'm unmanly. I'm too small/too fat/the wrong shape. I don't like my body.

Possible related beliefs
I'm fat. The body is less important/inferior. Luxury is wrong. Sex is an unfortunate necessity. Life is hard.

Life choices
Choose men/women who tend not to notice you. Choose more platonic relationships.

Ego advantage
I'm above bothering about the superficialities of appearance. My spirit/inner self is better. I'm special because I don't look good.

Judgment of others
Those who are concerned about how they look are superficial. They waste their time and money. They play silly games with the opposite sex. They make themselves nice on the outside to cover up what's inside. If they were nice inside they wouldn't have to bother with appearance.

Judgment of self
I don't look good. This really expresses my deeper opinion about myself: I'm no good. I'm scared of being looked at.

The illusion of safety

I don't have to worry about sexual tension or fear the complications and uncertainties of sexual relationships.

Less responsibility/work

You can't get me in the seduction game. I don't have to work at being attractive. I don't have to work at looking after my body. Sexless relationships are easier—I don't have to bother with any male/female battles.

Generalization from the past

My father didn't notice how I looked and he was the first man in my life. Therefore there is no point in bothering to look attractive to men.

I was teased about my appearance at school and the girls were never interested in me.

My parents often told me I was plain and I believed them.

Selective evidence from the present

Notice the times when you are not noticed. Do not notice, or minimize, the times when you are noticed. Notice all the things that you consider "wrong" with your body/appearance and ignore your positive assets.

Distortion of perception and interpretation

Distorted perception of face and body makes it seem unattractive in accordance with your belief.

Rationalization of contradictory evidence

If he notices me, it's because he wants to use me (the only thing men want is sex).

Justification by imagination of future results

They'll never really see me. Whatever I will do, will not help. I expect that I will not be noticed.

The manufacture of supporting feeling

A sad feeling of being unappreciated and a hopeless feeling that it will never change.

The self-fulfilling prophecy

1. I am not attractive. Therefore there is no point in making an effort to look good. Therefore I am not attractive.
2. I am not attractive. If he/she notices me it is abnormal and it scares me. Therefore I shrink away from him/her. Therefore he/she shrinks away from me. Therefore I am not attractive.

Opposite Belief

I am an attractive person. I am a beautiful expression of womankind/mankind. I like myself. I love myself as I am now. I respect myself. I accept myself.

The positive past

Remember a time when your appearance was appreciated. If you cannot, picture or feel your father or mother holding you as a child, saying with great warmth "you look beautiful."

Liberating imagination

See yourself dressed beautifully, looking great, being noticed and appreciated.

Liberating inner feeling

Openness, softness. Feel your enjoyment of other's appreciation and enjoy your own appreciation of yourself.

Positive action

Take care of your body in some way, for example, exercise, apply make-up, get a manicure, hair-cut, facial, etc. Wear a noticeable item of dress that looks good on you. Every day look at yourself naked in a mirror and deliberately focus on any aspect of yourself you like. As you look, tell yourself "I love you" even if you cannot feel it at all at first.

 **I'm Not Good Enough**

Similar beliefs
I'm not worthy of respect. I must be acceptable to others.
I've got to succeed in others' eyes. I must behave appropri-
ately. I don't have the right to express myself. I don't deserve
to be happy. I'm always left out. I'm wrong. I'm guilty. I'm
depressed. The authority knows better than I do. I have a
good behavior personality habit. I'm inferior. I'm a failure.
I'm a bad mother/father/lover/worker/friend.

Possible related beliefs
All limited beliefs carry a portion of "I'm not good enough."

Life choices
Choose less than your true capacity. Underachievement.
Choices may be determined by values of other people (such
as parents, authority figures). Or else, choose and fail at
unattainable tasks and difficult relationships.

Ego advantage
I'm special and different. I'm humble and unassuming. Poor
me. I'm patient. I'm a martyr. Look how I suffer.

Judgment of others
They're lucky. They're arrogant and presumptuous. They
are not so deep because they have not had to suffer.

Judgment of self
I'm no good.

The illusion of safety
I don't have to express myself and risk people's reactions to
me. I don't have to try very hard and risk change, success,
or failure.

Less responsibility/work
I don't have to work at being happy. I don't have to work
to do a task well, since I won't be good enough anyway. I
can't. It's not my fault.

Generalization from the past
The authorities I believed in told me I was not good enough. This happened through criticism, lack of respect for my wishes and appetites, ridiculing of my expressions of feeling such as anger or crying, and many other ways. If I was not good enough for them then, I will never be good enough for myself.

Selective evidence from the present
Notice the things that go wrong and especially the things that you think you *do* wrong. Minimize the useful and productive moments.

Distortion of perception and interpretation
If someone praises me I switch down my hearing. I see disapproval on other people's faces when there is no disapproval there.

Rationalization of contradictory evidence
If someone gives me something, it is only because they want something. They could not *want* to give me something. Expressions of appreciation of me are simply done out of politeness or pity.

Justification by imagination of future results
An endless struggle for approval or self-validation. Either imagine failing or else success in winning approval. Both feed the feeling of need for validation by another.

The manufacture of supporting feeling
Anxiety. Depression. Desperation. Loneliness.

The self-fulfilling prophecy
1. I'm always left out. Therefore I won't try to join in and I will resent those that do. Therefore I'm left out.
2. I'm guilty. I will brood over what I did wrong instead of making amends or at least learning from my mistake. Therefore I stay guilty.

3. I'm depressed. It therefore seems useless to take action to change my situation. Lack of action is depression.
4. I'm not good enough at doing X. Therefore I won't practice X and therefore I'll never be good enough at doing X.
5. The authority knows better than I do. Therefore I won't trust myself. Therefore the authority knows better than I do.
6. I'm not good enough. Therefore I try harder and harder to conform to other's ideas which are better. Therefore I get further away from my own inner impulses. Therefore I lose self-respect and feel that I'm not my own person. This judgment makes me feel I'm not good enough.
7. I cannot affect the world. This frustrates me because basically I want to do good. My frustration and my lack of power to affect change make it seem to me that there is an enormous unbridgeable gulf between my ideal of what people should be and my idea of selfish human reality. So anything I can do for the good seems so paltry that it's not worth doing. Therefore I won't do anything very much. Therefore I cannot affect the world.

Opposite Belief

I am worthy of respect. I respect myself. I like myself. I can do what I want. I have a free choice. I love myself as I am now. I am worthy of happiness. I am good and strong. I accept myself as I am now.

The positive past
Remember one incident or time when you felt good about yourself.

Liberating imagination
See yourself acting with confidence and pleasure in a situation you would have feared. See yourself giving to another or others with pleasure.

Liberating inner feeling
Calmness. Confidence. Self-acceptance. Peace of mind.

Positive action
Any positive action is better than self-criticism. If you feel so low that your physical energy feels depleted, do something physical, like a sport, exercises, walking, gardening, cleaning the house, painting a room, etc.

If you are feeling guilty, take action to amend or learn from what you chastise yourself for. It is almost never too late.

Practice expressing your thoughts and feelings to other people in a creative way (see chapter 17, page 193).

Self-criticism focuses on the self. Be of service to other people and self-deprecation disappears. There is no better antidepressant than giving something—it proves you are not empty, that there is something inside you.

I'm Shy

Similar beliefs
I don't like too many people around me. I'm a loner. I feel shy/awkward/lost in a crowd.

Possible related beliefs
The inner self is more important than the outer. I am boring. I'm not attractive. I must keep a low profile. They are against me.

Life choices
A few close friends, one friend, or no friends.

Ego advantage
My friends are real friends, not just acquaintances. I am deep. I don't need to be seen by a lot of people. It is up to

other people to make my acquaintance. I don't need to make the effort to get to know others—*I* should be sought out.

Judgment of others
Those who are at ease in crowds are superficial. Extroverts are inferior.

Judgment of self
I am a social misfit. I am weak. I am inferior. What I have within is unworthy of being expressed.

The illusion of safety
I don't need to take the risk of contact. I don't have to risk others' reactions.

Less responsibility/work
I don't need to do the work of getting to know people. I don't have the responsibility of much involvement with people.

Generalization from the past
When I opened up to people, I got my feelings hurt. I remember being made a fool of.

Selective evidence from the present
The moments of awkwardness while initiating contact are remembered. The pleasure from the contact initiated is forgotten or minimized.

Distortion of perception and interpretation
Facial expression and tone of voice misperceived as unfriendly or distant. Pleasure of contact with another distorted by the belief into difficulty/pain/awkwardness.

Rationalization of contradictory evidence
That moment of easy contact was unusual.

Justification by imagination of future results
Visualizing social contact going wrong.

The manufacture of supporting feeling
Expansiveness restricted by protective muscle tension. Feeling of smallness, inadequacy, awkwardness.

The self-fulfilling prophecy
I am shy. Therefore I will avoid social contact. Therefore I will have few chances to practice initiating contact. Therefore, since ease of social contact depends greatly on practice, I am shy and will stay shy.

Opposite Belief

I have the capacity to make contact effectively. What is inside me is worthy of being expressed. I am worthy. I have the right to speak up. I deserve to be taken notice of. I respect/ accept myself as I am now. I love myself as I am now.

The positive past
Remember a time when you enjoyed making contact with another person. Picture the scene and remember the feeling.

Liberating imagination
Visualize making contact and receiving a warm response. Imagine the pleasure from contact with others.

Liberating inner feeling
Warmth, pleasure, laughter. A full expression of any feeling.

Positive action
Practice taking the step of initiating contact each day.
1. Do this once each day with an acquaintance. This is easier if you focus on their concerns/interests rather than on your own belief in your shyness.
2. If there is someone you know better, practice each day saying something that the other person would not predict. Practice making the conversation more intimate.

I'm Unhappy

Similar beliefs
Life is bad. It's going to turn out badly. I don't deserve to be happy.

Possible related beliefs
I'm unworthy. I don't like myself. I'm unattractive. I am tainted with original sin. Life is hard. Pessimism.

Life choices
Situations and relationships which create bad feeling or failure.

Ego advantage
I see how life really is. I'm deep. Poor *me*—look how *I* suffer.

Judgment of others
They don't take life seriously. Happy people are superficial. They are not clever enough to see how life is—they live in a fool's paradise.

Judgment of self
I do not deserve to be happy. I am bad inside.

The illusion of safety
I know the unhappy feeling so well, it's comfortable. Working at being happy involves taking the risk of action.

Less responsibility/work
If I'm unhappy other people will take care of me whereas if I am happy I am responsible for looking after myself. I can avoid the work of making friends or doing anything well because I have the excuse of unhappiness. I don't have to work to succeed in being happy.

Generalization from the past
Unhappy moments—life will always be like this.

Selective evidence from the present
If something is going well, immediately change the focus of the mind to something that is not going well. Focus on difficulties and problems.

Distortion of perception and interpretation
Perception of pleasure distorted into mediocre or unpleasant sensations.

Rationalization of contradictory evidence
Motives for good results or feelings reinterpreted. For example, relaxation = shirking of responsibility.

Justification by imagination of future results
Imagine things turning out badly.

The manufacture of supporting feeling
Because of imagining things going to go wrong, feel bad preemptively.

The self-fulfilling prophecy
1. I'm unhappy. Things are going to go badly. Therefore I am tense or worried. Therefore I am less effective and things do go wrong. Therefore I'm unhappy.
2. I'm unhappy. I'm preoccupied with my own unhappy feeling. Therefore I am not open to positive events or feelings. Therefore I'm unhappy.
3. I'm not happy. Therefore my relationships with people are dampened. They will react by rejecting me. Therefore I'm not happy.
4. I'm unhappy. Because I am preoccupied with my unhappy state and because I am tense, I am disconnected from the inner source of relaxation and joy. Therefore I'm unhappy.

Opposite Belief

I'm happy. I like myself. Life is good. I am worthy of happiness. I like myself. I love myself. I accept myself as I am now. I respect myself as I am now.

Positive past

Remember a moment when you were very happy and carefree. Picture the details and remember the feeling inside.

Liberating imagination

Visualize yourself in a happy situation.

Liberating inner feeling

Feel the inner feeling of flowing energy and openness. Lightness. Self-respect. Pleasure.

Positive action

Give yourself something extra that you value. Take care of your body and how you look. Give something to somebody else—it gives you an inner sense of value and pleasure. Every day do the exercise on relaxing to the innermost pleasure (page 186). Do aerobic exercise at least once every forty-eight hours.

▶ I'm Weaker Than They Are

Similar beliefs

I'll always be bossed around by men/women/others. I'm a woman and the men in my life will always have the final say. My wife always makes the decision. They always put me down. I'm small. I am emotionally/intellectually/physically weaker. I cannot stand up for myself. She/he will always win.

Possible related beliefs
I can't help it. I'm dependent. I'm not good enough. People
are only out for what they can get. I must keep a low profile.

Life choices
Choose dominant partners/colleagues.

Ego advantage
I am reasonable, affable, kind, understanding. I am better
because I do not misuse power. If I were a leader, I would
be fairer/more intelligent/kinder/more spiritual than them.

Judgment of others
Those with power are unfair, overbearing, unreasonable, un-
seeing, insensitive. They misuse their power. Anyone who
does not see this has been fooled.

Judgment of self
I'm weak. I can't stand up for myself. I'm a lesser person.
I am a coward.

The illusion of safety
It's familiar. I'm looked after and taken care of. I don't have
to risk sticking my neck out. I never need to risk the threat
of independence.

Less responsibility/work
Since I'm the weaker, it's always his/her fault. My unhappiness is due to my partner or to the control of others. I don't
have to work at making my own life or fighting for myself.
It's the fault of the people with the power.

Generalization from the past
1. Remember, as a child, parents or other important adults
   avoiding fights.
2. Remember, as a child, a parent putting you down or
   competing with you when you expressed yourself freely

or strongly. Remember your father or mother being overbearing/controlling.
3. Remember, as a child, being bullied by older or physically stronger children. Remember yourself as a smaller or weaker child.

Selective evidence from the present
Notice especially the times when you give in or are overruled. Focus on the times you do not speak your mind rather than on the times when you do.

Distortion of perception and interpretation
Perception of the "stronger one's" voice as controlling, or angry or powerful even when it is not. When in conflict, feel and accentuate a sense of physical weakness/anxiety/verbal incoherence.

Rationalization of contradictory evidence
It's too good to be true. He/she only seems to respect me in order to get me to do something or agree to something.

Justification by imagination of future results
Imagine being put down. Or else imagine fighting successfully—the contrast between this daydream and reality feeds the lack of hope.

The manufacture of supporting feeling
Feeling small and resentful.

The self-fulfilling prophecy
1. I'm weak. Therefore I won't stand up to him/her. Hence I do not experience or practice my own strength. Therefore I'm weak. I'm weaker than they are.
2. Because I am weaker I need to be closed off emotionally in order to protect myself. Therefore I will argue stiffly, defensively, and with little energy. The lack of energy makes my argument weak. Therefore I am weaker.

3. I'm physically weaker. Therefore I'll avoid physical effort. Therefore I'll stay weaker.

Opposite Belief

I'm a big-hearted strong person full of self-respect. I am determined. I respect myself. I love myself as I am now.

The positive past
Remember a moment in the past, no matter how long ago, when you felt and used your strength and were proud of it! Remember the feeling within.

Liberating imagination
Imagine yourself as commanding. See yourself as arguing or making your point with love, rather than trying to put the other down. See yourself expressing yourself fully and at peace with yourself.

Liberating inner feeling
Self-respect. Strength. Flow of energy. Feeling your own energy/radiance even within the presence of the person you believed was more powerful. Laughing. Easy. Serene.

Positive action
Speak your mind firmly yet with love or respect for the other person. It is not a battle with the other person, it is a challenge for yourself to speak up. Start with something very small which will build your confidence.

I'm Lower Class

Similar beliefs
I will never be successful. I will always work for somebody else. Real work is physical. I will never employ anybody. I'm lower class. I'm of lower status.

Possible related beliefs
I'm poor. I'm not very intelligent. I am lazy. I can't help it.
I'm dependent. People (especially employers) are only out
for what they can get. My product will not sell. I'm not good
enough.

Life choices
Manual work. Avoidance of work which entails the responsibility of employing others. Avoidance of success.

Ego advantage
The lower class are the salt of the earth. Working with your
hands is the only *real* work. We are down to earth and practical. We are modest and unextravagant.

Judgment of others
Those who work with their minds are dodging real work.
Those who go to college are putting on airs. Bosses use real
workers like us for their own selfish ends.

Judgment of self
I'll never be a success. I'm lower and I always will be.

The illusion of safety
I don't have to try anything I don't already know.

Less responsibility/work
I don't have to take responsibility for others. I don't have to
worry about whether business succeeds or fails.

Generalization from the past
My father/mother was lower class.

Selective evidence from the present
Selectively tune in to incidents of failure.

Distortion of perception and interpretation
Misinterpret speech and facial expressions of the higher
classes as looking down from above. The micro-chip on the

shoulder distorts information into an (often preconscious) us–them battle.

Rationalization of contradictory evidence
I may be successful now but it won't last. He is successful now but he's not happy.

Justification by imagination of future results
Imagine the lower status quo continuing indefinitely.

The manufacture of supporting feeling
Bitterness or resignation about lower status.

The self-fulfilling prophecy
1. I'm lower class. Therefore I won't try for any position beyond my real status. Therefore I'm lower class.
2. I'm lower class. Therefore I cannot be a successful leader. If this begins to happen, it will feel so unnatural that I'll find a way to stop it. Therefore I'll stay lower class.

Opposite Belief

I have no class. I am beyond division. I am loyal to the spirit of my lower class friends/parents/ancestors, but not to their limitations of belief. I am a valuable part of the human family. When I give with my heart, my gift is immeasurable. I have the right to be successful. I accept myself as I am now. I respect myself as I am now. I love myself as I am now.

The positive past
Remember a time of accepting yourself fully without comparing yourself with others.

Liberating imagination
Imagine accepting yourself fully without comparison.

Liberating inner feeling
Feeling of inner warmth, love, and connectedness with all people.

Positive action
Talk to someone who, in your old belief system, would be of different status. Don't look down at them or up at them, but speak with the absolute knowledge that you are both equals in the face of the universe. Practice this as an exercise, and notice *their* attitudes change.

With full knowledge of the temptation to sabotage success, begin to take steps to follow what you want to do and what you are good at.

I Must Keep a Low Profile

Similar beliefs
I'll stay out of trouble. Don't get too involved. I won't give any reference points that people can hold onto. I don't want to share what I'm thinking. I can't communicate. I can't express myself. I'm an island.

Possible related beliefs
I am boring. Being assertive is dangerous. I'm shy. I'm weak. I'm not good enough.

Life choices
Jobs where verbal self-expression is not required. Relationships of distance.

Ego advantage
I'm strong—like a rock. It doesn't matter if anyone understands me or not. I'm lord of my own space. I'm on top. I'm above all the hysteria of human feeling. I am wise not to speak.

Judgment of others
They're neurotic, having to express themselves all the time. It's weak. It's vain—why would anyone else be interested?

Judgment of self
I'm held back. I can't express myself. I don't have the freedom of choice to speak out when I want to.

The illusion of safety
I can stay out of trouble.

Less responsibility/work
It is not necessary to make the effort to explain something or find out what the other really thinks.

Generalization from the past
Memories of speaking out creating hurt. "My parents couldn't really listen. So what's the point of communicating if I'm going to be misunderstood anyway."

Selective evidence from the present
Screen out the times when self-expression created a positive result.

Distortion of perception and interpretation
Anyone approaching too close is interpreted or perceived as attacking or intruding. "Talking with me" becomes converted to "Coming at me."

Rationalization of contradictory evidence
That communication went well because they/he/she were good at it.

Justification by imagination of future results
I will be embarrassed. They might laugh or think that what I say is not important.

The manufacture of supporting feeling
Closed off. Contracted.

The self-fulfilling prophecy
1. Communication does not work. So when I communicate my aim is to get out of a situation or away from too much involvement. Therefore communication does not work.
2. I must keep a low profile. The closer I get to someone, the more nervous I get which makes communication go wrong. Therefore I must keep a low profile.

Opposite Belief

It's good that people know where I stand. I am free to speak my mind. I am open. I am an open person. I respect myself. I accept myself as I am now. I love myself as I am now.

The positive past
Remember a time when honest communication created a good feeling and a positive result.

Liberating imagination
Imagine speaking honestly creating a positive result.

Liberating inner feeling
Warmth. Love. Self-acceptance.

Positive action
Practice speaking your mind each day. Say at least one little thing that you would not normally say.

► Insomnia

Similar beliefs
I need five/six/seven/eight/nine/ten hours sleep a night. If I don't sleep well, it ruins my day. I'm an insomniac.

Possible related beliefs
I'm at the mercy of my body mechanisms. The body is inferior. Life is random and material.

Life choices
More or less rigid sleeping hours, sometimes at the expense of pleasurable company, productive activities, etc.

Ego advantage
I am good because I try to rest myself properly. I am very sensitive.

Judgment of others
Those who burn the midnight oil will regret it later. They are undisciplined.

Judgment of self
I don't have much spare energy/resilience. I am weak.

Illusion of safety
My concern with the number of hours slept or my constant worrying about other things stops me from finding any deeper awareness which could endanger the ways that I know.

Less responsibility/work
I don't have to do so much or work so hard because I didn't get enough sleep.

Generalization from the past
Being told, as a child, to sleep at a certain time or for a certain number of hours.

Selective evidence from the present
After less sleep than usual, focus on moments of tiredness or poor performance and forget the good feelings.

Distortion of perception and interpretation
Good feelings after little sleep actually interpreted as signs of tiredness.

Rationalization of contradictory evidence
Those who manage without much sleep are lucky/will regret it later.

Justification by imagination of future results
Not being able to sleep. Having a bad day.

The manufacture of supporting feeling
Tension. Worry.

The self-fulfilling prophecy
If I don't sleep well it ruins my day. Therefore if I have less sleep than usual I worry about the next day. When I worry about the next day, it ruins my enjoyment. Therefore if I don't sleep well it ruins my day.

Opposite Belief

Depth of sleep is more important than length of sleep. I can trust my own natural processes. I can trust that my body will always take the rest that it requires eventually. I respect my body—I respect myself.

The positive past
Remember times when you slept very little and felt great.

Liberating imagination
A good day tomorrow however much or little you sleep. (Imagine something very boring for direct help in getting to sleep.)

Liberating inner feeling
Relaxation.

Positive action
Try getting physically tired (for example by strenuous exercise, digging up the garden, etc.). This often leads to greater physical relaxation and deeper sleep.

Try altering your sleep patterns, for example, deliberately going to bed very late but getting up at the same time.

Try to avoid sleeping. This will prove to you that your body will take its sleep when it is necessary.

If you sleep twice in twenty-four hours, perhaps by taking a one-hour nap after lunch, you may enjoy having less sleep altogether.

Make sure you get up the same time every morning, no matter how late you go to sleep—this prevents the sleep rhythm from moving later and later.

(These practices can prevent the need for sleeping tablets which are all more or less addictive and tend to interfere with the deepest sleep rhythms.)

Life Is Random and Material

Similar beliefs
All knowledge is mediated through the five senses. I am an accidental conglomeration of chemicals spawned by a meaningless universe, governed by chance. Life was created by chance. I have no purpose other than to perpetuate the species. The only useful thing I can do is to improve the material lot of myself or others. Science is the only real source of knowledge. Life is a series of physical/chemical reactions. ESP/the soul/spirit/God do not exist.

Possible related beliefs
The rational mind is best. People are only out for what they can get (the survival of the fittest). The end justifies the means. We are all insignificant. I can't help it.

Life choices
Scientific pursuits. Material gain. Avoidance of the emotional and spiritual.

Ego advantage
I am logical/rational/clear-thinking/scientific.

Judgment of others
Those who believe in inner meanings and purposes are ir-rational/self-deluded/stupid. Those who believe in an after-life lack courage and use this delusion to comfort themselves. Those who believe in God are childish.

Judgment of self
My life has no inner meaning.

The illusion of safety
I do not need to risk the uncertainties of feeling. I do not need to be threatened by spiritual ideas.

Less responsibility/work
I do not need to work at knowing or expressing my inner self.

Generalization from the past
1. Memory of experiences as a child of rational and scientific parent or other important adult who explained mysteries proficiently with logic.
2. Memory of mystical or religious people or institutions who used their beliefs in a dictatorial or negative and limiting way.

Selective evidence from the present
Read scientific books and papers. Avoid mystical literature or the literature of meaning. Notice and accentuate the first sign of trouble or disorder when control of the mind is not exerted.

Distortion of perception and interpretation
Evidence for anything beyond the material is misperceived or misinterpreted.

Rationalization of contradictory evidence
Evidences of phenomena beyond the material are not sci-entific. If they do seem to be scientific, the experiment was

a hoax. A very unlikely nonmaterial effect is explained as a coincidence.

Justification by imagination of future results
Imagination is limited to what can be understood in terms of cause and effect and likelihood. Therefore there is little room for "miracles," the joy of surprise, or great unexpected results. The imagination is grey.

The manufacture of supporting feeling
Lack of feeling on the surface. Inner (usually deeply hidden) anxiety or despair. Such feelings (both inner and outer) support the idea of a lack of meaning.

The self-fulfilling prophecy
Life is random. Therefore I will exclusively develop my mind and/or my material assets. Therefore I will not have experience of inner meaning or purpose. Since I am an empiricist and believe what I experience, there is therefore no meaning or purpose. Life is random.

Opposite Belief

Life has a purpose. My life has a purpose. My beliefs can change my reality. Materials are an expression of deeper and marvellous processes. I have free choice. I have the right to value and honor all aspects of myself. I have the right to value and honor my intuition. I have the right to greater depth and greater love. I love myself as I am now.

The positive past
Remember a time in the past when you were thrilled by the inexplicable.

Liberating imagination
Miracles, the unexpected, wonderful "coincidences" of meaning. Seemingly illogical or unlikely goals that you really want.

Liberating inner feeling
A sense of connectedness with all things. A sense of inner meaning.

Positive action
Develop your intuitive capacity by allowing yourself to free-associate on a problematic issue while under alpha rhythm. When your mind is as empty as you can make it, allow images to appear. Sometimes they provide intuitive solutions to problems that do not have an obvious logical answer. Seeing you have intuition challenges the old limiting belief in materialism.

▶ Life Is Hard

Similar beliefs
Life is full of sorrow. Suffering is worthy. Pain is a virtue. Life is unpleasant. Life should be hard. There is no hope for pleasure on this earth. Whatever life gives me, it will never be enough. Pleasure is an indulgence. Wealth is wrong. It is immoral to have when others have not. Life is about working and producing.

Possible related beliefs
Original sin. I am poor. I'm unhappy. Pessimism. The physical world is inferior. I'll grab what I can.

Life choices
Continuous hard work with little pleasure.

Ego advantage
There's more depth in suffering. The more you suffer, the better you are.

Judgment of others
Those who enjoy themselves are self-indulgent. They're not serious. They are shallow and unimportant.

Judgment of self
I am heavy. I'm not capable of much fun. I'm a killjoy.

The illusion of safety
It's comfortable and familiar this way.

Less responsibility/work
I do not have to go through the effort of changing my way of thinking. I do not have to work at creating pleasure. I do not have the responsibility of spreading happiness through my own example.

Generalization from the past
The Church/my family taught me that life is hard. Memories of life's difficulties accentuated. Memories of life's pleasures diminished.

Selective evidence from the present
Notice everything that goes wrong or causes difficulty. Ignore the things that go well or create good feeling.

Distortion of perception and interpretation
Interpretation of events darkened or even blackened to fit the belief.

Rationalization of contradictory evidence
You wait, it'll be tough in the end. It may be good for ten minutes, a week, even a year—but you'll see, it'll end up hard.

Justification by imagination of future results
See hurdles and difficulties ahead. Imagine things going
wrong; imagine poverty, hardship and suffering.

The manufacture of supporting feeling
A heavy feeling. Tension.

The self-fulfilling prophecy
1. Life is unpleasant. Therefore there is little point in trying
   to make it pleasant. Therefore life is unpleasant.
2. Life is hard. Therefore it makes sense that I'm bitter and
   critical. Others react to this by being defensive, or giving
   me very little or even by retaliating negatively. Therefore
   life is hard.

Opposite Belief

I have the right to be good/fulfilled/giving/deep, and happy
at the same time. Life is pleasant. Life is full of joy. I can
make life as happy as I want. I am worthy of having pleasure.
I am receptive to life's pleasures. I am kind to myself. I love
myself.

The positive past
Remember incidents when things went well and life felt good.

Liberating imagination
Imagine a scene of happiness, fulfillment, and pleasure. In
this scene everything goes well, with ease and lightness.

Liberating inner feeling
Lightness. Warmth.

Positive action
1. Deliberately, give yourself times of pleasure and sensuality. For example, eat out, and savor each mouthful

of gourmet food; smell the roses slowly. Enjoy all outward sensations.
2. Practice the exercises in chapter 17 so that you feel softer, more receptive, within.
3. Practice giving as a joy, rather than as a burden, and notice how much better *everyone* feels.

Men Are Brutes

Similar beliefs
Men only want one thing. A woman's lot is hard.

Possible related beliefs
People are only out for what they can get. They are against me. Men are insensitive. Women are weak.

Life choices
Attracted to men who are rough and uncaring.

Ego advantage
I, as a woman, am above them.

Judgment of others
Women who think otherwise about men have been fooled and are stupid. Men are stupid.

Judgment of self
I am only worth treatment by a brute.

The illusion of safety
I don't have to risk getting too close to a man.

Less responsibility/work
I don't have the responsibility and work of loving.

Generalization from the past
Father or other important male was sometimes hard or cruel.

Selective evidence from the present
Moments of tenderness and compassion from a man unnoticed or minimized.

Distortion of perception and interpretation
Words, tone of voice, facial expression all reinterpreted to fit the belief.

Rationalization of contradictory evidence
He's only tender to get his own animal way.

Justification by imagination of future results
Images of him treating her harshly.

The manufacture of supporting feeling
Hate/resentment of the man. Seemingly justified anger/outrage/suspicion.

The self-fulfilling prophecy
He's a brute. Therefore I hate/resent him; therefore he will not let himself be vulnerable and will not show tenderness, or else he resents me back and is angry. Therefore he's a brute.

Opposite Belief

My man has the capacity to be tender. I am worthy of being treated with care. I love myself. I respect myself.

The positive past
Remember a time when a man that was important to you was tender and loving. Remember how it felt.

Liberating imagination
Images of being caressed tenderly. Images of his eyes and face expressing love.

Liberating inner feeling
Respecting the man. Feeling cared for, loved, warm, melted.

Positive action
Treat him tenderly. If this consistently produces no change in either of you, you are free to choose a different man. If you do choose another man, beware the temptation to choose another brute. Initially a more tender man might appear dull and unexciting (because excitement has been bound with the passion of brutality). You can use this lack of excitement as a clue that you are on the right track! Perseverence with this seemingly unexciting man can lead to an acquired taste in a different kind of man.

Women Are Not to Be Trusted

Similar beliefs
Women are manipulative. She only wants my money. She only wants to achieve power through me. She wants to emasculate me.

Related beliefs
People are out for what they can get. People are against me. Women are . . .

Life choices
Marry manipulative untrustworthy women.

Ego advantage
I, as a man, am direct and trustworthy by comparison.

Judgment of others
Men who think otherwise about women have been fooled. Women can never be trusted.

Judgment of self
I am weak because I allow myself to be manipulated. I am
not capable of loving.

The illusion of safety
I don't have to risk getting too close to a woman.

Less responsibility/work
I don't have the responsibility and work of loving or too
much involvement.

Generalization from the past
Mother or other important female was sometimes manipulative, for example taking sides with her son to win against
her husband.

Selective evidence from the present
Moments of genuine feeling from a woman discounted. Moments of betrayal, or a feeling of being used by a woman,
maximized.

Distortion of perception and interpretation
Tone of voice, words, facial expression all reinterpreted to
fit the belief (see page 59).

Rationalization of contradictory evidence
She's only being nice to get something from me.

Justification by imagination of future results
Calculations of her "real" motives and imagination of her
designs succeeding.

The manufacture of supporting feeling
Tension from self-protection. Feelings of revenge, or seemingly justified anger or suspicion.

The self-fulfilling prophecy
Women are manipulative and not to be trusted. Therefore I
am rightly suspicious and I will avoid close contact. There-

fore she will get very little genuine feeling from me and eventually she will give up hoping for more from me. So then the exchanges we make are bartered for, based on convenience and what we can get. Since she goes for what she can get out of me, she is manipulative and not to be trusted. Women are manipulative and not to be trusted.

Opposite Belief

My woman can be tender. My woman can genuinely care for me. I am worthy of being loved by a woman. I respect myself. I love myself.

The positive past
Remember a time when a woman was warm and loving to you. Remember how that felt.

Liberating imagination
Being held tenderly. Images of her eyes and face expressing love.

Liberating inner feeling
Respecting the woman. Feeling warm, loved, melted.

Positive action
Treat her as if she is a good person. Speak out your suspicions but at the same time make it clear they are *your* suspicions, for example saying, "I am afraid that you don't really like me. I find it so hard to believe that I can be cared for." Give her love and tenderness even if you still feel suspicious and see what comes back. This is a way of breaking the vicious circle of the self-fulfilling prophecy.

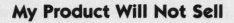

My Product Will Not Sell

Similar beliefs
No one will come to my course. No one will buy what I have to sell. No one will read my book. No one wants my product. I'm no good at business.

Possible related beliefs
I'm not good enough. I don't deserve success. Pessimism. My ideas are no good.

Life choices
Tend to choose products that are less likely to be wanted or else to choose poor or low-energy marketing.

Ego advantage
I don't need to sell my product. I already know it's good. I don't need affirmation. I am above selling. I am above money.

Judgment of others
Those who sell, dirty themselves or are of a lower order. The product or the person must be inferior if there is a need to market it.

Judgment of self
My product is not good enough. I'm not good enough.

The illusion of safety
I can avoid the trauma of trying and maybe failing.

Less responsibility/work
I don't need to work at selling since my product won't sell anyway.

Generalization from the past
Remember times in the past when you could not get what you wanted no matter how hard you tried to present yourself

well. Memories of unresponsive parents or schools creating an attitude of "well, it's not really worth trying."

Selective evidence from the present
Positive responses to your product minimized. Negative responses to your product remembered.

Rationalization of contradictory evidence
Positive results are seen as temporary.

Justification by imagination of future results
Imagine the product not selling and not being liked. Imagine only a few people buying/attending/reading.

The manufacture of supporting feeling
Feel low because of the presumed lack of success. (Then interpret the feeling as a sign of actual lack of success.)

The self-fulfilling prophecy
1. My product will not sell. Therefore it is not worth putting too much energy or money into marketing. Therefore my product will not sell.
2. My product will not sell. Therefore I feel a bit low. Since salesmanship depends on strong positive energy, my capacity to sell is as low as my mood. Therefore my product will not sell.

Opposite Belief

I am full of confidence about my product. I present my product beautifully. I enjoy presenting my product. I am worthy of using my talents fully. I have the right to express myself. I respect my work. I respect myself.

The positive past
Remember one time when you achieved what felt right to you through presenting yourself well. Remember the feeling of that.

Liberating imagination
Imagine people buying, using, and enjoying your product.

Liberating inner feeling
Imagine the feeling of success, especially your own inner sense of worth.

Positive action
Talk to potential buyers or your own staff about the quality of your product. If you still believe in the quality of your product, assess the market. If the market is open, spend the money and energy in marketing with the total assumption in your right to pleasure in selling.

▶ Original Sin

Similar beliefs
Humanity is guilty. People are basically bad. Morality is maintained only by obedience to external rules. There is no internal morality. The inner self/unconscious is basically aggressive and antisocial. You cannot change human nature. My natural impulses are selfish/chaotic/brutal/murderous/ at least, antisocial.

Possible related beliefs
The physical world is inferior. The body is inferior. Being assertive is dangerous. I am not good enough. I can't help it. Pessimism. I must keep a low profile. Sex is an unfortunate necessity. Consistency is essential. People are out of what they can get. Men are brutes. Women are untrustworthy.

Life choices
Rule-abiding positions. Rule-abiding people.

Ego advantage
I am better than most because I follow the rules of my church/society/philosophy, etc. I am aware of my guilt, bad-

ness, limitation: therefore I am more humble than most. I am more likely to go to heaven/be rightfully respected in society.

Judgment of others
Those who follow their instincts are untrustworthy/dangerous/evil/possessed by the devil.

Judgment of self
I am basically bad inside and whatever I do I can never be good enough.

Illusion of safety
Since I cannot trust my inner self, it is safer to rely on an outer authority.

Less responsibility/work
I do not need to do the work of finding out what is within me or trying to change within, so long as I obey the outer rules.

Generalization from the past
Parents or other important figures sometimes stressed the correctness of behavior and the distrust of intuition. Examples selected of instinctual responses having negative or disastrous results.

Selective evidence from the present
All the wrongs and sins of the world accentuated. When "correct" behavior hurts another's feelings, the hurt is not seen or is discounted.

Distortion of perception and interpretation
Misinterpret the expressions of those who do not hold to the rules as nasty or negative.

Rationalization of contradictory evidence
Instinctual responses that have positive results are lucky. When "correct" behavior has negative results on people, it

is because those people are negative/unbelieving/reaction-ary/stupid/primitive, etc.

Justification by imagination of future results
Expression of desire leads to social disaster. Expression of the inner self creates a mess.

The manufacture of supporting feeling
Hopeless longing for self-expression. Feeling of tension and holding in. Self-righteous indignation when others express themselves freely. Sense of "badness" somewhere deep inside.

The self-fulfilling prophecy
People are basically bad. Therefore they must repress their instincts. Therefore their instinctual feelings build up/become overpowering/become twisted. When they are eventually let out, they are therefore antisocial. Therefore inner desire and instinct are untrustworthy/bad. People are basically bad.

Opposite Belief

I am good inside. People are basically good. I have the right to express myself. My inner self is equally a gift of God. I am worthy of love. I love myself.

The positive past
Remember a time when you (or somebody else) expressed a seemingly negative strong feeling which resulted in a clearing of atmosphere, more contact, and more love.

Liberating imagination
Expressing the feeling you fear leading to positive results and more human contact.

Liberating inner feeling
Worthiness, inner warmth. Feeling good inside.

Positive action
Practice self-expression. Learn the art of expressing the many different aspects of yourself in such a way that you create contact with, rather than distance from, another (see the section in chapter 17 on creative expression, page 193). Do the exercises on relaxing to the innermost self (page 186) to prove to yourself that what is inside is good.

People Are Only Out for What They Can Get

Similar beliefs
People don't really care. The only way to get by is to beat the other guy. I'm distant. I'm controlled.

Possible related beliefs
Nobody loves me. I am alone. The world is an alien place. People are against me. Men are brutes. Women are not to be trusted. Pessimism. Life is random and material.

Life choices
Work in uncaring institutions. Uncaring acquaintances. Cynical "friends."

Ego advantage
Because I know this fact, I have a wisdom which prevents me from being disappointed by expecting too much from people. I am above the people that play at caring.

Judgment of others
Those who are fooled by people who pretend to care for them deserve their heartbreak. People who look like they care really only want something back and are therefore dishonest.

Judgment of self
I am incapable of loving.

The illusion of safety
The familiarity of distance and the avoidance of the threat of people getting closer.

Less responsibility/work
It's unnecessary to work at making relationships or to have the responsibility of caring for somebody.

Generalization from the past
Childhood, home, or school was sometimes cold/indifferent/heartless/competitive.

Selective evidence from the present
Moments of warmth unnoticed or minimized. Moments of indifference or rejection maximized.

Distortion of perception and interpretation
Kindness and genuine care are misperceived.

Rationalization of contradictory evidence
Although that act of kindness appeared genuine, it was only done to buy my goodwill/to manipulate me in some way.

Justification by imagination of future results
Calculations of the "real" negative motivations. Visualization of the negative results of others' selfishness.

The manufacture of supporting feeling
Tension from self-protection. Suspicion. Distance.

The self-fulfilling prophecy
People don't really care. Therefore I'll keep my distance from them and I'll have little involvement with people. Therefore they'll have little involvement with me. Therefore I'm right: they don't really care.

Opposite Belief

Some people really care. He/she really does care for me. I care for myself. I respect myself. I love myself.

The positive past
Remember one time in your life when somebody treated you with love. Picture the scene and remember the feeling.

Liberating imagination
Being cared for. Image of a loving person.

Liberating inner feeling
Feeling warm, melting (see page 186).

Positive action
Take care of somebody else, even in the smallest way (see page 195).

▶ Pessimism

Similar beliefs
It will never get better. Things will never change. In fact things are getting worse. I will never change. They will never change. I'll never have what I want. And it's too late anyway. I'm going to fail. A disaster is going to occur. I'm unlucky. When I hit the ball to the top of the net, it always comes down my side.

Possible related beliefs
The best part of my life is over. I'm unhappy. I can't help it. Life is hard. People are only out for what they can get. They are against me.

Life choices
Status quo. Situations of little change or risk. Choose people who have an investment in failure.

Ego advantage
I know about life. I'm realistic. I have a special tragic role.
I'm different. Poor me.

Judgment of others
They're unrealistic. They live in happy (and stupid) illusion.
They'll soon find out.

Judgment of self
I'm miserable/unhappy. I'm missing the spark of joy.

The illusion of safety
It's secure. I know this feeling. Nothing really terrible can
happen because I'm prepared for the worst.

Less responsibility/work
Since things will never change anyway, there's no point in
doing anything—and it's not my fault. There's no point in
working for success if I'm going to fail anyway.

Generalization from the past
Things never got better when I was a child, so why should
it be any different now. Look at all the feeling and inade-
quacies that I have now that are just the same as when I
was small. My father/mother failed/never changed.

Selective evidence from the present
See all the aspects of life that are unchanged and ignore
everything that has changed for the better. Focus on one
small aspect of a change that does not go so well. Focus on
the smallest things that go wrong (for example, the telephone
not working).

Distortion of perception and interpretation
Positive changes interpreted as negative.

Rationalization of contradictory evidence
It's good now but it won't last long. Every silver lining has
a cloud inside. You wait.

Justification by imagination of future results
Imagine nothing changing. Imagine failure. Unreal day-dreams of success contrast bitterly with seeming reality.

The manufacture of supporting feeling
Feeling heavy, unhappy, resigned, depressed, resentful.

The self-fulfilling prophecy
1. Things don't change, so I won't do anything, so things don't change.
2. Things get worse, so there's no point in doing anything. The longer I leave it, the more there is to clear up. Therefore things get worse.
3. Things usually go wrong. If things go well, I'll be over-confident and unreal, which will make things go wrong again.

Opposite Belief

Everything is changing for the better. My business goes well. My relationship goes well. I feel good about myself. Life is good and this day will be good. I am worthy of a good life. I respect myself. I love myself as I am now.

The positive past
Remember a time in the past when you acted positively to get change and you got it! Remember how that felt inside.

Liberating imagination
Experience part of your life that has seemed stuck changing for the better. Imagine a scene of success and hope.

Liberating inner feeling
Lightness, energy, hope, happiness.

Positive action
Set yourself goals of change that are so small that you cannot help but succeed.

Sex Is an Unfortunate Necessity

Similar beliefs
Sex is animal. I have better things to do. Sex is dirty. Sex is only for procreation. I hate sex. I don't like sex.

Possible related beliefs
Original sin. The body is inferior. The physical world is inferior. Pleasure is unimportant. Hard work is the only virtue. Life is hard.

Life choices
Choose sexual partners who do not enjoy sex.

Ego advantage
I am cleverer/higher/more spiritual than those who lust.

Judgment of others
Those who lust are more stupid/animal. They deserve the messes they get themselves into. They deserve venereal diseases.

Judgment of self
There's something wrong with me because I don't have very much sexual feeling.

The illusion of safety
Avoid risk of letting go; avoid the risk of strong feelings for somebody disrupting routines.

Less responsibility/work
Do not need to work at developing sexual intimacy. Avoid the responsibility of sexual involvement.

Generalization from the past
Sex was disapproved of or not talked about in the past. The subject of sex sometimes created embarrassment or distance.

Selective evidence from the present
Pleasurable moments during sex minimized. Misunderstandings, arguments and feelings of emptiness during sex maximized.

Distortion of perception and interpretation
Pleasurable sexual feelings altered by the belief into feelings of discomfort. Excitement may be reinterpreted as anxiety. Touch, smell, taste, hearing, and sight of the sexual partner may all become distasteful or even repulsive in accordance with the belief. The genitals may be perceived as dirty/offensive/smelly/ugly.

Rationalization of contradictory evidence
This good feeling is only transient.

Justification by imagination of future results
Imagine sex going wrong or creating emptiness or providing limited or no enjoyment.

The manufacture of supporting feeling
Disdain/disgust/distance/disapproval/emptiness.

The self-fulfilling prophecy
1. I don't like sex very much. Therefore I will get through it as fast as possible. Therefore my feelings are limited. Therefore I don't like sex very much.
2. I don't like sex. Therefore I worry about my incapacity and I think about my performance during sex. Therefore I don't feel very much. Therefore I don't like sex.
3. Sex is dirty. Therefore I do it with a feeling of repulsion. Therefore sex is dirty.

Opposite Belief

Sex is a gift of life. I have the right to enjoy my sensuality/sexuality if I want to. I have the right to be loved. I love my body. My body is worthy of being loved. I love myself. I respect myself.

The positive past
Remember a time in the past when sex was enjoyable/created intimacy. If you cannot remember an experience of this, imagine it.

Liberating imagination
Pleasurable/intimate moments.

Liberating inner feeling
Focus on inner body sensations. Imagine warmth/electricity travelling through your body (see page 187).

Positive action
Practice touching yourself (or if you have a partner, each other) sensually with absolutely no pressure to have sex, just purely for the experience of feeling the touch. Take turns in being the giver and the receiver. As the receiver, you have nothing to do except to tell your partner exactly what you want, how and where you want to be touched.

Go into alpha rhythm. Use one of the two exercises in chapter 16, pages 187—190, to help you relax deeply within. As you melt within, feel kind and loving towards yourself and then look at your partner with the same feeling.

The Best Part of My Life Is Over

Similar beliefs
Life is downhill after you get married, after you have children, after you are thirty-five/forty/fifty/sixty/seventy.

Possible related beliefs
I am at the mercy of my body. The physical world is inferior. Pessimism. I can't help it. The body is inferior.

Life choices
Choose less challenging and more boring situations.

Ego advantage
I am wiser because I know this reality. I've done it all. I know.

Judgment of others
Those who don't believe this will find out later when reality catches up with them. They are blind. Disdain and jealousy of those who are younger and have not yet reached the age of deterioration.

Judgment of self
I am deteriorating. I do not deserve continuing growth/fulfillment.

The illusion of safety
It's an easy, well-worn path.

Less responsibility/work
I don't need to do the work of keeping my mind and body fit. I don't need to take so much responsibility in work or relationships.

Generalization from the past
The example of important figures from the past: "My mother and father were miserable together." "After my mother had children, she gave up work completely and resented us for her lost ambition—she never got over this." "When my father was forty-five, he was disappointed about his work and thought it was too late for him to change." "My grandfather was alone and miserable."

Selective evidence from the present
All examples of the belief manifested are noted and accented from observations of society, friends, relatives and acquaintances.

Distortion of perception and interpretation
The smallest physical symptoms are misinterpreted as signs
of aging.

Rationalization of contradictory evidence
People who contradict the belief are seen as freaks/unusual/
lucky/strange. Their energy and hope is seen as temporary
or inappropriate.

Justification by imagination of future results
Deterioration mentally, physically, emotionally, and spirit-
ually.

The manufacture of supportive feeling
Loss of hope. Mood low or empty. Cynicism.

The self-fulfilling prophecy
Life is downhill since *X*. Therefore it is not worth trying to
change my lot. Therefore I will choose safer situations of less
challenge and interest. So I will be less stimulated and less
exercised in mind, body, and feeling. Therefore my mind,
body and feeling will deteriorate. Therefore life is downhill
since *X*.

Opposite Belief

My life is a continuous process of growth. When new parts
of myself grow, it is right and necessary that some old parts
die or change. I am growing. I am changing for the better.
I respect myself. I love myself as I am now.

The positive past
Remember times since this belief started when you felt vi-
brantly alive. Remember experiences with others who have
contradicted this belief.

Liberating imagination
See yourself as healthy, active, energetic, happy.

Liberating inner feeling
Worthwhile within. Energy flowing through the body.

Positive action
Take up a new activity which challenges your belief. Take
care of your body and enjoy how you look. Do some form of
exercise, even if it's only a little, which gently stretches your
capacity.
   Do hatha yoga or stretching exercises to loosen your muscles and joints. Exercise your mind every day with something
that interests you.

The Body is Inferior

Similar beliefs
The body is inferior to the mind. The body is inferior to the
soul. The body is insignificant/cumbersome/an unfortunate
necessity/disgusting. Feelings are connected to the body and
are also inferior.

Possible related beliefs
The physical world is inferior. Original sin. I'm weak. Sex
is an unfortunate necessity. I'm fat. I'm not attractive.

Life choices
Intellectual and/or spiritual pursuits. Intellectual people.

Ego advantage
I am above the body. I am a highly evolved spiritual being.
My mind is superior. I am more important than those who
enjoy their bodies. Mental work is superior to manual labor.

Judgment of others
Those who use and enjoy their bodies are stupid/lower/an-
imal.

Judgment of self
I feel physically/sexually/emotionally inferior. I am incapable of strong physical urges. I am weak.

Illusion of safety
Since my body and feelings are not felt very much, they are protected from being hurt.

Less responsibility/work
I don't need to work at developing my body or my feelings. I don't need to take the responsibility of compassion.

Generalization from the past
Possible memories of lack of physical contact as a child, or of coldness and distance.

Selective evidence from the present
The ills and discomforts of the body accentuated. Physical pleasure minimized.

Distortion of perception and interpretation
The feeling of pleasure can actually be changed by the belief to a feeling of unfulfillment, emptiness, or even pain.

Rationalization of contradictory evidence
Moments of pleasure never last long.

Justification by imagination of future results
The body is seen either as ugly or aesthetically ideal/unreal. The body may be visualized as becoming ill or weak.

The manufacture of supporting feeling
Little body feeling.

The self-fulfilling prophecy
My body is inferior. Therefore I will not take care of it/not exercise it/not feed it properly. I will even foster its illnesses through my imagination. Therefore my body is inferior.

Opposite Belief

My body is the source of feeling and pleasure. I love my body. My body is a unique expression of my spirit. My body is the temple of my soul. I respect my body. I respect myself.

The positive past
Remember a time when using your body gave you pleasure and uplifted you.

Liberating imagination
See the body as healthy and strong. Imagine the body as the container of your mind/spirit.

Liberating inner feeling
Feel the body as strong and full of energy. Feel warmth, pleasure or energy coursing through your body (see page 187).

Positive action
Eat an exquisite meal and enjoy every mouthful. Take time for sensuality. Play a sport or do some kind of physical movement that you enjoy. "Go inside" and experience the inner pleasure of the energy of the body. See also the positive action for "I'm not attractive," page 253.

The End Justifies the Means

Similar beliefs
Achieving my ideal justifies any or most means. All acts are really selfish. I will control you before you control me. Competition is the name of the game. I will be number one. Life is about power. You compete with someone of the same sex; you win someone of the opposite sex. Survival of the fittest is reality. The power-play personality habit. The seductive personality habit.

Possible related beliefs
People are only out for what they can get. They are against me. Women are not to be trusted. Men are brutes. Life is material.

Life choices
Join or lead movements for change. Politics. Positions of authority.

Ego advantage
I know what's best for others. My ideas are right. *I* am making the world a better place.

Judgment of others
Others know or understand less than I do. They are stupid/ blind/dependent.

Judgment of self
I am a manipulator. I am trying to change the world because I do not have the courage to change myself. I am frightened of being put down or of looking at my own weaknesses.

The illusion of safety
If I focus on what is wrong with the world and others I do not have the threat of looking at myself and how I relate to the world.

Less responsibility/work
I do not have the responsibility for changing myself. I do not have to be sensitive to other people's feelings.

Generalization from the past
Experience of the teaching that ideas are more important than feeling or experience of feelings being misused for the purposes of achieving power. Being put down by family or society and wanting to make amends/take revenge. Perhaps early training in family politics from forming an alliance with one parent against the other: "My father/mother competed

with me, therefore all men/women are competitive." "My father/mother was a political ally—therefore all men/women are political and out for what they can get."

Selective evidence from the present
Select instances of competition/fighting. Screen out all evidence of love and tenderness.

Distortion of perception and interpretation
Interpret assertion and independent energy as competitive and threatening.

Rationalization of contradictory evidence
If they are tender it's because they want to win something from me.

Justification by imagination of future results
See conflict and see either winning or losing. Imagine the campaign to win.

The manufacture of supporting feeling
Feel easily slighted and easily angry, combined with a sense of self-justification.

The self-fulfilling prophecy
1. Life is about who controls whom. Therefore I will control you before you control me, (because of course you are like me and want to control me). Naturally you defend yourself against my attempt to control you by fighting back. So you fight me: therefore you want to control me. Life is about who controls whom.
2. Men do not really love you. I don't want to be hurt so I'll seduce and control him first and I will never let him get close. So men never really love you.
3. Women do not really love you. I don't want to be hurt so I'll seduce and control her first and I will never let her get close. So women never really love you.
4. Life is about competition. Therefore I compete. When I

compete, you compete. Therefore life is about competition.

Opposite Belief

If I trust in love, I do not need to fight. I am worthy of being loved. I love myself. I love him/her/them. I respect our human rights. I respect my innermost self.

The positive past
Remember a time of genuine contact and warmth with your parent (of same sex). Remember times of genuine contact (with no ulterior motive) with others.

Liberating imagination
A scene of friendship or love with no ulterior motive.

Liberating inner feeling
Inner warmth.

Positive action
Play a game for pleasure alone (no scoring, no competition—just enjoyment of the interplay). Let someone else win without letting them know that you let them. Even if you are suspicious of someone's motives, assume they are coming from the best possible motive and act accordingly (see page 120—"the cure for case-building").

The Physical World Is Inferior

Similar beliefs
Life is bad. The world is a mess. People are untrustworthy. I want to get away from the world/people. The inner life is more important than the outer life. The spirit is more im-

portant than physical reality. Food is purely functional. I
don't like people. God has made a big mistake. People are
dangerous. The world is an alien place. The "up-in-the-
clouds" personality habit.

Possible related beliefs
Life is hard. Pessimism. Original sin. The body is inferior.
They are against me. Being assertive is dangerous. I am poor.
I must keep a low profile.

Life choices
Solitary positions. Avoidance of emotional contact.

Ego advantage
I'm more spiritual. I have the wisdom to understand how
bad things really are. I am above mundane reality.

Judgment of others
They're animals. If they enjoy other people/the world, they
are shallow and lack wisdom.

Judgment of self
I am incapable of warmth/involvement/love.

The illusion of safety
I do not have to risk involvement and the possibility of getting
hurt.

Less responsibility/work
I do not have to work at building relationships.

Generalization from the past
Because my parents lacked warmth/were rejecting/disliked
me, all people/the world are cold/rejecting/don't like me.

Selective evidence from the present
See all that is wrong/bad/hurtful. "The world is terrible—
just look at the news." Screen out the positive. Notice the
one dead petal in a beautiful bunch of flowers.

Distortion of perception and interpretation
A passive face seen as cold or even hostile. Sensations of touch, taste, smell, sight, and sound all distorted till they seem inadequate or even unpleasant.

Rationalization of contradictory evidence
What seems like love is only manipulation. You wait—it won't work. Hate/bad feeling/disappointment always win in the end.

Justification by imagination of future results
Imagine things staying cold, distant or not working out.

The manufacture of supporting feeling
Feel cold within. Literally reduce the blood supply to the extremities of the body which creates physical coldness.

The self-fulfilling prophecy
1. The world is an alien place. Therefore I will look down on it and only pretend to interact in worldly affairs. My lack of involvement causes the world to seem alien to me. Therefore the world is an alien place.
2. People are rejecting and untrustworthy. I therefore avoid them and am suspicious of them. They react by avoiding me and being indirect with me—so people are rejecting and untrustworthy.
3. People are full of bad feeling. I therefore dislike them. They react by disliking me. Therefore, people are full of bad feeling.
4. People are cold. I'll therefore withdraw my energy to the very center of my body. Therefore I'm cold and get very little reaction from people. Therefore people are cold.

Opposite Belief

I am a warm loving person. I am full of love. I have the right to enjoy touching/tasting/smelling/seeing/hearing. I am worthy of being touched. I am worthy of being held. I am worthy of being loved. I love myself as I am now.

The positive past
Remember moments of warm human contact.

Liberating imagination
Warm human contact.

Liberating inner feeling
Warmth throughout body.

Positive action
Practice touching. Feel the texture of objects. Touch, hold others for a short time. Practice tasting different kinds of food. Practice being more aware of smells. Practice expressing your thought or feeling. Practice enjoyable exercise.

They Are Against Me

Similar beliefs
People don't like me. You are trying to hurt me/reject me/damage me. You are against me. People are against me. No one likes me, that's why I'm so suspicious.

Possible related beliefs
I am unworthy of love. They are wrong. People are only out for what they can get. The physical world is inferior.

Life choices
Hostile people and hostile situations.

Ego advantage
I see more clearly than most people. I am justified in my anger with people/the world. I am unique in having so many people with such feeling about me, even if it's against me.

Judgment of others
Everybody is bad/wrong because they want to hurt me.

Judgment of self
People do not like me because I am unworthy of being liked.

Illusion of safety
I am safe from the risks of intimacy.

Less responsibility/work
I do not need to work at relationships.

Generalization from the past
Being hurt by insensitivity/aggression in the past.

Selective evidence from the present
The slightest innuendo magnified. Moments of care and love unnoticed or diminished.

Distortion of perception and interpretation
Facial expression and tone of voice misinterpreted as expressing hostility.

Rationalization of contradictory evidence
They only seem to be caring for me so that they can hurt me more. They're trying to suck me in.

Justification by imagination of future results
The imagined actions and plots of those seen as being hostile.

The manufacture of supporting feeling
Hurt, self-righteous anger, seemingly justified suspicion.

The self-fulfilling prophecy
People are against me. Therefore I'm against them and am justified in being angry with them. When I am angry and suspicious, people keep away from me or they try to stop me or get angry with me back. Therefore people are against me.

Opposite Belief

He did what he did for the best possible motives. People like me and care for me. I am worthy of being liked and cared for. I like myself. I love myself as I am now.

The positive past
Remember a time when you felt loved and you loved. Visualize the scene and remember the feeling.

Liberating imagination
Being cared for. Being loved.

Liberating inner feeling
Tenderness, loving another. Warmth and good feeling within.

Positive action
Actively assume that people are coming from the best motives and act accordingly. If they were, then you are right. If they were not, your good assumption will often change their heart positively towards you (see page 120—"the cure for case-building").

They Are Wrong—I Am Right

Similar beliefs
They are bad. He is wrong. She is wrong. The Chinese/ Americans/Jews/WASPS/whites/blacks, etc. are our enemies. They deserve to be put down.

Possible related beliefs
They are against me. (All limiting beliefs have an element of "I'm right—they're wrong.")

Life choices
Situations of conflict.

Ego advantage
I am right. I or we are better than they are. We know better.
I have the truth.

Judgment of others
They are stupid/dirty/of evil intent. Anyone who doesn't
agree with me about them is gullible/stupid/has been misled.

Judgment of self
I am wrong to be so judgmental. I am limited in my understanding. I am narrow, prejudiced, and lacking in wisdom.

The illusion of safety
It feels secure to know I'm right. I do not have to suffer the
anxiety of questioning myself.

Less responsibility/work
I do not need to work at challenging my own thoughts,
motives and actions. I have no responsibility at all for
"them."

Generalization from the past
I remember all the past evidence of their mistakes or when
their intention was questionable. I forget the times when they
were right or had good intentions. I remember others from
the past who were just like them.

Selective evidence from the present
I focus on every slip. I ignore the positive points.

Distortion of perception and interpretation
Alter the perception of their facial expressions so that they
seem malevolent or confused or belligerent.

Rationalization of contradictory evidence
Reinterpret their intentions; for example, "he was kind in
that instance in order to get that person on his side," or "they
are only doing that to win/put our side down."

Justification by imagination of future results
Envision them doing wrong things to you or others.

The manufacture of supporting feeling
Feelings of distrust and suspicion ("I have to keep watching out with them") or of seemingly justified anger. Self-righteousness. Indignant rage. Hate.

The self-fulfilling prophecy
1. He is wrong. Therefore I am suspicious of his every action and I judge him. Therefore he will protect himself from my suspicion or even retaliate against my judgment. Since I do not approve of how he does this, he is wrong.
2. I dislike them and put them down. Therefore they retaliate and act against me, often with anger. When I see their angry reaction, I know they are lower than me and deserve to be put down. I dislike them.
3. I hate them. Therefore they hate me. Therefore I hate them.

Opposite Belief

He has a right to his opinion. She has a right to her way of life. They have a right to their choices/color/interests/politics/limitations. At heart we are the same. I respect myself. I respect them. I respect them as they are now. I respect myself as I am now.

The positive past
Remember a time of loving reconciliation with someone who you had judged as wrong. If it is a group you judge, remember a member of that group who contradicts your judgment. Focus on that person and your feeling for her/him.

Liberating imagination

Imagine him or her as a good person. Imagine them as good people. Focus on their hearts or their innermost centers essentially the same as yours, with the same longing for love.

Liberating inner feeling

Ignoring all the outside "wrongs" and distractions, focus your heartfelt feeling on anything that connects you with the person/people you judged.

Positive action

If you are endangered by the "wrong" person, protect yourself in a practical, effective way. Otherwise treat the person as if he or she is good; be kind to them and they may react very differently. If being kind consistently has no effect, don't spend too much time with this person. If you judge a group as bad, get to know one member personally and note down the similarities this person has with yourself (see page 120—"the cure for case-building").

▼

WHEN *DO* YOU NEED
A THERAPIST?

*S*ometimes it is hard to believe that we hold a narrow belief. Our intellect tells us that we could not possibly subscribe to such a simplistic generalization. A man brought up with a mother of limited capacity, for example, may make the generalization that women are limited. But, having a good mind, he realizes that such a generalization is ridiculous. And yet his actions toward women (for instance, condescension, unwarranted protection) clearly state his assumption about their limitations. Often it is our actions that give away our beliefs, and sometimes we only realize the peculiarities of our actions when we get feedback from somebody else. So this is the first area in which a therapist or a non-judgmental friend can be useful: giving feedback.

Sometimes a limited belief is all too apparent but we simply cannot see the advantages of such a belief. This is illustrated by the example of a woman of twenty-five who believed she was unhappy.

"So what are the advantages of being unhappy?" she was asked.

"Advantages?"

"Yes, advantages."

"Well," she said, "I suppose it's kind of familiar. I feel safe. I know how to act. I can't think of anything else."

"What about your ego?"

"My ego?"

"Yes, your ego."

She smiled. "It makes me feel bad about myself."

"What are the advantages to your ego?"

"Advantages? . . . Mm . . . I can't think of any."

"What do you feel about people who are happy?"

"I envy them."

"What's your judgment about them?"

"Oh—they don't take life seriously. They're superficial. In fact, they're stupid—they're not clever enough to see how life is."

"So what does that make you?"

"Aha—I'm clever; I see that life is not nice. I'm deep. Yes. I'm deep."

"Any other advantages?"

"If I were happy I would have to do it on my own. I'd have to take care of myself. Being unhappy, I can ask for help—like I'm doing now. I don't have to struggle to make friends or do well because I'm unhappy. It feels like I'm working hard because I'm so tense. I'm always flapping around, but I don't have to do any real work at changing things because I'm unhappy and I can't help that. It feels like I'll always be unhappy."

"But how do you keep that belief up?"

"If something is going okay, I immediately focus on something that's gone wrong. If I'm having a good time with my boyfriend, I worry about not having contacted a friend. If I'm feeling good, I see a pimple on my face. I can say: "Ah, there's something wrong there." If things are good, I think I'm being too controlling. If I'm relaxed, I think I'm shirking responsibility or the real facts."

As she looked back at the session so far, she added: "I hadn't realized it's such a list—being unhappy is a full-time job!"

Love and the Nonjudgmental Approach

It is possible to analyze our beliefs and limits in such a judgmental way that we end up with the conviction that we are small, limited, and awful. Sometimes it is useful to have someone else present who helps us see more clearly yet with kindness and respect to ourselves. Clarity of vision about our little limits need not be belittling. On the contrary, the purpose of seeing the limits we impose on ourselves is to transcend them. This does involve care, self-respect, and love. Sometimes guilt and self-deprecation get in the way, and it is at such times that a nonjudgmental and caring therapist can help change our view from *against* us to *for* us. The therapist may accept us as we are now and that can help us accept ourselves as we are now. Self-acceptance is so important: If we have it, then change becomes an adventure; if we don't, then change is an unpleasant pressure born out of a feeling of not being good enough.

Techniques

Many excellent psychotherapeutic techniques, with the help of the therapist, can help us discover hidden aspects of ourselves which we would otherwise avoid.

For example, the limited beliefs of the mind may get frozen into family "reflections." When everyone in your family agrees with your limiting ideas, it may sometimes be very hard to shift your individual pattern without looking at the whole family pattern, perhaps with the aid of a family therapist.

The fixed beliefs of the mind may also get frozen into patterns of body tension. Various forms of bodywork, such as bioenergetics, can be excellent means of releasing these patterns of body/mind holding, especially for those who have difficulty expressing feeling.

When our progress is stuck and the issue that blocks us is

too cleverly disguised for our own belief analysis, the advice of a therapist can be extremely useful. Such therapies do not usually need to be long term. Once we have the mental, emotional, and physical understanding, then it is time to practice an alternative reality.

Self-Generated Effort

Using this self-help book takes a great deal of effort, even dedication. It requires the initiative to get started and the energy and self-motivation to follow through. It requires self-questioning and the discipline to carry through exercises and unfamiliar actions.

There is no doubt that some of this can be easier with a therapist. It is much easier to motivate ourselves if we know we have a session in a week's time when someone is going to ask us what we have done or how we are doing. It is easier in some ways to be questioned than to question ourselves. It is more difficult to give up our self-searching, when someone else has expectations of us. And it is harder to daydream or to pretend to ourselves when there is someone else present.

Nevertheless, self-generated effort is necessary whether we use a therapist or not. Therapy is useless without putting the insights into action. Even changing a belief system internally requires practice every day for which some kind of discipline is necessary.

Preference

Some people prefer working alone and some prefer to work with somebody else. Your own preference, which may change from time to time, is an important factor in whether or not you need or want a therapist. But whether you choose a therapist or not, there is a great deal of work that can be done without one. Then, if you do decide to have therapy sessions, you can make far more profitable use of them. For me as a psychotherapist, it is a particular pleasure to meet people who have worked things out for themselves but who might come for a certain period to deal with a particular hurdle. It is great to have the two of us, therapist and client, working together in an atmosphere of mutual respect and interested exploration.

▼

Chapter 21

HOW FAR CAN YOU GO?

SO, WHAT IS REAL?
WHERE DO YOU DRAW THE LINE?

The whole area of limiting beliefs brings up a logical and philosophical question. When is a belief a mind-set that limits our capacity, and when is a belief a statement of how things really are? If you believe that you cannot be professor of mathematics at Harvard, for example, you may well be right.

Of course, there are limitations that are sensible for most of us to accept. You cannot usually fly without an airplane and you cannot usually live without food. Where exactly we draw the line between changeable belief and "reality" is a personal matter. Analytical observations on some Eastern Yogis completely overturned some Western ideas of the "realities" of the human body (for example, that heart rate was uncontrollable by will). How many other "realities" are simply embedded assumptions? Dr. A. Mason reported in the British Medical Journal the cure of a completely "incurable" and fatal inherited disease known as *crocodile skin*. To avoid critics calling it coincidence, he told his subject under hypnosis that the disease would initially disappear on one arm only—which it did. Extraordinary teachers of great faith and belief have been reported as performing "miracles" in most religious traditions. Jesus is quoted as saying that if your faith is strong enough, you can move a mountain. Who knows what are the limits of belief?

Since Einstein, science has accepted that all matter is simply a particular dense form of energy. Some people believe that the energy patterns which create the appearance of matter are maintained, or at least influenced, by our thoughts. Experiments on psychokinesis have verified many times that human thought can affect matter.

Yet even when we believe this "scientifically" it may still be hard to *really* believe. Developing belief in the unlimited seems to take time. This book helps us see that it is indeed we who have made our world narrower than it need be. When we see how we create our various everyday perceptions, we *know* that we can also create something different. We know that far more is available.

How Far Can We Go?

Practicing our unlimited beliefs expands our capacities and improves our confidence. Yet there are some inner doors which cannot be opened and depths within that cannot be reached by any amount of analysis and practice. How do we go further? How far can we go? Can we really reach the unlimited?

In the seventeenth century, Angelius Silesius said that to reach the highest it is first necessary to find yourself. Then it is necessary to lose yourself. This book is about the first part—knowing yourself and understanding yourself. Much of this can be done without a guide or a therapist, though a therapist may be very helpful.

When it comes to the second part, however, no book can be very useful as a guide to losing ourselves in the limitless. The sage, Swami Nityananda said to Swami Muktananda who was immensely well-read and who was carrying an important book under his arm: "Do you know how this book was made? It was made by a brain. The brain may make any number of books but a book cannot make a brain. You had better throw it away and meditate." The limitless cannot be circumscribed. We cannot tell it what to do—we can only be led by it. Paradoxically, this second stage of losing ourselves nearly always requires a guide—and the guide needs to be someone who is totally unfamiliar and immersed in the joy of the unlimited, in other words, someone who has transcended limited beliefs. But here, we are in the realm of spiritual masters, which is far beyond the scope of this book.

READING LIST

Bandler, Richard, *Using Your Brain for a Change* (Utah: Real People Press, 1985).

Barnett, Wincoln, *The Universe and Dr. Einstein* (New York: Bantam Books, 1948).

Blake, William, *Complete Writings* (Oxford: Oxford University Press, 1966).

Browne, Mary T., *Love in Action* (New York: Simon & Schuster, 1990).

Downer, John, *Supersense* (London: BBC Books, 1988).

Eysenck, Hans J. and Carl Sargent, *Explaining the Unexplained* (London: Book Club Associates by arrangement with Weidenfeld and Nicolson, 1982).

Fischer, Louis, *The Life of Mahatma Gandhi* (London: Panther Books, 1982).

Fay, Allen, *Prescription for a Quality Relationship* (New York: Simon & Schuster, 1990).

Gillett, Richard, *Overcoming Depression* (London: Dorling Kindersley Publishers Ltd., 1987).

Goodall, Jane van Lawick, *In the Shadows of Man* (Glasgow: William Collins, 1971).

Gregory, R. L., *Eye and Brain* (London: World University Library, 1966).

Grindler, John and Richard Bandler, *Trance-formations* (Moab: Real People Press, 1981).

Hayes, Peter, *The Supreme Adventure* (New York: Delta, 1988).

Magee, Bryan, *Popper* (London: Fontana, 1973).

Muktananda, Swami, *Where are you going?* (New York: Syda Foundation, 1982).

Palmer, J., Chapter in B. B. Wolman (Ed.), *Handbook of Parapsychology* (New York: Van Nostrand Reinhold, 1977).

Patterson, J. H., *The Man-Eaters of Tsavo* (London: Fontana Books, 1973).

Roberts, Jane, *The Nature of Personal Reality* (London: Prentice-Hall International Inc., 1974).

Russell, Bertrand, *Mysticism and Logic* (London: Penguin Books Ltd., 1953).

Siegel, Bernie M., *Love, Medicine and Miracles* (New York: Harper & Row, 1988).

Watts, Alan W., *Psychotherapy East and West* (London: Penguin Books Ltd., 1973).

INDEX